# HOW TO SURVIVE
# MIDDLE SCHOOL
# WORLD HISTORY

Visit us on the Web! rhcbooks.com

Educators and librarians, for a variety of teaching tools, visit us at RHTeachersLibrarians.com

Library of Congress Cataloging-in-Publication Data is available upon request.

ISBN 978-0-525-57145-2 (trade)

ISBN: 978-0-525-57150-6 (e-book)

Printed in the United States of America

10 9 8 7 6 5 4 3 2 1

First Edition

Writer: Elizabeth M. Fee

Curriculum and Equity Consultant: Amit Shah

Sideshow Media Editorial and Production Team: Dan Tucker, Julia DeVarti

Penguin Random House Publishing Team: Tom Russell, Alison Stoltzfus, Brett Wright, Emily Harburg, Eugenia Lo, Katy Miller

Produced by Sideshow Media LLC

Illustration and Design by Carpenter Collective

# HOW TO SURVIVE
# MIDDLE SCHOOL

## A DO-IT-YOURSELF STUDY GUIDE

# WORLD HISTORY

# ELIZABETH M. FEE

BRIGHT
MATTER
BOOKS

NEW YORK

# TABLE OF CONTENTS

# CHAPTER 6     289
## LATE MODERN HISTORY II

# CHAPTER 7     343
## THE POSTWAR WORLD

# CHAPTER 8     383

## CHALLENGES TODAY

# CHAPTER 9     419

## HOW TO THINK LIKE A HISTORIAN

# ADDITIONAL READING     458

# TEXT CREDITS     465

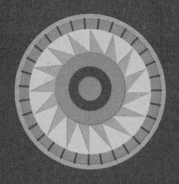

# WHAT IS HISTORY?

Take a look at the word "history." Do you see how the word "story" is hiding in there? It's actually good to think of history as a story. It's the story of humans—from our earliest beginnings all the way up to this moment. On the pages ahead, you'll read many, many stories. You'll see how humans throughout the ages have fought, failed, grown, and learned. You'll also learn why history matters—why it always has, and always will.

## CHAPTER CONTENTS

# ABOUT HISTORY

Here's a tip right up front: History is often about power—who has it, who doesn't and what happens as a result. We'll come back to this again and again. History can also tell you what people believed, how they lived, and how they invented amazing things to improve their lives. Sometimes history is bloody and terribly unfair. But you can always, always learn something from it.

## THE REAL DEAL ABOUT HISTORY

If you want to know the real deal about history, keep two things in mind: (1) There's not just one story, and (2) whatever story is being told, it matters who is telling it.

Let's look more closely at these two big concepts.

## BIG CONCEPT #1: THERE WILL NEVER, EVER, BE JUST ONE VERSION OF FACTUAL HISTORY.

Please don't think this study guide—or any book—will give you the whole history of the world. It's not gonna happen. We can never say: "Here is what exactly happened. This is all of it, and it's all true."

As you'll see in the chapters to come, archaeologists and historians are constantly discovering new artifacts and sources of information. Sometimes, a fact that everyone accepted as true turns out to be wrong!

## UNTOLD STORIES

But more often, the challenge of history is to get the *complete* story. Many people in the past have written about events and ideas, but way *more* people never wrote one word. Why? Because they didn't know how to write, or they didn't have time, or they weren't allowed to. For a very long time, the experiences of whole groups of people (like women, native people, people who were enslaved, and the poor) were basically left out of history books because they did not seem important to scholars.

*Archaeologists look for artifacts, the physical evidence of history.*

# BIG CONCEPT #2: IT MATTERS WHO IS TELLING THE STORY.

For most of history, very few people in the world could read and write at all—like, not even the alphabet. Those few people who could read were mostly males in powerful positions. In ancient times, scribes, kings, priests, and monks wrote history.

Lucky for us, modern historians are filling in the gaps they left. For instance, historians might find, say, a diary from a wealthy, literate woman (most poor women were uneducated) or a letter by a slave who managed to learn to read and write, and they give us information.

And a few powerful people wrote on behalf of those who didn't have a voice. For example, after Columbus arrived in the New World, a Spanish monk named Fra Bartolomeo de las Casas wrote about the horrors endured by enslaved people.

The human story is gradually correcting itself and going deeper, but historians will need to keep uncovering the stories of those who have been silenced.

## POINT OF VIEW

Also bear in mind that whoever is telling the story—whether it's a king or a peasant—will see things from their own point of view. For example, if two people watch a soccer game and they focus on different players, they will tell two slightly different stories about the game. You could even say that everyone in the stadium might see a slightly different game.

They will watch for different things, and depending on which team they are rooting for, they are likely to tell the story of the game from that point of view. Considering point of view is HUGE if you ever want to understand history. That's why we have equipped you with powerful binoculars.

## HOW DO WE EVER KNOW ANYTHING?

So, what are you thinking now? Maybe it's something like: Sheesh! So if only *some* people are telling the story, and people tell stories from *their* point of view, how do we ever figure out what really happened? Good question. Read on!

# WHAT IS A HISTORIAN'S JOB?

Historians today are also telling a story, just like historians who came before. They write about facts, but they don't just say what happened (remember, that's dicey!).

Historians look for patterns. They try to understand why things happened as they did, and how events connect to each other and to our experience now. It's their job to fill in the blanks about whose point of view might be missing, and to make sense of events so that we can all understand where we've triumphed and where we've failed.

Historians have to keep learning, keep asking questions, and keep digging for the truth. And before they decide if something is true, historians look for convincing evidence from several sources.

## UNDERSTANDING YOUR SOURCES

What do we really mean by sources? A source is anything that provides historians with information about a certain event or time period. There are two kinds.

Primary sources are things that people wrote or made back during the time period being studied. These sources are the most direct route to the past because we get to see through the eyes of people who were actually there.

Secondary sources are articles, books, videos, and websites created by people who have studied the time period later but were not actually there.

# A LOOK AT SOURCES

| EXAMPLES OF PRIMARY SOURCES | EXAMPLES OF SECONDARY SOURCES |
|---|---|

**EXAMPLES OF PRIMARY SOURCES**

- Oral histories
- Pamphlets
- Diaries
- Pottery, weapons, tools
- Speeches
- Artwork from the time period
- Letters
- Photos
- Maps, songs, films, and newspaper articles from the time period
- Interviews
- Eyewitness accounts
- Twitter, TikTok, and other social media

**EXAMPLES OF SECONDARY SOURCES**

- Encyclopedias
- Biographies
- History books (they often quote from primary sources, though)
- Articles and videos online by historians
- Articles in current newspapers and journals

## ORAL HISTORIES

Some cultures had, and continue to have, rich oral traditions, meaning people pass down history by memorizing it and saying it out loud to others in poems and songs. For example, in some Western African countries, respected members of society called **griots** serve as community historians, and use poetry, song, and music to pass down stories and historical accounts.

# THINKING ABOUT PRIMARY AND SECONDARY SOURCES

Do you think it's more important to pay attention to the point of view of the author when you read a primary source or a secondary source? (Hint: there's no right answer to this, just good reasons for your own answer.)

_____

_____

_____

_____

_____

_____

_____

You'll learn more about how to evaluate sources in Chapter 9.

# WHAT OTHER SUBJECTS INTERSECT WITH HISTORY?

Spoiler alert: most of them!

| | |
|---|---|
| **GEOGRAPHY** | Where people live determines how they live and who influences them. Resources determine what and how they trade. You'll see how people managed to cross mountains and oceans, and how fighting over what land belongs to who continues to happen. |
| **ART, MUSIC, DANCE, AND LITERATURE** | Artistic expression reveals what people care about and how they live. Artists and writers are often the people to bring about change in their societies. |
| **RELIGION** | What people believe about God and the unknown has been important in every time period and every location. You'll see how religion has unified and divided people throughout history. |
| **SCIENCE AND TECHNOLOGY** | Big changes occur through scientific discoveries and advances. Beginning with the wheel, advances in technology continue to move societies forward. |
| **ARCHITECTURE AND ENGINEERING** | The structures people build and how they build them tell us about the values of a culture, as well as the extent of its knowledge. Historians continue to debate how ancient people created structural wonders like Machu Picchu in Peru and the pyramids of Egypt. |

# WHY DOES HISTORY MATTER?

You will eventually figure this out for yourself if you stick with studying history. You'll realize that people from the past were still people, and you can actually relate to people who lived hundreds, even thousands, of years ago.

We think that's pretty cool. For instance, if you're into science, you can understand how much Galileo wanted to see the stars and planets. It's amazing to think that a person with no computer, no cell phone, and not even a calculator, could build a telescope that allowed him to see objects millions of miles away. Still, Galileo was just a person, like you. History helps you see yourself and others as part of the human race's big story.

## A LONG, WILD RIDE

History also helps us understand how we got to where we are today. Ever wonder how the environment got off balance to begin with? A historian might say it all started with the invention of the steam engine in 1698. It took hundreds of years for the environment to get this out of whack, but once you know the starting point, you can trace how one thing led to another, and see where humans might have taken a wrong turn.

Albert Einstein

## HUMANS CAN BE FOOLISH

Albert Einstein once supposedly said, "The definition of insanity is doing the same thing over and over and expecting different results." It turns out Einstein never said that, but it's still a pretty smart thing to say. History shows us that humans are sometimes insane. We mess up and then a few decades later we mess up again in pretty much the same way.

## LEARNING FROM PATTERNS

We might do some really smart things in between, but a lot of historians have pointed to some patterns we should just stop—like racism or denying girls an education. Anyone who lived through the 1918 Influenza Pandemic might wonder how people in 2020 let COVID-19 get out of control. The more people know about those "over and over" wrong moves, the more we can learn to avoid them.

## BENEFITS OF HISTORY

So by studying history, by seeing what's great about our story, and also taking a hard look at what's horrible, we can make better choices. Here's a quote from the famous writer, Maya Angelou.

*"History, despite its wrenching pain, cannot be unlived, but if faced with courage, need not be lived again."*

After all, you'll be shaping history pretty soon, and the old folks are counting on you young folks to get it right.

Are you down for a wild ride through world history? Let's pack up and go!

# PACKING UP (OR... HOW TO USE THIS BOOK)

Hold your horses! Don't flip the page just yet! We have some gifts for you to take along, and this is why:

When you read any text for any reason, you are the one understanding it, right? Someone else can't understand it for you. They could read it to you, and that can help, but teachers in middle school don't read aloud much. And in high school? Forget it.

That's why we are here to help! We are not only giving you the tools below, we will remind you to use them! In the pages ahead, you'll see the tools pop up, along with some questions and ways to think about what you're reading. Check 'em out:

## YOUR MIDDLE SCHOOL SURVIVAL TOOLS

| SYMBOL/ TOOL | WHAT IT IS | HOW TO USE IT WHILE YOU READ |
|---|---|---|
| | People use a GPS so they don't get lost. It helps them figure out where they are, get directions, or explore a new area. | When you see the GPS, stop and pay attention to the big picture. You might... <br><br>• Ask yourself some big picture questions before you read <br><br>• Preview the text by skimming the headings, timelines, charts, and illustrations |

| | | |
|---|---|---|
| | Boots give hikers sure footing, even on rocky paths. All serious hikers pull on their boots before setting out. | Think of boots as knowledge you already have that supports new knowledge. When you see the boots, it's time to…<br><br>• Think back on what you already know about the topic<br><br>• Recall something you've already read about |
| | A pickaxe is a digging tool. Notice how it has a sharp point to get into small places! | Your pickaxe will help you dig deeply for meaning. Take it out when you need to…<br><br>• Dig out important words or phrases that help you understand the text<br><br>• Find evidence and important details |
| | People use binoculars to see things that are far away. But people in different places will see the same thing differently. | Binoculars will remind you to consider point of view in a text. You will need to think about things like…<br><br>• Who is telling the story?<br><br>• Whose story is NOT told?<br><br>• How would someone else see this?<br><br>• When and why was this text written? |
| | People use a magnifying glass to examine something up close. | The magnifying glass will remind you to stop and focus on one thing. You can magnify your understanding by…<br><br>• Thinking about how one part is important to the whole.<br><br>• Paying attention to new vocabulary. |

## AND HERE'S THE THING. . .

It's up to you to use the tools. You could flip through this book, glancing at the pictures so your parents think you are reading it. But what's the use? Teachers and researchers have figured out that these strategies work. So when you see a question or a strategy prompt, stop and try it. See if it works to keep you interested, clarify things, or go deeper into the subject. You really don't have much to lose. In fact, as you get great at learning and thinking, you'll be set for middle school—and you'll kill it in high school, too.

You got this. Onward!

# CHAPTER VOCABULARY

Each chapter in this book has a list of vocabulary terms like this one (only longer) at the end. To make life even easier, we also included pop-out definitions on the page where the term first appears. Vocabulary terms are in bold, and the definition appears in a box nearby.

**Griot:** Griots are community historians, and use poetry, song, and music to pass down stories and historical accounts.

**Primary sources:** These are historical sources that people wrote or made during the time period being studied.

**Scholar:** A person who completed advanced studies in a certain area. Historians are scholars of the lives, events, and stories of past peoples.

**Secondary sources:** These are articles, books, videos, and websites that act as historical sources about a time period but are created by people who have studied the time period later but were not actually there.

# NOTES

# 1
# ANCIENT CIVILIZATIONS

Early humans had to work hard to survive. In this chapter, you'll learn how we advanced from picking berries in the wilderness to building majestic pyramids. The key? It all starts with food.

## CHAPTER CONTENTS

# EARLY HUMANS AND THE AGRICULTURAL REVOLUTION

## YOU ARE FROM AFRICA

On a hot July day about 60 years ago, an archaeologist named Mary Leakey, was digging for artifacts in Tanzania, East Africa. She and her husband Louis made an important discovery that day. She found a rock with fossilized bone inside. Then another, and then another. When pieced together, the bone fragments formed part of an early human's skull. When scientists tested them, they discovered that the fossils were more than 1.75 million years old.

### WHY DOES THIS MATTER?

If you go back far enough, to your ancestors' ancestors' ancestors (do that about 50,000 times), you can say with some certainty that you are connected to all of us and we all started out in Africa, probably on the eastern side, toward the south in the area known today as Tanzania. You can see from the map (turn the page) where it all began.

**Before we move on, see what you can deduce on your own.**

What do you think this map is showing? What might the arrows mean? What does it make you wonder?

_____

_____

_____

_____

_____

# CAUSES OF MIGRATION OUT OF AFRICA

Why did early people migrate out of Africa and keep spreading around the world? (It's a lot of work to walk across **continents**!) No one exactly knows, but here are historians' main theories:

 To escape droughts and other extreme climate changes

 To find new food and water sources

 To escape attacks by neighboring bands of people

 To explore!

**Archaeologist:** Archaeologists are scientists who study human history by digging up and excavating sites and analyzing the artifacts they find there. It's a lot of digging in the dirt and learning secrets about ancient societies!

**Artifact:** An artifact is an old item that holds cultural or historical significance. Artifacts can help historians learn what life in the past looked like.

**Ancestor:** An ancestor is someone from whom you're descended. They could be a great-grandparent, a great-great-grandparent, or someone even further back.

**Continents:** Continents are geographic divisions larger than countries. There are only seven continents: North America, South America, Africa, Asia, Europe, Australia/Oceania, and Antarctica.

# HUMAN MIGRATION
## from
## AFRICA

TANZANIA

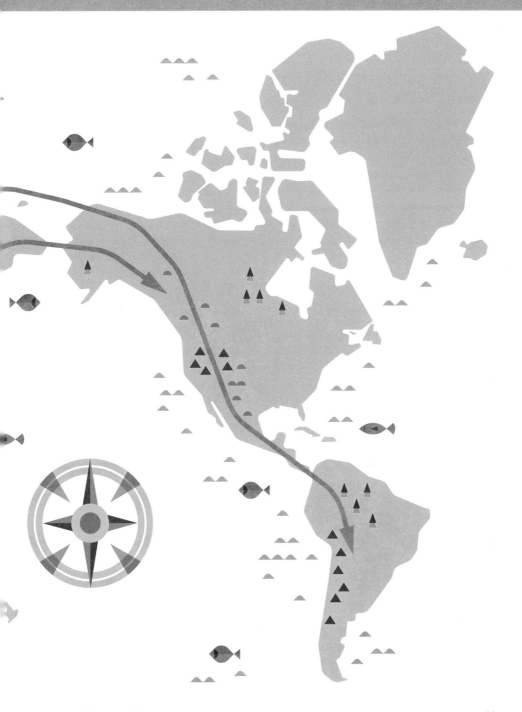

Historians believe that early humans spread throughout the world from that area of Africa.

As they came to populate the world, early humans invented all sorts of stuff, including spoken language, but they did not figure out how to write things down until about 3200 BCE. This was a huge, huge deal, and we will keep coming back to this.

But for now just know that once people could keep detailed records of events and exchanges, by writing down stories, speeches, poems, letters, and logs, we could know tons more about their lives. So scientists divided human history into prehistory (before writing) and regular history (after writing was invented). Then they broke the millions of years of human prehistory into sections as well. Check out this timeline:

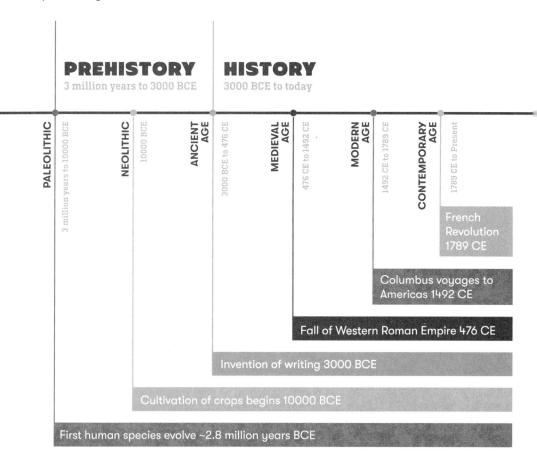

# ANCIENT AGES

| STONE AGE | DATES | DEFINING FEATURES |
|---|---|---|
| **PALEOLITHIC** (Old Stone Age) | 2.5 million years ago to 10000 BCE | Basic stone tools, hunted with stone axes; end of last Ice Age |
| **MESOLITHIC** (Middle Stone Age) | 10000–8000 BCE | Smaller stone tools, sometimes sharpened, attached bones and antlers to make spears and arrows |
| **NEOLITHIC** (New Stone Age) | 8000–3000 BCE | Polished stone axes, adzes for tilling soil |
| **BRONZE AGE** | 3000–1300 BCE | Metal tools and weapons, plows, wheel |
| **IRON AGE** | 1300–900 BCE | Invented ways to heat and forge iron—steel and iron tools. Advances in architecture |

Keep in mind that these dates are basic estimates. Scientists keep discovering new artifacts and revising their theories. The main thing to remember is that developments happened at different times in different parts of the world.

Look closely at the names of the different ages and what defines them. Then zoom out and think: What's the big idea here? What made the difference from one age to the next?

_____

_____

_____

_____

_____

_____

_____

If you are thinking tools, you are on to something. There is another name for this that you might know: technology. Yep, even though there were no iPhones (or even electricity!) at this time, whenever humans make something better, which helps them do something else better (or more easily) we call it technology.

# BC, BCE, AD, CE EXPLAINED

So what does BC mean? Or AD or BCE? CE? People (like you) who read about ancient history run into all of these abbreviations, depending on who the author is and when they were writing. Here's what the letters stand for and how they're used:

BC = Before the birth of Jesus Christ

AD = Anno Domini ("the year of our Lord")

BCE = Before the Common Era

CE = in the Common Era

## TELLING TIME

Wondering why the birth of Jesus determines time measurement? Here's a simple answer: Because the Christian church, through the Romans (more later on them), controlled much of the world right around the time.

## BC, AD, AND MORE

The Romans made Christianity a state religion and spread their version of keeping time throughout their huge empire. But they spread this system of calendar years way after Jesus's time, probably around 800 "Anno Domini" (to use their words), or 800 years after Jesus lived.

The "Common Era" language came along later to unify all the different calendars in the world. As far as the monthly time measurement goes, the Roman emperor Julius Caesar first introduced the Julian calendar (similar to ours) for the Roman Empire in 46 BCE.

Remember that when you're in BC or BCE time, the bigger the number, the longer ago it was, and the smaller the number, the more recent. Think of it as a number line, with BCE years being negative:

| 50 BCE | 25 BCE | 1 CE | 25 CE | 50 CE | 75 CE |
|--------|--------|------|-------|-------|-------|
| -50    | -25    | 0+1  | +25   | +50   | +75   |

If you read about one event in 25 BCE and one in 50 BCE, which happened more recently?

## THE CENTURY NUMBER RULE

Here's another hint: A lot of times when you're reading about history, you'll come across two ways that historians refer to centuries. For example, if you are reading about an event that happened in the 1800s, the source could say it took place in the nineteenth century. It doesn't seem to make sense because the numbers don't match, but it's actually right. Notice how it works out when you count out centuries:

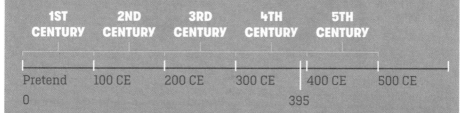

| 1ST CENTURY | 2ND CENTURY | 3RD CENTURY | 4TH CENTURY | 5TH CENTURY | |
|-------------|-------------|-------------|-------------|-------------|---|
| Pretend 0   | 100 CE      | 200 CE      | 300 CE      | 400 CE      | 500 CE |
|             |             |             |             | 395         | |

There was never a year 0! The BC/AD system was only just invented in 545 AD.

## SO WHEN DID THE EMPIRE BECOME TWO?

Let's say you are reading about the split of the Roman Empire into East and West. That occurred in the year 285 CE. Even though the year starts with a 2, it falls within the third century, doesn't it? So whenever you run into the number of century, remember to increase the first digit by one for a 3-digit year. For a 4-digit year, increase the first two digits by one. 1848, for example, is in the nineteenth century—18 plus 1.

Let's try it. What century are we in now? Yep, the twenty-first century, not the twentieth. Got it?

# ON THE MOVE

During the Old Stone Age and the Middle Stone Age, early humans survived by moving around. Early people ventured out from Africa, and spread to new lands over the course of thousands of years.

## YES-MADS OR NO-MADS?

People and animals don't live very long without food and water, so early humans clustered in areas where there was a water source, food they could gather, and animals they could hunt and eat. Then they would move to a new place (near water) when they needed new supplies of food. They carried temporary huts with them, or they might crash in a cave for a while.

These people, called nomads, survived by gathering food from wild plants (nuts, berries, and maybe tree bark when things got rough) and by hunting animals (antelopes, woolly mammoths, and cave bears). They learned it worked better to live together, especially for hunting large animals. So they traveled around in groups of twenty or thirty. They were living off the land, so nobody owned anything.

## GREAT INVENTIONS

Nomads had to figure out the most basic things, like how to use fire to cook, how to preserve meat, make tools, draw and paint, and make clothing from animal skins. They also had to survive when it was really, really cold. You might have heard of the Ice Age. There were actually five in the Earth's history. Humans were around for the last one, beginning about 2.6 million years ago and ending 10,000 years ago.

## CHALLENGING CONDITIONS

Scientists think temperatures consistently remained around 10 degrees Fahrenheit, and no higher than 40, creating hardships that may have sped along human development by forcing early

humans to create shelters, stitch clothing, and fashion tools.

*What an early nomad might have looked like.*

Early people had to step up their survival game to stay warm, feed themselves, and fend off wild animals. One of their most important inventions was the bone needle, which allowed them to stitch together animal skins and use them as coats.

**Nomads:** Nomads are people who don't have a permanent physical home. They move from place to place.

# WHAT KIND OF ARTIFACTS AND REMAINS DO ARCHAEOLOGISTS USE TO LEARN ABOUT THE PAST?

FOSSILS
BONES
BITS OF TOOLS
POTTERY
WEAPONS
ART
JEWELRY
COINS

Scientists studied digested food inside the stomach of a frozen mummy discovered on a mountainside between Austria and Italy. Wondering what was in there? Something similar to beef jerky. It's true! Such a discovery proved that the people living 5,000 years ago knew how to cure meat.

# GEOGRAPHY AND THE DEVELOPMENT OF CIVILIZATION

## SETTLING DOWN

Eventually, people learned how to grow their own food instead of chasing it. Maybe by accident at first, someone discovered that you could plant a seed and food would grow from it. In fact, you could plant a lot of seeds. . . and they would grow. You didn't have to go anywhere.

## THE NEOLITHIC REVOLUTION

People could now settle down, build a house (their places got nicer and nicer), and have a farm nearby. You could also have some animals inside of a fence and raise animals for food, instead of having to go out and hunt them.

*Sedentary*

*Animal husbandry*

This move was HUGE for humans and we refer to it as the Neolithic (neo=new, lithic=stone) Revolution, or New Stone Age. Finally, people had a dependable supply of food so life got better.

## STONES AND SOIL

*rivers*

What mattered most was where you planted those seeds. To grow well, most plants need soil with lots of nutrients (fertile soil), and, of course, water. Such ideal conditions existed in a few river valleys: in the Middle East between two rivers, along the Nile River in northern Africa, along the Indus River in present-day India and Pakistan, and along the Yellow River (Huang He) in China.

## THE FIRST CIVILIZATIONS

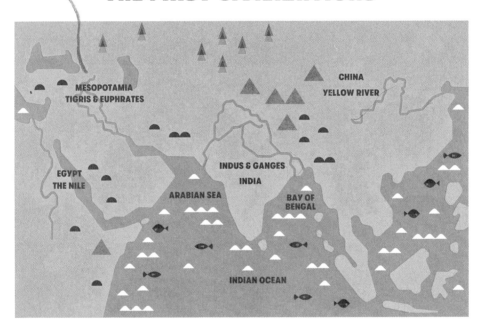

MESOPOTAMIA
TIGRIS & EUPHRATES

CHINA
YELLOW RIVER

EGYPT
THE NILE

ARABIAN SEA

INDUS & GANGES
INDIA

BAY OF
BENGAL

INDIAN OCEAN

## FANTASTIC FLOODS

A few times a year the rivers would flood and the rising water would carry and deposit silt along the banks of the river. This silt was like powdery rock so it drained well and contained nutrients. The crops loved it! Even when the rivers receded, farmers figured out how to dig canals to bring water to the farmland. This is called irrigation and it was crucial to the functioning

*Super importante*

of early farms. Many of the crops first produced thousands of years ago are still important to the present-day societies in those areas.

**Neolithic:** If something is Neolithic, that means it is related to the New Stone Age. That's a direct translation; "neo" means new and "lithic" means stone!

**Fertile:** Fertile soil is soil with lots of nutrients and is ideal for growing crops.

**Silt:** Silt is a deposit of sediment, often found beside rivers.

**Irrigation:** Irrigation is the system that farmers use to get water to all of their crops.

## ANCIENT FOODS STILL IMPORTANT TODAY

| AREA | FOODS |
| --- | --- |
| India | rice, wheat, dates, lentils |
| China | rice, wheat, millet, barley |
| Middle East | wheat, barley, figs, dates |
| Mesoamerica | corn, beans, squash |

# STEP BY STEP: FROM HUNTING AND GATHERING TO CIVILIZATION

**1** Steady food supply (farming)

*Neolithic Revolution*

**2** Increase in population (more babies!) leads to cities

**3** Surplus food (not everyone has to farm because there is extra)

**4** Some people start to have specialized jobs, such as artisans

**5** People have shared beliefs, religion forms

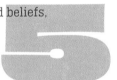

**6** Government forms to keep order

**7** A system of writing develops

**8** Social classes form based on power and wealth

# MESOPOTAMIA AND THE FERTILE CRESCENT

 Take out your magnifying glass and let's look closely at an area of the Middle East called the Fertile Crescent.

It's called "fertile" because it had all those perfect conditions we learned about. Notice how that fertile area between the Tigris and Euphrates Rivers is in the shape of a crescent. Now you know why it's called Mesopotamia—because that's Greek for "the land between the rivers." In this pastry-shaped region, over the course of a couple thousand years, a number of cities grew up, crowded and noisy, just like ours.

## DAILY LIFE

There were no cars, phones, skyscrapers, or subways, but people were busy doing things we do, like going to work and school, tending to their animals, cooking dinner, and relaxing on their rooftops in the evening.

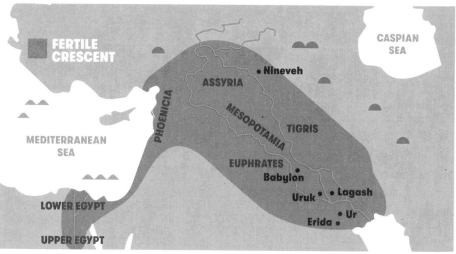

*Mesopotamia*

Check out the names on the map—Babylon, Uruk, Eridu, Ur, Lagash, and Nineveh. Some are mentioned in the Bible. A historian who translated their ancient writings started calling the whole region Sumer, but that's not what they called themselves. It's been discovered that one group, the Akkadians, called themselves *sag-gig-ga* or "Black Heads."

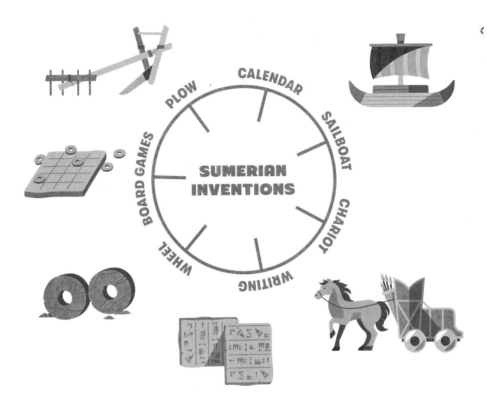

**THE WHEEL**—allowed them to carry things more easily for longer distances

**THE CHARIOT**—being pulled by two to four horses was faster than riding one (or walking!)

**THE PLOW**—dug the ground quickly so they could plant more crops

**THE SAILBOAT**—wind-powered sea travel

**THE CALENDAR**—kept track of time, mainly for business purposes

**WRITING**—called cuneiform, for recording calculations—and history!

**BOARD GAMES**—including checkers

## GILGAMESH THE HERO

1st Epic

The Sumerians also wrote long, symbolic stories, known as epics. The Epic of Gilgamesh tells the story of a hero's quest for the secret to immortality. He had a sidekick named Enkidu who starts out as half-human, half-beast, but evolves to be Gilgamesh's trusted friend and guide. So the story (like many timeless stories we'll encounter) is also about what it means to be human.

# HAMMURABI'S CODE

Mesopotamia continued as a kind of mishmash of different cities until the Babylonians started attacking other cities and winning. They were led by their king, Hammurabi. During Hammurabi's lifetime (1792–1750 BCE), he unified the area and it became one Babylonian kingdom. Hammurabi was a powerful, ambitious leader, and he meant business.

## AN EYE FOR AN EYE

He developed one of the first legal codes, based on the concept of retribution in justice, meaning if you did something to someone, it also got done to you. For example, if you broke someone's arm, your arm would be broken. If you put someone's eye out, your eye would be put out. Yes, for real. It got pretty gruesome. But the severity of the penalty often depended on the social class of the offender, as well as the victim. So, if you broke the arm of someone in a social class lower than yours, you'd pay a fine instead of having your own arm broken.

Here's a direct quote from the Code of Hammurabi:

"The first duty of government is to protect the powerless from the powerful."

Based on some of the examples above, do you think Hammurabi's Code protected the powerless from the powerful?

_____

_____

_____

_____

_____

_____

_____

# EGYPT AND THE NILE RIVER

Mesopotamia is typically thought of, at least by people from the Western Hemisphere, as the "Birthplace of Civilization." But as we've seen, civilizations sprang up in other areas of the world right around the same time with similar accomplishments.

## EARLY CIVILIZATIONS

| CIVILIZATION | ACCOMPLISHMENTS |
| --- | --- |
| THE FERTILE CRESCENT (MESOPOTAMIA) | Writing with symbols (cuneiform), code of law, and advances in farming |
| YELLOW RIVER VALLEY (CHINA) | Writing with symbols, bronze, and ceramics technology |
| INDUS RIVER VALLEY (INDIA/PAKISTAN) | Writing with symbols and sounds Indus script*, urban planning—sanitation systems, transportation networks<br><br>*Indus script still hasn't been deciphered! |
| NUBIA (NORTHERN SUDAN, SOUTHERN EGYPT) | Writing with alphabet (Meroitic), advances in science and medicine |
| EGYPT | Writing with symbols (hieroglyphs), complex religion, and architecture |
| OLMEC (CENTRAL AMERICA) | Writing with symbols, highly advanced art |

# ANCIENT EGYPT

The ancient Egyptians were smart, organized, and basically peaceful. Their wealth stemmed from abundant resources, most especially the Nile River.

Read this excerpt from a hymn (or song to the gods) sung by the ancient Egyptians during the flooding of the Nile. It was probably recorded by an unknown scribe around 2100 BCE.

## Hymn to the Nile

*If the Nile smiles, the Earth is joyous*

*Every stomach is full of rejoicing*

*Every spine is happy*

*Every jawbone crushes its food.*

What might this excerpt tell us about the Egyptians' feelings about the Nile? Why do you think it was so important to people?

_____

_____

_____

_____

_____

_____

_____

_____

_____

# MANY GODS

The ancient Egyptians worshipped hundreds of gods, who often appeared in their art as partly human and partly animal. Their mythology did what all mythologies do from various cultures. When people don't understand something, like why the sun comes up each day, or where a person goes when they die, a story gets created to explain it.

Isis: Goddess of the underworld and wife of Osiris. Isis was said to bring him back to life after he had been cut to pieces by his evil brother Set. For years, she searched the Nile for his body parts, and when she found them, glued them together with wax, and breathed life into him with her love.

Osiris: God of the underworld. Osiris was one of five Egyptian gods, said to be born from the union of earth and sky. Egyptians worshipped Osiris for giving Egypt law, harmony and cultural values.

Horus: Sky god. Horus was the son of Isis and Osiris. Part falcon, his right eye was the sun and his left eye was the moon. In a fight with Set, to avenge his father's death, Horus injured his left eye (this explained the phases of the moon).

# THE GOOD LIFE

The Egyptians loved life and most people in Egypt lived well, whatever their station in life. The Egyptians also cared *a lot* about death. Many of their myths are about death. And various businesses developed, centered around death, including the craft of mummification.

The Egyptians believed in an afterlife for everyone, and the more prepared you were for it, the better. But it depended on your social class how fancy your afterlife would be and how many goods you'd have. If you were a royal or well off, you could afford a high-end mummification by a professional embalmer. (You had to pay him in advance!)

## MAKING A MUMMY

| | | |
|---|---|---|
| The body is rinsed → | Rubbed with sweet smelling oil → | Internal organs removed and put in jars ↓ |
| Body is left to dry out ↓ | Brain pulled out through the nose with a hook ← | Heart left in (center of intelligence and emotions) ← |
| Rinsed again → | Wrapped in linen → | Body placed in tomb, sometimes inside a sarcophagus (fancy coffin) |

Egyptologists estimate that during Egypt's three thousand year history, more than 70 million mummies were made. Some still exist in museums, so some day you can go see the body of a famous Egyptian king like Ramses II or King Tutankhamen.

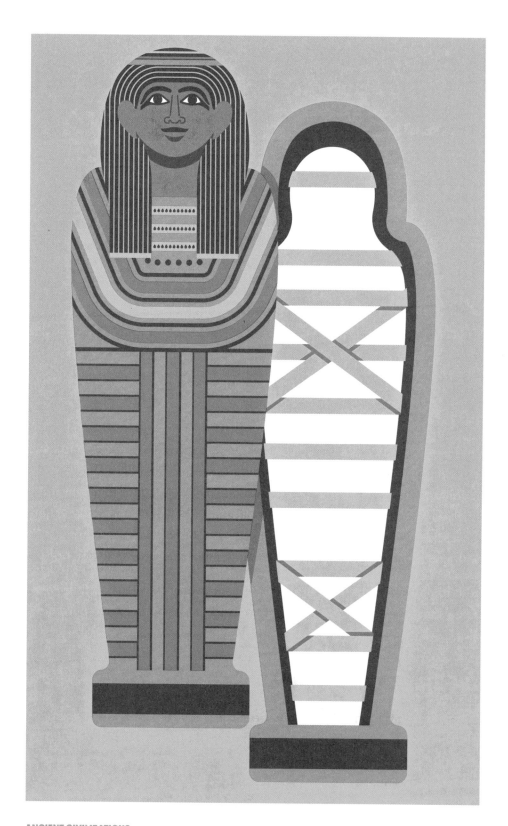

## EGYPTIAN TOMBS

Your mummy would then need somewhere to go to start its journey to the afterworld. Often, this would be an underground tomb. If you were in the royal family or close to the top of the social hierarchy, your tomb would be filled with food, beer, jewels, even furniture. The Egyptians believed you CAN take it with you when you die. They thought you needed to bring stuff with you into the afterlife, and the more you brought, the more you had.

Your tomb also might have statues inside, beautiful paintings on the walls, secret passageways to fool the tomb raiders, and maybe even a pyramid on top of it so that all could see your burial site for miles around.

## THE ETERNAL PYRAMIDS

The pharaohs had the biggest and best pyramids. The most famous, and also the oldest and biggest, is Khufu's pyramid at Giza, finished around 2560 BCE. It's one of the Seven Wonders of the Ancient World and the only one still standing.

Wrap your head around these other amazing facts about this unreal (but real) accomplishment:

- 481 feet high

- The base is a perfect square, each side being over 750 feet long (like, 7½ football fields)

- The measurements are so exact that the sides differ in length by only 1¾ inches!

- Constructed of 2,300,000 blocks of limestone

- Each block weighed 2.5 tons (a midsize car weighs about two tons, an eighteen-wheeler semi-truck weighs forty tons)

- Egyptologists think it took about twenty years to construct

- The builders and laborers had no mechanical machinery

## ASK QUESTIONS

If you pictured all this and let it roll around in your mind, you most likely wondered, "How and why would these people do such a thing?"

*How* they did it is what everyone still debates. Historians marvel at the advanced engineering it took to make these structures happen, and they guess that the workers used pulleys and rollers to pull rocks up those hundreds of feet. As you can imagine, it took thousands of people and animals working together.

## A CLASS OF LABORERS

Historians no longer think that only slaves built the pyramids. They have found burial evidence that indicates otherwise. It could be that an entire class of laborers worked through generations to construct these tombs, and most likely considered it an honor to do so.

## BURIAL FOR EVERYONE ELSE

We know about burials and tombs for royalty, but what about everyone else? As we see from the social pyramid, lots more regular folks lived in ancient Egypt than higher-ups.

Middle-class Egyptians were often buried in tombs, called *mastabas*, perhaps lined with dried brick and usually comprised of two chambers. They often had small chapels on top, rather than pyramids. Common people were usually just wrapped in cloth and buried in the desert by their relatives, with a few possessions and some food.

## EGYPT'S SOCIAL HIERARCHY

The Egyptians worshipped their kings as gods. They believed the king, or pharaoh, had special powers and, of course, absolute power. The pharaoh was top dog of the social hierarchy. So, if the pharaoh said, "Go build me a pyramid and spend your whole life doing it," people got to work. The pharaoh had numerous advisers and managers, but ultimately, he owned the entire land and called the shots no matter what.

# THE SOCIAL HIERARCHY IN ANCIENT EGYPT

PHARAOHS

VIZIERS AND PRIESTS

SCRIBES

ARTISANS

PEASANTS

SLAVES AND SERVANTS

**Hierarchy:** Hierarchy is a system in which people or things are ranked by their authority or significance. In Ancient Egypt, Pharaohs were at the top of the hierarchy.

**Artisans:** Artisans are craftsmen (or craftswomen!) who practice a trade or handicraft. They might make plows or pottery or something else that could improve life.

**Peasants:** Peasants mainly did the work of farming for ancient Egyptian society, but they also helped construct pyramids and irrigation systems.

**Pharaoh:** A pharaoh was the king of ancient Egypt. Egyptians worshipped their pharaohs as gods.

**Priests:** Priests had an important religious role, keeping order between the gods and the ancient Egyptians. They oversaw rituals and sacrifices.

**Scribes:** Scribes were the only Egyptians who were trained to read and write. They helped keep records and manage taxes.

**Slaves and Servants:** Slaves and servants did the hardest labor for ancient Egypt, and many were captured from neighboring societies.

**Viziers:** Viziers were the highest officials serving the pharaoh. They oversaw the courts and the treasury.

 ## FAMOUS PHARAOHS

Hatshepsut was the most famous female pharaoh. She first took power because her stepson, Thutmose III, was too young to become pharaoh. Hatshepsut sometimes wore a false beard as a sign of authority. During her twenty years as pharaoh, she accomplished much: a successful trade expedition to a place called Punt, and lots of big construction projects, including a temple dedicated to—you guessed it—herself.

## LITTLE EVIDENCE REMAINS

Unfortunately, we don't have much evidence of Hatshepsut's grandeur today. When she died from a dental infection in her fifties, Thutmose III took power, assumed credit for her achievements, and tore down most everything she had built.

*Hatshepsut sporting her false beard*

## RAMSES II AND NEFERTARI

Ramses II held power for sixty-six years, one of the longest reigns in Egyptian history, and lived to be 90 years old. (Most Egyptians died in their forties.) He, too, accomplished amazing designs and structures in architecture. Ramses is said to have had over 200 wives and fathered over 100 children.

His first and favorite queen, Nefertari, ruled alongside him for twenty-four years. Ramses built his beloved wife a beautiful tomb in the Valley of Queens, filled with exquisite and well-preserved wall paintings, including a blue ceiling painted with stars.

## AKHENATEN AND NEFERTITI

Akhenaten held power for only seventeen years (1353 BCE–1336 BCE), but tried to do a huge thing: change the entire religion of Egypt! Akhenaten and his queen Nefertiti worshipped only one god called Aten, who was associated with the sun, but all other Egyptians believed in many gods (or polytheism).

Akhenaten and Nefertiti set about destroying the temples and art devoted to any other god but Aten. They built shrines to Aten, and a new capital city called Amarna. This symbol of Aten can be found in much of the art of Akhenaten's time:

## DEVOTION TO ATEN

Akhenaten and Nefertiti made the widest road in the ancient world so that hundreds of chariots could speed up the move into the new capital. But that day never came.

Egypt grew weaker under Akhenaten. He was so busy with religion that enemies started to invade Egypt. Also, the people of Egypt were not convinced about this one god. They worried about their afterlife and their jobs. Many earned their living as priests and artists connected to the worship of many gods.

# NUBIA

Just south of Egypt lay the civilization of Nubia, which stretched from the Nile to the Red Sea, in what is now the country of Sudan. The area became settled earlier than Egypt, around 5000 BCE. The Nubian and Egyptian civilizations existed side by side, sometimes peacefully, sometimes not. Around 745 BCE, the Nubian King Piye (reigned from ca. 750 to ca. 719 BCE) took control of Egypt. A succession of Nubian pharaohs held power in Egypt for the next hundred years.

# KANDAKES: POWERFUL WOMEN

Nubia was similar to Egypt in culture, religion, and social structure, except that the priests had even more power, enough to depose a ruler. The Nubians worshipped Isis, the mother goddess, above all other gods. They believed Isis gave birth to all women, giving them her power. This set Nubia apart from the ancient world in that women had status and influence. Nubian queens were revered as much as kings and they were known as Kandakes or "mothers of the nation."

## IMPORTANT NUBIAN QUEENS

The earliest known African queen was Queen Shanakhdakete, ruling from 170 to 150 BCE, who figured prominently in religion at the time. Another queen, Amanirenas, was a warrior queen. Ruling from 40 to 10 BCE, Amanirenas led the Kushites in battle against the Romans from 27 to 22 BCE, and defeated three groups of Roman soldiers. She lost one eye in battle and became known to the Romans as the "One-eyed Kandake."

*A mask of Amanirenas, warrior queen*

# NUBIAN ECONOMY AND CULTURE

Nubia's chief resources were gold and iron. Nubia also served as a trade gateway to precious materials that came from areas southward. For example, the Nubians traded heavily in ivory, ebony, and incense, as well as gold. The Nubians were famous for their prowess as great archers. Nubia has often been called "Land of the Bow."

The Nubians developed their own languages and systems for writing, separate from Egypt. Instead of using hieroglyphs, which required hundreds of picture symbols, the Nubians developed an alphabet with only twenty-three symbols to form words, similar to the way our alphabet works.

# THE HEBREWS AND JUDAISM

It took a special person to bring monotheism to the world, and that person was Abraham. We don't know exactly when he lived because most of our information about Abraham comes from the Bible, a religious text of the Judeo-Christian tradition. The authors of ancient religious texts didn't keep time in the way we do. Stories got passed down for centuries, then got written down by various folks, most likely. Even though we're not sure of every detail, the story of the Hebrews is vital to the world, as we'll see as we move through history. For now, here is one basic version of the history of Abraham and his people:

**Monotheism:** Monotheism is a belief in only one God.

## THE FATHER OF HIS PEOPLE

Abraham was from the City of Ur in Mesopotamia. His father had been a seller of items for idol worship. Ironic, but not surprising, because the Mesopotamians worshipped many gods, just as the Egyptians did. One day, as the Bible tells us, God revealed himself to Abraham and made a covenant with him.

> *"I will make nations of you, and kings shall come forth from you.... And I will establish my covenant between me and you and your descendants after you throughout their generations for an everlasting covenant, to be God to you."*

—Book of Genesis

## A PATH TO MONOTHEISM

And so began a promise between the Hebrew people and their one and only God. As long as the Israelites stayed close to Yahweh, as they first called their god, that force would protect them and guide them. The curious thing is, the Hebrews (later known as Jews) came up against all kinds of trouble throughout history, but they held to their faith.

Abraham and his family migrated to a place called Canaan (roughly where Israel is today), and there, many shepherd families gathered and shared in this unusual belief in one God. They formed a community known as the Israelites and continued to hold to their belief in one God—all-knowing, all-powerful, yet invisible and difficult for humans to understand.

## A DROUGHT BRINGS HARD TIMES

But the land in Canaan was not ideal for farming, and when drought came it forced Abraham's family and many others to migrate to Egypt. According to the Bible (known to Jews as the Torah) the Jewish people became slaves in Egypt.

# HEADING OUT OF TOWN

This is where the Exodus story from the Bible kicks in. The Greek word "exodus" means "the road out," and that's actually what happened. As the Biblical story goes, Moses, the next great patriarch of Judaism, led his people out of enslavement in Egypt and back to Canaan. He said to the pharaoh at the time, "Let my people go."

As you might imagine, the pharaoh didn't budge, so the Israelites' God sent ten plagues upon the Egyptians. Horrible things like invasions of frogs and locusts, and even the death of their firstborn children.

# MOSES LEADS THE EXODUS

Finally, Moses led the Israelites out of Egypt and God helped out by parting the Red Sea, and doing other things to clear the way. People had to leave right away, so they didn't even have a chance to let their bread dough rise. They just took it with them. So, to this day Jewish people who celebrate the Passover holiday eat unleavened bread, or *matzah*, to commemorate the Exodus (or exit) from Egypt.

## SO IS WHAT THE BIBLE SAYS TRUE?

It depends on who you ask. Many religious people would say, yes, it's all true. Others say it's all myth, just stories to illustrate deeper truths and explain things people could not understand.

Many historians and archaeologists say the truth is somewhere in the middle. They can confirm some locations, based on historical records, like the city of Pi-Ramses. They think Exodus occurred during a certain time frame (around the thirteenth century BCE). In fact, the pharaoh in the Exodus story might have been our friend Ramses II.

# A BIBLICAL TIMELINE

Many events involving Jerusalem are referenced in sources in addition to the Torah (the holy book of the Jews). Here is a basic timeline of the destruction and rebuilding of the Jewish Temple, which is both historically verified and central to the story of the Jewish people.

| 1010–970 BCE | 960 BCE | 720 BCE |
|---|---|---|
| King David unifies the Israelites. Captures Jerusalem. The city and the Jews thrive. | David's son Solomon builds First Jewish Temple (said to have housed the Ten Commandments). | Assyrians attack Israel and Judah (the two kingdoms of Israel). |

| 586 BCE | 539 BCE | 516 BCE |
|---|---|---|
| Babylonians destroy the Temple, capture Jerusalem, take Israelites to Babylon. | Persians led by King Cyrus conquer Babylon. | King Cyrus allows Jews to return to Jerusalem. |

| 515 BCE |
|---|
| Second Temple is built. |

 Viewing this timeline, why do you think the building of the First and Second Temples is so important to Jewish history and religion?

_____

_____

_____

_____

_____

_____

# MESOAMERICA

Mesoamerica means "middle" America. It refers to the bridge of land between North America and South America, shown in the map near the end of this chapter. Early civilizations developed in this area, much as they did in other parts of the world.

Indigenous people in the Americas built complex communities with advanced technology that rivaled that of Europe and Asia. Often these ancient communities are called Pre-Columbian because they existed before Columbus's voyage.

After Columbus arrived in the Americas, many European explorers followed, who conquered the Indigenous civilizations and attempted to erase their traditions.

> **Indigenous:** If a group is indigenous, that means they are the original natives of a place. Some examples of Indigenous nations you'll read about here are the Aztecs, Incas, and Maya.

## THE OLMECS

As far as archaeologists have been able to determine, the oldest American civilization was established on the southeastern coast of Mexico and thrived between 1200 and 400 BCE. These people, known as the Olmecs, lived in a highly ordered society with religious rituals and powerful ruling families.

They forged extensive trade routes and developed as "Olmecs," meaning "rubber people" in the Aztec language. No, they weren't people made out of rubber! They learned to make rubber from certain trees.

The Olmec's religious art still exists today, and their customs made their way into the Mesoamerican cultures that came after them. They are well known for carving gigantic heads out of forty-ton stones. No one knows how they could possibly transport these stones to their religious sites, but they did it somehow.

## INVENTORS OF SPORTS!

The Olmecs used their knowledge of rubber production to make rubber balls for playing a sport known as the ballgame and sometimes called *ulama*. The rubber ball was smaller than a soccer ball, very heavy, and very dangerous. The ballgame had rules (can't use your hands), equipment (gloves), and teams.

Ulama was played for hundreds of years throughout Mesoamerica and was even brought back to Europe by the Spanish explorers. The game had religious meaning and connected to beliefs about the movement of planets and the sun. Sometimes opposing tribes played a ballgame instead of fighting a battle.

Archeologists have unearthed more than twenty huge rectangular ulama fields, where teams challenged each other—often to the death!

# THE MAYA

The Maya are famous for their amazing accomplishments in astronomy and math. They watched the heavens and took careful measurements for years and years, which allowed them to develop an accurate and complex 365-day calendar (like ours) and also a 260-day calendar based on the orbits of Venus.

How did they do all this without a telescope? It's still a mystery. Most Mayans were farmers of corn and other crops. Many lived in large cities like Chichén Itzá, which at its height had a population of 50,000. Overall, about 19 million people made up the Mayan civilization.

# FIVE AMAZING FACTS ABOUT THE MAYANS

They understood the concept of zero before the Greeks did.

They constructed some of the largest pyramids in the world.

They made books called codices out of tree bark where they recorded their calculations.

They spoke and wrote in many different languages—some of the languages are still spoken by people in Central and South America.

They invented chocolate!

## A MYSTERIOUS DECLINE

Historians debate why Mayan cities were rapidly abandoned around 900 CE. Many think that deforestation (cutting down trees for firewood and to clear land for farming) was one big cause. Their environment and climate might have gotten out of balance and caused food shortages. Or perhaps constant warfare took a final toll. Mostly likely a combination of causes led to the fall of the Mayan civilization.

# THE AZTECS

A few hundred years after the Mayans began to decline, the Aztec Empire grew to cover most of present-day Mexico. The powerful Aztec government ruled over millions of people who lived in well-planned cities and traded with tribes far and wide.

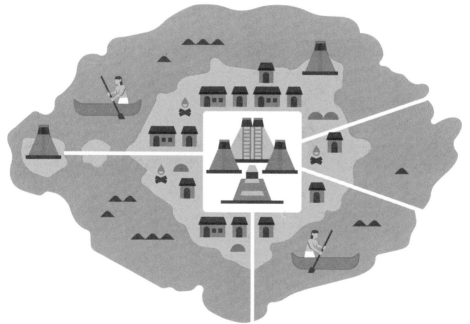

*Aerial view of Tenochtitlán, set in Lake Texcoco*

## TENOCHTITLÁN, THE AZTEC CAPITAL CITY

Does it look like this city is in the middle of a lake? It is! The Aztecs managed to build a city five miles wide onto a swampy area of Lake Texcoco. The city had a complex system of roads, canals, aqueducts, and bridges. At its center were palaces, temples, schools, and marketplaces. Tenochtitlán reached a population of 200,000.

## INVENTORS, ASTRONOMERS, FARMERS—AND WARRIORS

Like the Mayans, the Aztecs were great inventors, astronomers, and farmers. The Aztecs were also fierce in battle, expanding their territory and taking prisoners of war who became slaves. In Aztec society, slaves could own land and sometimes buy their freedom. But sometimes they were killed during religious ceremonies.

Although the Aztecs recorded their history (and made predictions of the future), we have very few of their writings today. Conquerors arrived from Spain in the 1500s, burned their books, destroyed Tenochtitlán, and brought about the fall of the mighty Aztec culture.

## WERE THERE REALLY HUMAN SACRIFICES IN MESOAMERICA?

The answer is yes. Archaeologists have found huge numbers of human bones on the sites of temples. Mayan and Aztec art also depicts human sacrifices. The Aztecs believed sacrifices were required by the gods to keep the world in balance. Human sacrifice also scared their enemies!

# THE INCAS

Technically, the territories of the Inca Empire were not located in Mesoamerica. As you can see from the map on the following page, the Incas inhabited present-day Peru and also spread southward along the west coast of South America. The Inca culture shared many aspects with the early cultures of Mesoamerica. They also distinguished themselves with unique advancements:

- At their height in the 1400s, the Incas developed an organized government that collected the harvests and spread food among the people.

- Farmers figured out how to farm in the mountains by digging terraces that kept the rain from flowing down the hillside.

- They performed brain surgery, and knew how to use anesthesia well before the Europeans.

- The Incan road system was so advanced and so extensive that scholars agree it surpassed that of the Romans.

*The Inca city of Machu Picchu, high in the Andes Mountains*

- The Inca Empire was unified under one ruler and one language.

- The Incas did not develop a full system for writing. Instead, they used knots on strings to represent numbers so that they could compute taxes, population, and even record historical events.

- Incan culture only lasted about one hundred years. Civil war, disease, and Spanish conquerors led to its fall around 1530.

# THE MAJOR CIVILIZATIONS OF MESOAMERICA AND SOUTH AMERICA

LAKE TEXCOCO
(MODERN DAY MEXICO)

YUCATÁN
PENINSULA

CHICHÉN ITZÁ

MACHU PICCHU
(TERRACED INCA CITY)

LIMA
(MODERN DAY CITY)

CUSCO

AZTEC

MAYA

INCA

# CHAPTER VOCABULARY

**Ancestor:** An ancestor is someone from whom you're descended. They could be a great-grandparent, a great-great-grandparent, or someone even further back.

**Archaeologist:** Archaeologists are scientists who study human history by digging up and excavating sites and analyzing the artifacts they find there. It's a lot of digging in the dirt and learning secrets about ancient societies!

**Artifact:** An artifact is an old item that holds cultural or historical significance. Artifacts can help historians learn what life in the past looked like.

**Artisans:** Artisans are craftsmen (or craftswomen!) who practice a trade or handicraft. They might make plows or pottery or something else that could improve life.

**Continents:** Continents are geographic divisions larger than countries. There are only seven continents: North America, South America, Africa, Asia, Europe, Australia/Oceania, and Antarctica.

**Cuneiform:** Coming from the Latin word cuneus (which means "wedge" in English), cuneiform is an ancient writing technique that involved pressing wedge-shaped marks into clay tablets. It likely took a lot longer than sending a text on a modern cell phone, but cuneiform tablets are one of the ways we know so much about ancient history!

**Fertile:** Fertile soil is soil with lots of nutrients and is ideal for growing crops.

**Hierarchy:** Hierarchy is a system in which people or things are ranked by their authority or significance. In Ancient Egypt, pharaohs were at the top of the hierarchy.

**Indigenous:** If a group is indigenous, that means they are the original natives of a place. Some examples of Indigenous nations you read about here were the Aztecs, Incas, and Maya.

**Irrigation:** Irrigation is the system that farmers use to get water to all of their crops.

**Monotheism:** Monotheism is a belief in only one God.

**Neolithic:** If something is Neolithic, that means it is related to the New Stone Age. That's a direct translation; "neo" means new and "lithic" means stone!

**Nomads:** Nomads are people who don't have a permanent physical home. They move from place to place.

**Peasants:** Peasants mainly did the work of farming for ancient Egyptian society, but they also helped construct pyramids and irrigation systems.

**Pharaoh:** A pharaoh was the king of ancient Egypt. Egyptians worshipped their pharaohs as gods.

**Polytheism:** Polytheism is the religious belief in multiple or many gods.

**Priests:** Priests had an important religious role, keeping order between the gods and the ancient Egyptians. They oversaw rituals and sacrifices.

**Scribes:** Scribes were the only Egyptians who were trained to read and write. They helped keep records and manage taxes.

**Silt:** Silt is a deposit of sediment, often found beside rivers.

**Slaves and Servants:** Slaves and servants did the hardest labor for ancient Egypt, and many were captured from neighboring societies.

**Technology:** Technology is anything that humans invent to make a process easier. That's everything from a wheel to a computer.

**Viziers:** Viziers were the highest officials serving the pharaoh. They oversaw the courts and the treasury.

# NOTES

# 2 CLASSICAL CIVILIZATIONS

As civilizations grew bigger and more powerful, people had the time and resources to explore new ideas, create more complex governments, and invent new technology. "Golden ages" of classical civilizations brought art, music, literature, and architecture to new heights. But what happens after a golden age?

Take a look at this graphic that illustrates the elements of classical civilizations:

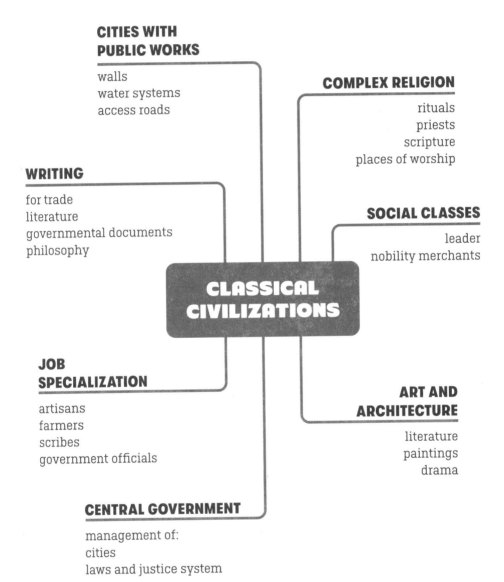

# WHAT MAKES UP CLASSICAL CIVILIZATIONS

**CITIES WITH PUBLIC WORKS**

walls
water systems
access roads

**COMPLEX RELIGION**

rituals
priests
scripture
places of worship

**WRITING**

for trade
literature
governmental documents
philosophy

**SOCIAL CLASSES**

leader
nobility merchants

**CLASSICAL CIVILIZATIONS**

**JOB SPECIALIZATION**

artisans
farmers
scribes
government officials

**ART AND ARCHITECTURE**

literature
paintings
drama

**CENTRAL GOVERNMENT**

management of:
cities
laws and justice system

Which elements do you remember from ancient civilizations? What new elements do you notice here?

_____

_____

_____

_____

_____

_____

As civilizations enter a classical period, the basic elements from ancient times (and those were a big deal to establish) develop into more complex, more sophisticated forms of organization, production, and artistic expression.

People in classical times, at least those in the upper classes, had time to get educated, create new products and tools, develop their belief systems, and experiment with new art forms. Life wasn't just about survival anymore, it was about living a good life. Empires rose to power and grandeur, fought with one another, and ultimately fell. The cycle then repeated itself, as we will soon see.

Store this knowledge away. You'll need it later.

**Empire:** An empire is an extensive territory or set of territories under one imperial control or rule. Throughout history, many empires have risen and fallen. Try to keep track of all the ones you'll meet in the next few chapters!

# ANCIENT GREECE

## THE LANDS OF ANCIENT GREECE

By analyzing this physical map of Greece, you can make some inferences and conclusions about how and why their civilization developed. What do you notice?

_____

_____

_____

_____

_____

_____

_____

_____

_____

_____

# SEPARATE COMMUNITIES

You don't see any big rivers running through Greece as we saw in Mesopotamia and Egypt, do you? Instead, this is a rather small area surrounded by water on three sides (that's called a peninsula). You also can see many islands and many mountain ranges.

So, from the start, we can conclude that it was tough to get around in ancient Greece. People were separated by mountain ranges as well as water. It makes sense, then, that separate communities developed—on the mainland as well as on the islands.

## CITY-STATES

These communities were called city-states, and folks in these separate areas developed their own ways of life, their own beliefs, and their own economies. In addition, there were not a lot of resources to go around. So, that's a recipe for conflict.

The Greeks fought a lot with each other, and they got very good at it. This served them well when the biggest enemy of all came along—the Persians. The Greeks had a way of persisting so that a bad thing (separation, lack of resources) became a good thing (expertise in warfare and at sea).

City-state: A city-state is a single city that serves as the political and social hub for its connected territories. One example you'll read about in this chapter is Sparta, an independent city-state in Ancient Greece.

Peninsula: A peninsula is a landmass that is surrounded on THREE sides by water but is still connected to the mainland. It's almost an island, but not quite! Some peninsulas you might recognize are Italy, Florida, and Baja California.

# TRADERS AND TRAVELERS

Let's look at another way the Greeks ended up making lemonade from lemons, taking advantage of what they had. Unlike Egyptians and Mesopotamians, the Greeks had to endure some pretty crummy farming conditions. The soil was dry and rocky. People did farm, but only olive trees, grapes, and barley grew very well.

## OVERSEAS TRADE DEVELOPS

So, they began to export the things they had lots of (olive oil and wine mainly) and trade them for things they needed (like grains and meat). Being surrounded by water, the Greeks became skilled mariners. They developed robust trade with people both near and far.

**Export:** Exports are goods and commodities that countries or empires are selling and sending to other countries. The opposite, what countries receive, is called an import. So, Greeks would EXport olive oil, for example, and for the countries buying it, olive oil was an IMport.

**Mariners:** Yoho, it's a mariner's life for me! A mariner is a sailor or seaman who can take on any number of responsibilities aboard a ship.

# GREEK TRADE, 500 BCE

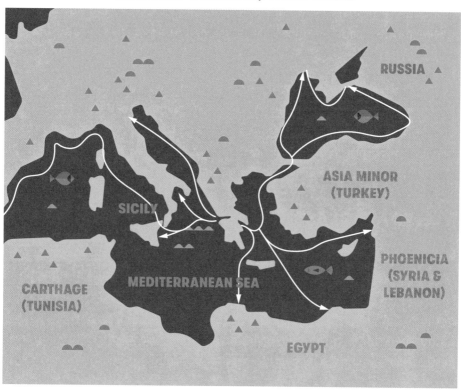

## LOOKING AT ANCIENT MAPS: WHAT'S CHANGED?

Land masses don't change and natural resources don't change. What changes are the political arrangements between people, the names of things, and the lines that are drawn between peoples and territories. On this map right here, nothing has changed about the shape of land and water, but there are a few new names:

| NAME ON THE MAP | IS NOW CALLED. . . |
|---|---|
| Asia Minor | Turkey |
| Carthage | Tunisia |
| Phoenicia | Syria and Lebanon |

Looking at the map of Greek trade routes, you can see that the Greeks ventured as far east and north as present-day Russia. In addition to goods, such extensive trade brought in new knowledge, which led to cultural advancement.

For example, the Phoenicians were expert writers. Their alphabet, with twenty-two letters, each representing a sound, influenced that of the Greeks and led to greater advances in written records and expression. Even our own English alphabet borrows elements from the Phoenicians' alphabet, developed over thirty-five hundred years ago.

## SLAVERY IN CLASSICAL GREECE?

There is one more important resource that war and trade brought to the Greeks: slaves. Slavery was a common and accepted feature of ancient Greek life. In the city of Athens, historians estimate that 30–40 percent of the population was enslaved. In the city-state of Sparta, slaves outnumbered free citizens seven to one. Slavery provided free labor in the fields and the mines, which led to greater productivity and greater wealth.

# THE GOLDEN AGE OF ANCIENT ATHENS

Even though Greece was still not unified, by 500 BCE it was thriving, and Athens was the wealthiest of all the city-states. Around this time, the Persians had amassed a huge empire, stretching from Asia Minor (present-day Turkey) all the way to India.

# THE PERSIAN EMPIRE IN 500 BCE

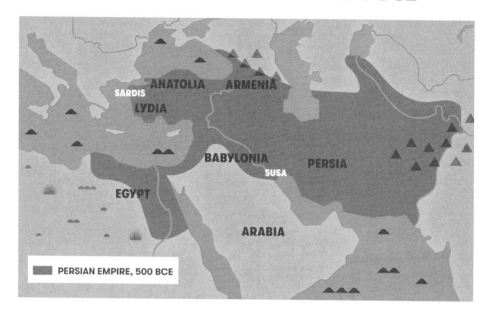

ANATOLIA ARMENIA
SARDIS
LYDIA
BABYLONIA PERSIA
SUSA
EGYPT
ARABIA

PERSIAN EMPIRE, 500 BCE

## GREECE AND PERSIA

The Ionians, who lived on the coast of Asia Minor, detested being ruled by a foreign empire. They tried to rebel, and Athens sent them money in support, but they failed. The Persian king Darius vowed to conquer Athens next, in revenge for their support of the Ionian rebellion.

The Persian army sailed for Greece, landing at a place called Marathon, where an amazing thing took place. The Persians far outnumbered the Athenians, but by some miracle the Athenians emerged victorious.

## THE ORIGINS OF A WORLD-FAMOUS FOOT RACE

According to legend, Themistocles, the Athenian general, knew that the Persians would persist, so the Greeks sent their fastest runner to Athens to tell people about the victory and warn them of a further attack. (Remember, they had no phones or Internet for spreading news!) He ran for 26.2 miles to Athens, delivered the message, and dropped dead. So, when you hear about the Boston Marathon, or the New York City Marathon, the twenty-six mile races people run today, you'll know that marathons started in Ancient Greece. The story is most likely a myth, but it has persisted to this day.

# THE PERSIAN WARS

The Persian Wars continued for about twenty more years, with other city-states joining in the effort to repel the Persians once and for all. Athenians, Spartans, and Ionians fought with all their heart, and won a great sea battle in 480 BCE, even though the Persians had superior ships and a much larger force.

A year later the Greeks won again, this time on land, in Asia Minor. After that, when the Persians and Greeks fought, the Greeks were on the offensive and never on defense. The Persians never again tried to invade Greece.

## HERODOTUS: FATHER OF HISTORY

Much of what we know about the Greco-Persian wars comes from the writings of a highly educated man from Asia Minor called Herodotus. Herodotus lived from about 484 to 430/420 BCE, a century after the Golden Age of Athens. He traveled widely and was a great storyteller. He was the first person in the West to write down detailed historical records, which today's historians agree are mainly accurate.

Let's think about how the Athenians might have felt after those big wins. Pretty thrilled with themselves—and for good reason. They had wealth and confidence, and they knew they were special. Many special things started to happen, and special people came on the scene. Pericles was one of these.

# ATHENS' GOLDEN AGE

Many historians think it was mainly Pericles who brought about the Golden Age of Athens. Pericles wanted a united Greece so that they could continue to win against the Persians. Athens was an important member of a confederation of city-states called the Delian League. Pericles managed to move the treasury for the league from Delos to Athens, which made it easy for the Athenians to dip into those funds for their own projects.

# PERICLES, THE PARTHENON, AND DEMOCRACY

One of these projects was the Parthenon, which cost big bucks. The other city-states didn't like it, but Athens was so powerful there wasn't much they could do about it. Pericles wasn't shy about pushing around the other city-states, but he did NOT want Athenians pushing their fellow Athenians around. He wanted all people (well, all *men*—more on that later) to have a say in government.

To do this, he strengthened the Athenian assembly, where about six thousand men—rich, poor, and in between—met several times a week to debate issues and cast their votes for decisions. Sound familiar? Yup. We learned a lot from the Athenians about government. Their assembly provided a model of democracy for us to follow.

**Confederation:** When several groups, parties, or countries come together, that's a confederation. Usually, some political power is given to a central authority. Throughout history, confederations have served as stepping stones on the way to establishing a national state.

**Democracy:** Democracy is a system of government where a group or a country is governed by its own people. That can be through elected representatives, voting, and more.

Read these two excerpts from primary source documents, and analyze them.

*"Our constitution is called a democracy because power is in the hands not of a minority but of the whole people... what counts is not membership of a particular class, but the ability the man possesses."*

—Pericles, *Funeral Oration*, 430 BCE

*"... that this nation, under God, shall have a new birth of freedom—and that government of the people, by the people, for the people, shall not perish from the earth."*

—Abraham Lincoln, *The Gettysburg Address*, 1863

Both of these quotes are from speeches in praise of soldiers who died in battle. Notice that Lincoln's speech took place more than two thousand years after Pericles's.

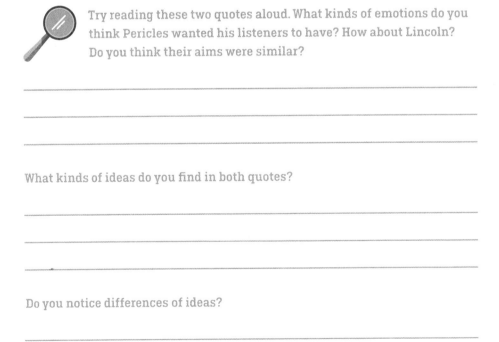 Try reading these two quotes aloud. What kinds of emotions do you think Pericles wanted his listeners to have? How about Lincoln? Do you think their aims were similar?

_____

_____

_____

What kinds of ideas do you find in both quotes?

_____

_____

_____

Do you notice differences of ideas?

_____

_____

## RELIGION IN ANCIENT GREECE

If you noticed that Abraham refers to (one) God, while Pericles in this quote does not, you're on to something. Remember the idea of monotheism, belief in one god, took a while to catch on in the world. So the ancient Greeks were polytheists, believers in many gods, just as the Egyptians and Mesopotamians had been.

*Zeus, the god of sky and thunder, was the ruler of all gods in Greek religion.*

*Hades was the brother of Zeus and the powerful king of the underworld.*

But the Greek gods had only human characteristics—no animal parts. In fact, they were so similar to humans that they fell in love, got angry, jealous, vengeful, and even silly. Greek mythology helped to explain the natural world, as well as what it meant to be human. The gods would interact with regular mortals (people), and some very extraordinary people (heroes), and use their superpowers to either instruct or protect them.

## GREEK PHILOSOPHY

People who think about big questions like "What is the meaning of life? Why are we all here? What is truth?" are called philosophers. Every classical civilization had its own philosophers who taught and wrote about the big questions in life.

*Athena, the goddess of wisdom and warfare, was born from the forehead of Zeus, according to Greek mythology.*

During the Golden Age of Athens, a man named Socrates loved to question people about the things they thought they knew, to the point where they would realize for themselves that they didn't know much at all. Socrates did not claim to have the answers either. And yet, his questioning made powerful people feel threatened.

## SOCRATES MEETS HIS FATE

The Athenians accused him of disrespecting the gods and leading young people in the wrong direction with his ideas. When he went to trial, Socrates was found guilty and sentenced to death. In those days, people were executed with a poisonous drink, made from an herb called hemlock. Socrates defended himself in a speech, but in the end accepted the verdict and drank the hemlock peacefully.

Socrates's ideas live on, even though he never wrote anything down. What we know about his teachings was recorded by his student, Plato. Plato added to Socrates's ideas and passed them on to his student, Aristotle.

# FAMILY TREE OF GREEK PHILOSOPHERS

SOCRATES     PLATO     ARISTOTLE

## SOCRATES

Considered one of the founders of Western philosophy.

*"The unexamined life is not worth living."*

## PLATO

Student of Socrates, founded the Athenian Academy, considered the first university in the Western world. He is famous for writing *The Republic*, in which he describes an ideal and wise society.

*"The society we have described can never grow into a reality... until philosophers become rulers in this world, or until those we now call kings and rulers really and truly become philosophers."*

## ARISTOTLE

Student of Plato, Aristotle came up with ways to organize scientific knowledge, and founded his own school called the Lyceum.

*"We are what we repeatedly do. Excellence, then, is not an act, but a habit."*

# GREEK LITERATURE

Stories and myths in any ancient culture, including the Greek culture, were first passed down through an oral tradition. People would learn the story by heart and retell it through the generations. Actually, the stories were more like poems and people often sang them.

> Oral Tradition: Oral tradition is the collection of history, culture, and mythology passed down by word of mouth, rather than through written documentation.

# HOMER'S EPICS: THE *ILIAD* AND THE *ODYSSEY*

This is definitely true of the two greatest epic poems of ancient Athens, the *Odyssey* and the *Iliad*. They are epic because they are long. An Ionian poet named Homer, living in about the ninth century BCE, about four hundred years before the Golden Age, started to sing longer poems and eventually people wrote them down.

You can learn a good amount about them by reading the Percy Jackson series. But don't miss reading the real stories, too. Actually, you'll probably have to read at least one of them in high school. Both epics tell the story of the struggles, journeys, and victories of warriors.

The *Iliad*, set during the Trojan War, tells of the adventures of the half-human, half-god warrior Achilles and his quest to defeat the Trojan prince, Hector. In the process, various women are fought over and traded around, and the gods make appearances as well.

The *Odyssey* contains even more fantasy. We follow the hero Odysseus through a long journey home from the Trojan Wars. He gets diverted, distracted, tricked by the gods, and nearly killed several times, but finally makes it home to his kingdom of Ithaca and his faithful queen, Penelope.

These two stories actually formed huge parts of the belief systems of western civilization. They influenced thinkers and artists throughout history, including those of the Roman Empire, the Byzantine Empire, and the Italian Renaissance. If you are a Percy Jackson fan, you're in good company.

# GREEK ARCHITECTURE

The ancient Athenians were imaginative architects and builders, but they also followed certain rules that governed the style of a building and how all the parts fit together. You've probably seen how many government buildings today have columns with a wide triangle on top, called a pediment. This style of architecture was invented by the ancient Greeks.

The Greeks built many temples to their gods, the most famous being their temple to the goddess Athena, called the Parthenon. Ruins of the Parthenon, and other temples, remain on the Acropolis, a hill in Athens, where over a million tourists flock to view them every year.

> **Acropolis:** An acropolis was an easily defensible settlement built on a hill in ancient Greece. It might serve as a political or religious center. Although it wasn't the only acropolis of its time, the Acropolis in Athens is one of the most well-known and best preserved.

*The Parthenon was built in the fifth century BCE atop the Acropolis in Classical-era Athens. Yes, it was painted in bright colors!*

# GREEK DRAMA

Every Greek city, not just Athens, held festivals for the god Dionysus, where thousands of people attended dramatic performances and playwrights competed for prizes. The Greeks loved the entertainment, and they also believed that theater was important for mental health.

Aristotle, a Greek philosopher, wrote that when people watched a play full of emotion and meaning, it helped them get their feelings out and process their own life and emotions. He called it catharsis. Famous playwrights (Aeschylus, Sophocles, and Euripides) wrote some pretty heavy stuff (called tragedies), as well as some comedies, about death, families, moral issues, the individual versus society, and relationships with the gods.

## THREE GREAT GREEK PLAYWRIGHTS

| NAME | WHEN DID THEY LIVE? | WHY ARE THEY IMPORTANT? |
|---|---|---|
| AESCHYLUS | 525–456 BCE | Aeschylus wrote almost one hundred plays, and won awards at Greek festivals. Some say Aeschylus invented what we think of today as theater. He was the first to write plays (tragedies) with multiple characters. He also added costumes and dance to performances. |
| SOPHOCLES | 496–406 BCE | Sophocles wanted to show that humans can't control what happens to them, but they can choose to do the right thing. In high school you might read the play *Antigone* about a young woman who insists on giving her brother, considered a traitor, a proper burial, even though the king forbids it. |
| EURIPIDES | 484–406 BCE | Most plays by Euripides (like *Medea*) are intense and sad. Euripides' plays helped people confront the dark, complicated side of human beings and the pain of life. |

# ATHENS, SPARTA, AND THE PELOPONNESIAN WAR

Athenian values spread and influenced other city-states, but Sparta remained a world unto itself. Due to their very different values, and the fact that Greek city-states were always competing, Athens and Sparta became enemies, which led to a twenty-seven-year-long war.

## SPARTA

Located about one hundred miles southeast of Athens, on the Peloponnesus (see sidebar "Pelopo-What?"), the Spartans were literally all about war. Men could only be soldiers, and boys started military training at the age of seven. So, how did anything else get done? Who did the farming, building, and day-to-day commerce? Slaves. When the Spartans (then called Dorians) first came down from the northern mountains, they conquered and enslaved the people living there.

## PELOPO-WHAT??

The Peloponnesus is the area of southern Greece separated from the mainland by water. (Check it out on the map of Ancient Greece on page 72) "Peloponnesus" means "island of the Pelops" in Greek. The Pelops were an ancient people, who had a mythological King Pelops. Look back to the map to find where the Peloponnesus is located.

The Spartan form of government was called an **oligarchy**. They had two kings and then a small group of powerful men who advised the kings and also voted on state decisions. This is yet another way in which Spartan society was so different from Athenian society. Women's lives in the two city-states also show us a contrast in values.

Oligarchy: Oligarchy is the opposite of democracy. It's when just a small group of people have authority over a country or group.

## THE HELOTS

They called the slaves Helots, and these folks kept the farms tended and systems running so that the Spartans could focus only on preparing to win battles. There were huge numbers of Helots, far outnumbering the free citizens. The Spartans lived in fear of a slave revolt, so they valued strict control and harsh discipline. Here is how Plutarch, a Greek historian, described education in Sparta:

*"They learned to read and write for purely practical reasons; but all other forms of education they banned from the country....All their education was directed toward prompt obedience to authority, stout endurance of hardship, and victory or death in battle."*
—Plutarch, *Moralia*

Compare that to this quote about education in Athens:

*"The object of education is to teach us to love what is beautiful."*
—Plato, *The Republic*

# COMPARING THE ROLES OF WOMEN IN ANCIENT GREECE

## SPARTAN WOMEN

Received a public education

Joined in athletic competitions

Required to exercise (so that their bodies were strong for giving birth to many sons who could become warriors)

Could own and manage property

Responsible for home and family

Did not participate in the military

Could not have careers

Were thought to need protection

Stayed in the home, could not go out of the home unless in the company of a male

Errands were done by slaves or children

Not formally educated (some girls in upper classes got instruction at home)

Could not attend the Athenian assembly

Could not vote

## ATHENIAN WOMEN

# THE DEMISE OF ATHENS

A bunch of factors came together to bring about the fall of Athens. For one thing, the problems with the Delian League came back to bite them. The sketchy financial moves made by Athens earned them several enemies among the city-states. Some city-states also didn't want to be democratic and Athens was pushing hard for that.

## FORMATION OF THE PELOPONNESIAN LEAGUE

Anti-Athenian folks sided with Sparta and formed the Peloponnesian League in response to the Delian League. In 431 BCE war broke out and it dragged on for twenty-seven years.

## GEOGRAPHY AND DISEASE PLAY A ROLE

Geography was another problem that couldn't be helped. Sparta was located inland, away from the shore. This meant that Athens couldn't deploy its powerful navy because Sparta couldn't be attacked from the sea. The Spartans were comfortable on land. All they had to do was march north to encroach on Athens.

Finally, disease wiped out about a third of the Athenian population, including Pericles. He had allowed people from outside the city to come inside the city walls when the Spartans were attacking. It got overcrowded and plague spread through the city. The leaders who came after Pericles weren't nearly as effective, and even undermined democracy.

## THE RETURN OF THE PERSIANS

The ultimate blow came when the mighty Persians (remember them?) joined up with the Peloponnesian League and the city of Athens was captured. Athens and its culture held on for some years after, but it never regained the power and influence it had enjoyed during the golden age.

# THE RISE OF ALEXANDER THE GREAT

Mighty warriors from the northern region of Macedonia took over most of southern Greece in 338 BCE. They were led by their king Phillip II, but when Phillip was assassinated, his son Alexander took over as military commander at the age of twenty.

Alexander the Great, as he came to be called, was a military genius and never lost a battle. He ended up conquering most of the Middle East and Asia, establishing an empire that stretched over three thousand miles, all within thirteen years. Alexander had been a student of Aristotle and is believed to have carried the works of Homer with him on his conquests.

# ANCIENT ROME

When you think about Rome, think big. Rome, at the height of its power and glory (117 CE) was the largest city in the world, ruling the largest empire in the world, which extended all the way around the Mediterranean Sea, up into northwestern Europe, over to the Middle East, and down into Egypt.

## THE ROMAN EMPIRE IN THE SECOND CENTURY CE

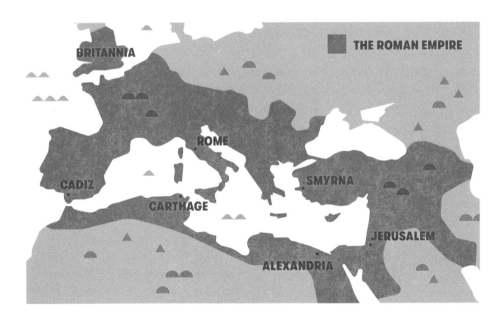

THE ROMAN EMPIRE

BRITANNIA

ROME

CADIZ

CARTHAGE

SMYRNA

JERUSALEM

ALEXANDRIA

## BUILDERS EXTRAORDINAIRE

The Romans built and built and built. They conquered and conquered—and conquered some more. They were superb organizers and expert engineers. Borrowing knowledge from many cultures, they knew how to take an idea and run with it. Above all, they knew how to get things done.

# FROM REPUBLIC TO EMPIRE

It all started with a river, as we've seen is often the case with ancient cities. Rome began as a small city-state on the banks of the Tiber River in Italy. The traditional date of its founding is 753 BCE, right around the time when Homer was writing the *Iliad* and the *Odyssey*. Take a look at the map on the previous page and you'll notice how early Rome was surrounded by various Mediterranean civilizations.

To the immediate north were the Etruscans, the Carthaginians lay to the southwest, and the Greeks were to the south. All of these cultures affected Roman civilization, but none more than the Greeks, as you'll soon see.

## FORMING THE REPUBLIC

Early on, the Romans were ruled by an Etruscan king and they hated him. In 509 BCE they drove him out and set up a republic (a democratic government with elected officials). At first, the Roman senate was composed only of upper-class landowners, called patricians. All the other folks, and there were a lot of them—artisans, farmers, merchants— were known as plebeians and had zero say in government decisions. But they did speak up. In time, the plebeians won the right to elect their own officials, called tribunes. Eventually plebeians could serve as consuls, the high-ranking officials.

> **Patricians:** Patricians are upper-class landowners. Early on in the Roman Republic, much of the ruling power was in the hands of patricians, rather than held by all the other folks, or plebeians.

# CITIZEN ASSEMBLIES DURING THE ROMAN REPUBLIC

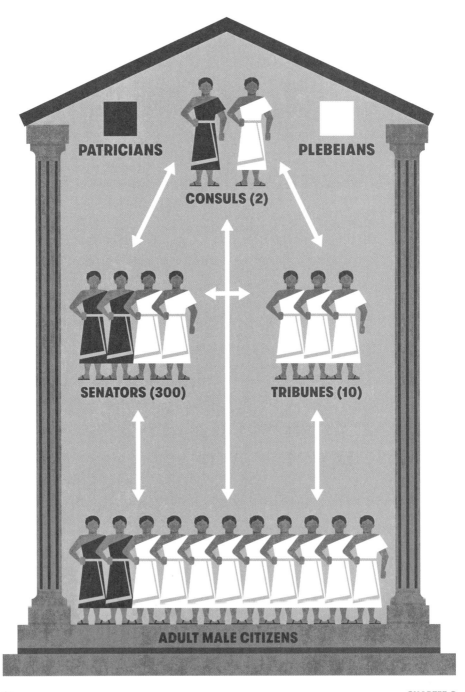

Let's grab onto a big idea here. Why does this evolution of Roman government matter? Be specific, and refer back to page 93! How has it influenced our own government?

_____

_____

_____

_____

## WOMEN IN ROME

Roman women had more freedom than those in ancient Greece. They engaged in public life, and lower-class women worked as farmers, midwives, and artisans. Roman women could attend public events and parties, and socialize at the baths and in the marketplace.

# EXPANSION OF THE REPUBLIC

The Roman army was huge, but highly organized and well trained. Soldiers of the Roman Republic were known to be extremely disciplined and committed. In fact, Rome was the first civilization to pay its soldiers full-time wages. With each territory conquered, more resources, slaves, goods, food, and wealth poured into Rome. But these riches went only to the wealthier class.

# SLAVE LABOR AND WAR WEAKEN THE REPUBLIC

With free labor, the wealthy, slave-owning farmers could produce food more cheaply than common farmers could. The regular farmers couldn't compete, and so they grew poorer and poorer. Civil wars broke out. A series of wars with Carthage in northern Africa (the Punic Wars) dragged on for many decades. Different Roman armies started to compete for power. Things were going from bad to worse, until Julius Caesar came on the scene.

## JULIUS CAESAR

Julius Caesar was a relentless and shrewd warrior. He traveled around for nine years, taking even more territory for Rome and subduing rebellions. He conquered all of Gaul (which we now know as France) and is said to have lost only two battles. Caesar was a hero of the Roman people, but he did have enemies who were either jealous of him or didn't trust his ambitions.

## CIVIL WARS AND THE FALL OF CAESAR

Civil wars erupted again, but once Caesar subdued his main rival, Pompey, the senate made him dictator. Caesar proved to be an effective ruler. He made many reforms for the good of the people but the senators feared he would try to make himself king, overrule the senate, and rule as a tyrant. A group of senators got together and secretly planned to get rid of him. In 44 BCE, Caesar's enemies stabbed him to death as he arrived at the senate.

## THE AGE OF AUGUSTUS

After more chaos and various power struggles, the senate named Caesar's grandnephew, Augustus, as the first Roman Emperor in 27 BCE. And so the Republic came to an end and the Roman Empire began.

## THE PAX ROMANA

Things got much better for the Romans, at least for about 200 years. Under Augustus, life in Rome was peaceful, stable, and prosperous. The time was called the Pax Romana. People enjoyed all kinds of entertainment at public arenas, festivals, and parties of all sorts. They congregated at public baths and in the forum (marketplace). The arts and literature also blossomed. They borrowed ideas from many cultures, but none more than the Greeks. Roman art, philosophy, architecture, literature, and religion all echo the Athenians. The Roman gods and goddesses were pretty much the Greek gods with new names.

**Dictator:** A dictator, at least in ancient Rome, was a chief ruler with absolute power.

**Tyrant:** A tyrant is a powerful, cruel and oppressive leader.

**Emperor:** An emperor is the supreme sovereign ruler. Try to see how many emperors you can identify throughout the chapter!

## ROMAN AND GREEK GODS

| GOD/GODDESSES | GREEK NAME | ROMAN NAME |
|---|---|---|
| King of the gods | Zeus | Jupiter |
| Goddess of marriage | Hera | Juno |
| God of war | Ares | Mars |
| Goddess of love | Aphrodite | Venus |
| God of the sea | Poseidon | Neptune |
| Goddess of wisdom | Athena | Minerva |

# ROMAN ACCOMPLISHMENTS: PUBLIC WORKS GALORE

## ROADS

The Romans built an extensive and advanced system of roads. The roads enabled the military easy passage in and out of Rome, but also made it easier for them to communicate across their vast conquered territories. Any messages had to be delivered on foot or by horseback and smooth (sometimes paved) roads were much easier to travel.

A Roman aqueduct

## AQUEDUCTS

The Romans were not the first to invent aqueducts, but they did them bigger and better than anyone had in the ancient world. Almost five hundred miles of stone bridges, canals, tunnels, and pipes, winding around and outside the city, brought in fresh water from lakes and springs in the mountains.

The aqueducts were so well constructed that they are still standing in many areas of Europe. Rome needed lots of water for drinking, irrigating crops, and supplying hundreds of public fountains. Plus, the Romans loved to take baths.

## BATHS

The Romans built public bathhouses where people would go to relax and socialize. The Greeks had built baths, too, but nothing like the Romans.

By 1 CE, Roman bath centers resembled our own posh health spas, with steam rooms, massage rooms, heating-up rooms, cooling-off rooms, exercise rooms, open-air swimming pools, and beautiful mosaic floors. Not bad for ancient folk. Again, their skill with engineering, and talent for taking things to a new level of excellence allowed Romans to blow bathing out of the water.

Rome is sounding pretty luxurious, right? Here's another take on it from the historian Mary Beard:

> The institution of slavery disrupted any clear idea of what it was to be a human being (neither Greeks nor Romans ever worked out whether slaves were property or people). The filth of the place was, in our terms, shocking. There was hardly any reliable system of refuse collection in ancient Rome, or in any ancient city, and there were revealing stories about stray dogs walking into posh dinner parties clutching in their mouths human body parts they had picked up in the street.

—Mary Beard, *SPQR: A History of Ancient Rome*

Is she talking about the same place?? Yup. Notice how the facts historians include or exclude can paint an entirely different impression of a place. As we've said, there is no single, objective history telling or history reading. The information you get colors your interpretation. Let's return to two of our earlier questions: Whose story is being told?

Whose story is not being told?

# ROMAN SOCIETY GOES DOWNHILL

Around 200 BCE, the Roman civilization began to get shaky. Problems from the days of the Republic still hung around and got worse. For instance, the gap between rich and poor got wider and wider. Some people had grand villas with fountains, gardens, and marble statues, and ate exotic foods and drank wine at lavish banquets, while others had hardly enough to eat.

In addition, the whole culture became hooked on entertainment, and some of it was pretty shocking. People of all types would flock to a

*Usually, the gladiator battles in the Roman Colosseum were fights to the death.*

gigantic stadium called the Colosseum to watch people called gladiators engage in bloody battles, or get ripped apart by wild animals.

Mosaic: Mosaics are pictures made from many smaller colored pieces of glass, marble, or stone.

Gladiator: Gladiators were men who trained to fight against either other gladiators or wild animals. These fights would happen in arenas in front of huge crowds!

## TRUE OR FALSE?

Sometimes so-called factual history is in fact false! For many years people thought that the Romans had special rooms called vomitoriums where they would go to barf after stuffing themselves, so they could eat even more. Not true! It was a misunderstanding, dating back to the 1800s, about an architectural term. Vomitoriums were actually passageways in stadiums and amphitheaters that allowed audience members to "spew forth" easily, to enter or exit quickly.

The ruling class in Rome got more and more selfish. Politicians started to serve themselves instead of the community. They often lied or stole money. They made harsh laws to keep people in line so that they could hold onto their power. They made people pay high taxes to fund the huge government and military. Plus, reliance on slave labor slowed down technology. If someone was doing all the work for free, why invent more efficient ways for it to be done? Farmers started to abandon their fields because the earth was over farmed and they couldn't make a living.

## BREAD AND CIRCUSES

We saw in the earlier Republic stage that the plebeians demanded their rights and the patricians eventually listened. You may be thinking the lower classes and slaves revolted when the wealthy people had unfair amounts of luxury. But that's not how it happened.

The government gave away food to the poor and also provided free entertainment. Many scholars describe this as the government's plan to encourage addiction to entertainment by making it free so that people would stay satisfied, or at least distracted, and not demand deeper change. This kind of tactic came to be known as the "bread and circuses" policy. A poet named Juvenal, who was critical of Romans' lack of responsibility and seriousness, wrote this about the policy:

This quotation from Juvenal is a challenging primary source. You'll need at least three tools. So get ready with your PICKAXE, your MAGNIFYING GLASS, and your BINOCULARS! We'll help a little with new vocabulary, but be sure to read it two or three times. Each time, try to catch Juvenal's attitude toward this policy.

> *"Already long ago, from when we sold our vote to no man, the People have abdicated our duties; for the People who once upon a time handed out military command, high civil office, legions—everything, now restrains itself and anxiously hopes for just two things: bread and circuses."*

—Juvenal, *Satire* 10.77–81, Roman poet

What do you think is the "long ago" time he is talking about?

_____

_____

_____

_____

What in his opinion is the effect of giving away food and keeping people entertained?

_____

_____

_____

_____

Do you think people today are addicted to entertainment?

_____

_____

_____

# WHO WAS THE WORST ROMAN EMPEROR?

There is some debate about this, but Caligula is almost always on the short list. Check out these weird facts about someone who was actually in charge of an empire for, well, four years.

- He loved his horse so much he wanted it to be a part of the Roman senate.

- He liked to dress up like the gods in costumes, and made people call him Jupiter (the king of the gods).

- He hated his real name Gaius and his nickname, Caligula.

- He punished severely anyone who called him Caligula.

- He loved gold so much he liked to wallow in baths of gold coins.

- He had huge pleasure boats built, called Nemi ships, with baths, heating systems, banquet rooms, gardens and statues.

- He spent so much money on entertainment that Rome was almost bankrupt.

# WHY THE ROMAN EMPIRE FELL

| ECONOMIC TROUBLES | POOR LEADERSHIP* |
|---|---|
| The empire overspent on the military. Gap between rich and poor widened. Wealthy people moved to the countryside rather than pay taxes. | Many weak emperors came and went during the decline of Rome. They cared more about their own pleasure than the good of the empire. |
| Labor shortage—the Romans were too dependent on slave labor. When the empire stopped expanding, fewer wars meant fewer prisoners of war to use as slaves. | The empire was not managed well. Poor decisions were made. People lost respect for their leaders. |
| **MILITARY BREAKDOWN** | **FOREIGN INVASIONS** |
| Loyalty to emperors declined—soldiers instead became loyal to different generals. | The Huns (see sidebar "Who Were the Huns," following) invaded northern regions and pushed Germanic tribes into Roman areas. |
| Armies fought in civil wars rather than on behalf of the empire against invaders. | Weakened Roman forces couldn't defend such a huge empire. |

*see previous sidebar "Who Was the Worst Roman Emperor?"

# WHO WERE THE HUNS?

The Huns were fierce nomadic warriors who came from Central Asia and swept through Eastern and Western Europe on horseback. They launched surprise attacks that devastated cities and drove whole tribes of people southward.

The Huns' famous leader, Attila, amassed an empire in only ten years and was feared for his brutal war tactics. Attila claimed that he invaded Gaul to gain a wife (though he had many). Her name was Honoria, and she had sent him a message asking him to save her from an unwanted marriage to a Roman senator.

A Germanic leader named Odoacer captured Rome in 476 AD, overthrew the last Roman emperor, Romulus, and ended the empire.

# ANCIENT CHINA

What do historians consider first when they study the beginnings of civilization?

Geography, you say? Well then, you're starting to think like a historian. Yes, we need to examine the lay of the land first to understand how and why ancient China developed in the way it did.

## THE MIDDLE KINGDOM

The ancient Chinese called their civilization the Middle Kingdom (*Zhongguo* in Mandarin). They assumed they were at the center of things, and in a way they were. They were surrounded by geographical barriers that isolated them for much of their history. Take a look:

## THE MIDDLE KINGDOM OF CHINA

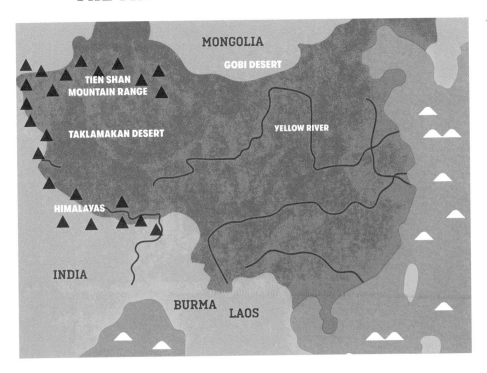

# TALL, TALL MOUNTAINS

Those aren't just regular mountains you see. There are several ranges, and the Himalayas are the highest mountains in the world. Pretty much impossible for ancient people to cross. Then you've got a couple of giant oceans, and the forbidding Gobi desert.

For centuries almost no one got into China, and very few ventured out. It took until 130 BCE for trade routes to be established, which meant the Chinese did not receive new ideas from others until later. They had their own game going though. We'll find a few similarities to other early civilizations and a lot of differences.

# CHINA'S RIVERS

So, where did the Chinese first settle? Are you thinking rivers? Right! The banks of the Yellow and Yangtze rivers provided good conditions for farming. The "Yellow River" got its name from deposits called loess that blew around in barren areas and settled in the river, making it look yellow. The loess is like the silt of the Nile, which collected on the riverbanks and provided good soil for farming.

But the Yellow River behaved differently from the Nile that we learned about in Egypt. When the Yellow River flooded, which was every three or four years, it flooded suddenly and often caused disaster. Crops got destroyed, homes got swept away, people drowned. For this reason, it was nicknamed the "River of Sorrows."

**Loess:** Loess is a sediment that is distinctive for two reasons. First, its color is a unique yellow-gray; and second, loess soils make for some of the most fertile soils in the world!

# CHINESE DYNASTIES

As with the Egyptians, Chinese history is most easily organized into time periods marked by whichever group or family was in power at the time. There were thirteen dynasties in all. We'll look at the first four, which take us from ancient history through the classical period.

| SHANG | ZHOU | QIN | HAN |
|---|---|---|---|
| 1570–1045 BCE | 1045–256 BCE | 221–206 BCE | 206 BCE–220 CE |

## SHANG DYNASTY

The Shang people first held power in that valley of the Yellow River. A social structure developed similar to that of Egypt and other early civilizations. At the top of the hierarchy was a class of royalty, then nobles, warriors, on down to artisans and farmers. Artisans become increasingly skilled at bronze work, ceramics, silk making, and jewelry making from jade and other precious stones. The Shang got very good at making weapons from bronze, rather than stone.

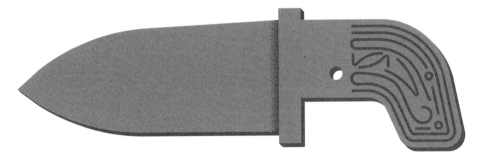

Shang innovation: a dagger with a gun-like handle

## THE LATEST WEAPONRY

The dagger-axe was the first weapon to be used only for battle, and not for other purposes as a tool. It had the blade of a knife, but a handle like a gun. Sometimes dagger-axes were decorated with jewels. Many were found in ancient tombs.

# ZHOU DYNASTY

The Zhou dynasty lasted a very long time. The Zhou people came from the west and overthrew the Shang. They brought with them an idea called the Mandate of Heaven that allowed them to keep power for almost 800 years, and remained important to the Chinese culture into the nineteenth century CE. According to the Mandate of Heaven, rulers were given power by the gods and would retain their authority as long as they were governing well. When they began to fail, heaven would withdraw its support and the reign would end. Natural disasters were a sign that the gods disapproved of the leader.

Feudalism was a governmental and economic system that also allowed the Zhou to stay in power and expand its territories. In a feudal society, a ruler grants land and self-government to landowners who then supervise peasants who work the land.

**Feudalism:** Feudalism is a system of government and economics where the ruler grants land and self-government to landowners, who then owe military service and (probably) taxes to the central government.

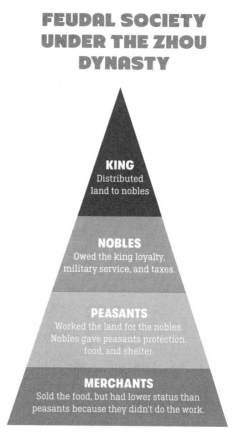

**FEUDAL SOCIETY UNDER THE ZHOU DYNASTY**

**KING**
Distributed land to nobles

**NOBLES**
Owed the king loyalty, military service, and taxes.

**PEASANTS**
Worked the land for the nobles. Nobles gave peasants protection, food, and shelter.

**MERCHANTS**
Sold the food, but had lower status than peasants because they didn't do the work.

The territory of the Zhou expanded hugely under feudalism, which was a good thing, until it wasn't. Just as the Romans found, keeping a huge territory unified wasn't easy. The Zhou's feudal lords began to stray from being loyal and began to fight among themselves. The time following the Zhou dynasty is aptly called the Warring States period.

*A small section of the Great Wall of China*

# QIN DYNASTY

Out of the chaos of Warring States came a time of strict order imposed by a leader named Shi Huangdi. His dynasty lasted only fifteen years, but a lot got done.

Shi Huangdi, considered to be China's first emperor, made huge changes in order to unify and protect China. He:

- abolished feudalism and set up military districts

- gave land to the peasants (but charged them huge taxes)

- repaired roads and canals

- created a common system for weights, measurements, and currency

- built the Great Wall of China by connecting existing walls

# AN OPPRESSIVE RULE

How did so much happen so fast? Sheer, brutal force. Shi Huangdi killed, tortured, or jailed anyone who disagreed with him. He destroyed any kind of writing that was critical of his regime. Soldiers, criminals, and common people were forced to work on the Great Wall in the harshest of conditions.

# LEGALISM

Similar to the way the Zhou had the Mandate of Heaven to help them hold onto power, Shi Huangdi had a philosophy to back him up, too. It was called legalism, and it depended on a certain view of human nature.

> **Legalism:** A system of legalism puts the focus on rules and laws, rather than trusting humans to be naturally moral.

Take out your binoculars and check out these quotes from the *Hanfeizei*, a book named after Han Feizi, considered to be the founder of legalism:

*"... the nature of man is evil. His goodness is acquired."*

*"When the [wise man] rules the state, he does not count on people doing good of themselves, but employs such measures as will keep them from doing any evil."*

Do you agree that people will most likely do wrong and they need to be forced to do right?

_____

_____

_____

_____

_____

Legalism was all about law and order, rules, and punishment—and the punishments were severe. For a serious offense, the accused could have their feet cut off, or their nose, or their head!

Later generations of Chinese came to hate legalism, but aspects of it remained even after Shi Huangdi, especially when the government needed to force people to work on public projects.

## SHI HUANGDI'S SURPRISE LEGACY

Shi Huangdi died in 210 BCE. Almost two thousand years later, in 1974, a farmer who was digging a well discovered Shi Huangdi's tomb. Amazingly, the tomb contained more than eight thousand life-sized statues of warriors, each one unique down to facial features. The clay soldiers stand in formation to this day. Every year, thousands of tourists flock to the first emperor's grave to see them.

*Terra cotta (clay) warriors stand at the ready in Shi Huangdi's tomb more than 2,000 years after the emperor's death.*

## HAN DYNASTY

In 206 BCE, the Chinese government underwent another huge shift, away from legalism and into Confucianism, with new values, new rulers, new expansion, new trade routes, and much progress.

## A GOLDEN AGE UNDER THE EMPEROR WUDI

The famous emperor Wudi brought forth a long period of strength, considered to be one of China's golden ages. Wudi brought back feudalism and set up a strong central government. He wanted his advisers and officials to govern according to the philosophy of Confucius.

He even set up a university at Xian, the capital, to train scholars in Confucian principles, history, music, and poetry, and he required potential government workers to pass exams that tested their knowledge of Confucian thought. The revolutionary part was that anyone (well, any man—women were excluded) could try to prepare for and take the tests. This created opportunities for lower class citizens to reach for prestigious positions. It also kept Confucianism alive in the culture, even after the Han rulers were long gone.

## ABOUT CONFUCIUS

Confucius (551–479 BCE) was China's most influential thinker and statesman. He taught principles for living a good, moral life and creating a moral government. Confucius believed that education could transform society, and called for an educated governing class. He thought respect for one's parents ("filial piety") would ultimately lead to harmony in society. For Confucius, every person had their place in the hierarchy of society. He thought people on the lower levels should be loyal and obedient to those above them, and that those at the top had a duty to set a good example.

Do you think people in our society would agree with Confucius's ideas or oppose them?

_____

_____

_____

_____

_____

_____

_____

_____

What kind of evidence would you give for either side?

_____

_____

_____

_____

_____

_____

Here's a quote from Confucius about learning:

*"He who learns but does not think is lost.*
*He who thinks but does not learn is in great danger."*

What do you think Confucius is talking about? Can you think of ways that people learn without thinking or think without learning?

_____

_____

_____

_____

_____

_____

_____

Why do you think he says that thinking without learning is dangerous?

_____

_____

_____

_____

_____

_____

**PRODUCTS THAT FLOWED FROM WEST TO EAST:**
fruits, glassware, wool carpets, camels, horses, spices

**RELIGIONS OF THE SILK ROAD:**
Buddhism, Zoroastrianism, Christianity, Islam

**From Rome to China:**
**glassware**

**From the Middle East to China:**
**wool carpets, camels**

**From the Mediterranean to China: fruits**

## THE SILK ROAD

Wudi also opened up a network of trade routes that eventually stretched four thousand miles, all the way to the Mediterranean Sea. As the Chinese sent out silk as fast as they could to the West, new ideas, foods, animals, and materials flowed back into China. Historians have named all of these routes the Silk Road, and it changed the world. Take a look at all the things and ideas that were exchanged on the Silk Road.

At the time of the Han dynasty, China was the most technologically advanced civilization in the world. Here are some Han inventions that changed the world forever:

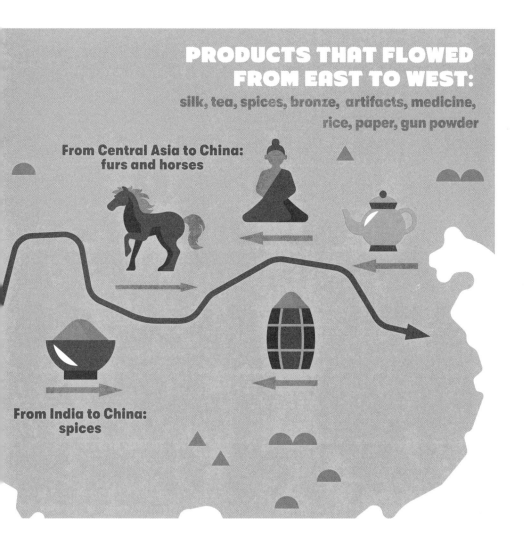

## PRODUCTS THAT FLOWED FROM EAST TO WEST:
silk, tea, spices, bronze, artifacts, medicine, rice, paper, gun powder

**From Central Asia to China:**
**furs and horses**

**From India to China:**
**spices**

- paper
- the wheelbarrow
- the compass
- suspension bridges
- the blast furnace
- stirrups for horseback, saddles
- rudders for steering boats
- acupuncture
- herbal remedies for illnesses

The Han were also great astronomers, and could measure the movement of planets and stars, which helped them make accurate calendars and clocks. In the arts, the Han created advanced architecture, bronze work, and poetry.

# DECLINE OF THE HAN DYNASTY

*"The empire, long divided, must unite; long united, must divide. Thus it has ever been."*

—Luo Guanzhong, *Romance of the Three Kingdoms*

After a few hundred years of success, the Han dynasty began to fail. Looking back on the rise and fall of the Han and many other dynasties, historians noticed a pattern that they've named the Dynastic Cycle.

 Study the diagram closely with your pickaxe and then we'll do some big thinking.

After many years, the new dynasty becomes a corrupt old dynasty

**THE NEW DYNASTY**
- Restores peace and prosperity
- Rebuilds walls, canals, and roads
- Gives land to the peasants

**THE OLD DYNASTY**
- Lets things go
- Doesn't protect the people
- Charges high taxes
- Lives in luxury while the peasants get poorer

**THE CHINESE DYNASTIC CYCLE**

A new dynasty is believed to acquire the Mandate of Heaven

The old dynasty is believed to lose the Mandate of Heaven

**PROBLEMS ARISE**
- Peasant revolts
- Floods
- Earthquakes
- Invasions by enemies

Please don't skip these questions, they're important!

(Remember what Confucius said about learning but not thinking.)

Based on what you've learned about the beliefs of ancient people, why do you think the Mandate of Heaven was so important to the dynastic cycle?

_____

_____

_____

_____

_____

_____

How do the problems of the aging dynasty relate to Confucianism?

_____

_____

_____

_____

_____

_____

How is this cycle similar to the causes of the fall of the Roman Empire?

_____

_____

_____

_____

_____

_____

# ANCIENT AND CLASSICAL INDIA

 When you think about India, what comes to mind? Maybe not much, given that we in the West are far removed from eastern cultures because we're still learning about them. But think hard. Maybe you know someone who practices Hinduism or Buddhism, two of the world religions that originated in India—or maybe you've just heard or read about them. Maybe you know someone who does yoga—that originated in India as well! These are all clues to the culture and history of this vast area.

## THE INDUS VALLEY CIVILIZATION

Early people first settled along the Indus River. On the map (opposite) you can see that it's a long one, running from the Tibetan plateau (where it is fed by melting snow) all the way down to the Arabian Sea. Around 2500 BCE, two cities grew up along its banks, and they were called Harrapa and Mohenjo-Daro. These early cities were remarkably well-planned, with orderly street layouts, public water systems, and stable governments. But get this—Western historians did not even know about the early period of this civilization until about one hundred years ago!

### AN OUTDATED THEORY GIVES WAY

For many years historians thought that civilizations did not take hold in the Indus valley until people called the Aryans migrated across Europe and came down into the Indus River valley around 1250 BCE. But in the 1920s, this theory was proved wrong.

Plateau: A plateau is an area of highly elevated level ground.

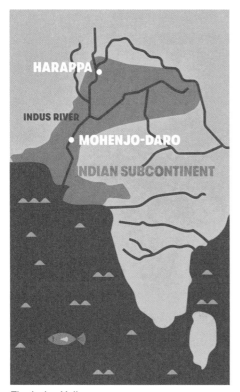

*The Indus Valley*

Archaeologists started to unearth ruins of buildings, household items, weapons, toys, pottery, etc., providing evidence that this civilization had developed at least one thousand years before the Aryans had even arrived. Historians do agree that the Indus valley civilization ended around 1500 BCE, but they don't know exactly why. Some think environmental changes, like deforestation, flooding, or even an earthquake caused people to abandon the area.

## A VAST GEOGRAPHICAL AREA

For convenience, we will call these "Indian" empires, but let's get straight about historical regions versus present-day nations. The area we are referring to as ancient "India" or "the subcontinent of India," is now in fact six countries: India, Pakistan, Bangladesh, Sri Lanka, Nepal, and Bhutan (see map on the following page).

# MODERN-DAY INDIA AND SURROUNDING COUNTRIES

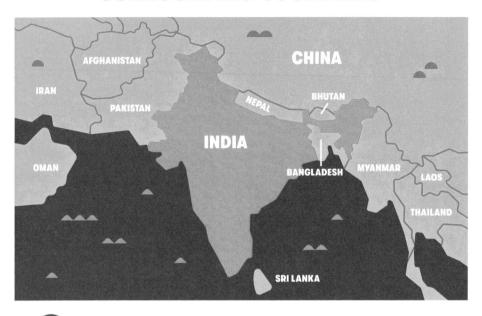

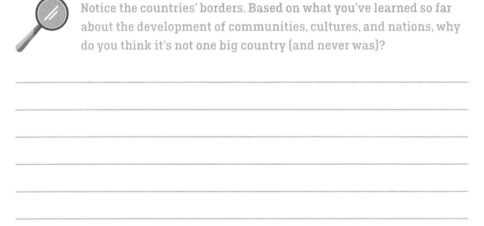

Notice the countries' borders. Based on what you've learned so far about the development of communities, cultures, and nations, why do you think it's not one big country (and never was)?

_____

_____

_____

_____

_____

If you are still thinking along the lines of geography, you're on the right track. We know from our studies of China and Greece that things like deserts and mountains divided people into smaller, usually isolated communities. This happened in the huge Indian subcontinent as well. Many, many languages sprung up and communities developed their own customs and values. In addition, as trade developed, new ideas came through and intermingled with established traditions.

# CLASSICAL INDIAN LITERATURE AND RELIGION

Certain aspects of language, literature, and cultural life, brought down by the Aryans, held strong. Remember the Greek epics of the *Odyssey* and the *Iliad*? Like those epics, the *Mahabharata* and the *Ramayana* of ancient India were passed down orally for thousands of years before being written down.

## THE GREAT EPIC POEMS

Along with prayers, poems, and songs brought by the Aryans, the *Mahabharata* and the *Ramayana* are central to the religion of Hinduism, still practiced by about 80 percent of India's population. If you want to understand every belief of Hinduism (as well as some history) you could read these epics, but it would take you a REALLY long time. With over two hundred thousand lines, the *Mahabharata* is THE LONGEST epic poem ever written!

## THE CASTE SYSTEM

As with many cultures, religion in ancient India ended up shaping the way society was organized. Think back to the social hierarchy we

## IS HINDUISM POLYTHEISTIC OR MONOTHEISTIC?

Hindu rituals involve worship of many deities—for example Shiva, the destroyer, and Vishnu, the Preserver, and thousands of other gods and goddesses. And yet, Hindu texts proclaim that the universe in reality is One or Brahman, which shows itself in many forms. Can you wrap your head around that? Monotheism and polytheism at the same time?? If not, a Hindu guru (or teacher) would say "Good! Your mind can't know Brahman. You can only know the one reality through meditation."

*The Hindu god Shiva*

learned of in ancient Egypt. India's caste system was similar, but much more strict. People could not move among levels. They could not marry people from a different caste.

At the top of the hierarchy were the priests and holy men (yes, usually men); at the very bottom were people thought to be impure, called "untouchables." These hapless folks were excluded from society and given the worst jobs, like cleaning up human waste and clearing away dead animals. However, because the Hindus believe (still) in reincarnation, there was hope. People who fulfilled their duty within their present caste could hope to be born into a higher level for their next life.

The caste system shaped Indian society for thousands of years, and it still influences its culture and economics today.

Caste: In the Indian caste system, a caste was a specific social class that determined what parts of society a person had access to.

Reincarnation: Reincarnation is the belief that a soul can come back to life in a different body or being, even after it dies in one body.

## THE CASTE SYSTEM

**BRAHMINS**
Priestly, academic class

**KSHATRIYAS**
Rulers, administrators, warriors

**VAISHYAS**
Artisans, tradesmen, farmers, merchants

**SHUDRAS**
Manual laborers

**DALITS**
Street cleaners, menial tasks

Do you think our society has layers also?

_____

_____

_____

How about your school?

_____

_____

_____

Or your friend group?

_____

_____

_____

How are these layers similar to and different from the caste system?

_____

_____

_____

Do you think layers of power happen naturally in groups of people or do you think layers are not natural?

_____

_____

_____

# THE FOUNDING AND SPREAD OF BUDDHISM

During the 500s BCE, just as the Roman Republic was getting going, a new religion grew out of Hinduism. Its founder was a prince named Siddhartha Guatama. According to legend, Siddhartha lived inside of luxurious palaces, never seeing pain or suffering or anything sad. But when he grew up and ventured into the real world, he started to see people who were sick, poor, and miserable.

# SIDDHARTHA'S REVELATION

He realized he had to find out why humans had to suffer—and if they had to suffer. So Siddhartha went off to meditate in the forest. After many weeks, Siddhartha realized his true "Buddha" (enlightened) nature. He knew he had risen beyond suffering, and began to teach others what he had learned.

*A depiction of the Buddha, with characteristic hand gestures*

# BUDDHISM: THE FOUR NOBLE TRUTHS

1. Life is full of pain and suffering.

2. Suffering comes from wanting things and not knowing about the ultimate reality.

3. The cure for suffering is to let go of desire and understand one's true nature.

4. It is possible to let go of desire and become enlightened by following the teachings of the Buddha.

Buddhism rejected the caste system, as far as religion and spirit were concerned. It promised any person, at any level of society, the possibility of enlightenment. It also did away with Hindu rituals that Buddhists thought interrupted a direct experience of **nirvana**, or perfect peace.

**Nirvana:** In Buddhism, the central goal is to reach nirvana, which is a state of perfect happiness, free from suffering.

## THE MAURYAN EMPIRE AND THE SPREAD OF BUDDHISM

Buddhism grew slowly in India until the emperor Ashoka took power over much of the Indian subcontinent around 268 BCE and built the Mauryan Empire. Ashoka's strict grandfather, Chandragupta Maurya, had ruled for about fifty years before him. Ashoka started out as a ruthless warrior, leading bloody conquests that killed more than one hundred thousand people.

## ASHOKA'S BUDDHIST CONVERSION

But when he learned about Buddhism he changed his ways. He then sought to spread peace and well-being to his "children" (citizens). He built hospitals, shrines, and better roads. He made Buddhism the state religion, but also tolerated other traditions. Under Ashoka's reign, Buddhism spread throughout the Mauryan Empire, which by then extended over most of what is now the huge country of India. When Ashoka died around 238 BCE, the Mauryan Empire declined and disunity ensued once again.

## THE GUPTA EMPIRE

About 500 years later, just as the Roman Empire was collapsing, the Gupta came to power in India. Scholars consider the Gupta Empire (lasting about 200 years) to be India's golden age. It was a time when farming flourished, artistic expression reached new heights, and learning accelerated. In addition, the people of the empire's many villages were largely self-governing.

## A GOLDEN AGE

The Guptas were inventors, much like the Greeks. They created the Arabic numerals and decimal system that we use today. They also found new ways to treat illnesses with herbal remedies, surgical techniques, and vaccinations.

During Gupta times, people practiced both Hinduism and Buddhism, and other religions as well. Buddhism started to decline, mainly because Hinduism adopted some of its concepts, and Buddha became one of the Hindu gods. Buddhism kept spreading eastward into Asia and southward, down to Sri Lanka and Indonesia.

# SPREAD OF HINDUISM AND BUDDHISM FROM 500 BCE TO 600 CE

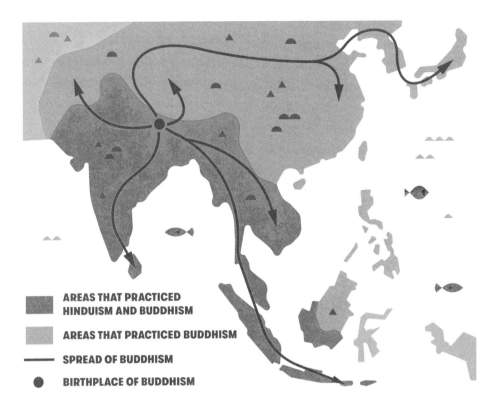

AREAS THAT PRACTICED
HINDUISM AND BUDDHISM

AREAS THAT PRACTICED BUDDHISM

——— SPREAD OF BUDDHISM

● BIRTHPLACE OF BUDDHISM

# CHAPTER VOCABULARY

**Abdicate:** When someone refuses to do their duty, they are abdicating, or giving up, responsibility.

**Acropolis:** An acropolis was an easily defensible settlement built on a hill in ancient Greece. It might serve as a political or religious center. Although it wasn't the only acropolis of its time, the Acropolis in Athens is one of the most well-known and best preserved.

**Caste:** In the Indian caste system, a caste was a specific social class that determined what parts of society a person had access to.

**Catharsis:** A word we get from ancient Greek, "catharsis" means the release of strong emotions.

**City-state:** A city-state is a single city that serves as the political and social hub for its connected territories. One example you read about in this chapter is Sparta, an independent city-state in Ancient Greece.

**Confederation:** When several groups, parties, or countries come together, that's a confederation. Usually, some political power is given to a central authority. Throughout history, confederations have served as stepping stones on the way to establishing a national state.

**Democracy:** Democracy is a system of government where a group or a country is governed by its own people. That can be through elected representatives, voting, and more. As Abraham Lincoln said, democracy is "of the people, by the people, for the people"!

**Dictator:** A dictator, at least in ancient Rome, was a chief ruler with absolute power.

**Empire:** An empire is an extensive territory or set of territories under one imperial control or rule. Throughout history, many empires have risen and fallen.

**Emperor:** An emperor is the supreme sovereign ruler.

**Export:** Exports are goods and commodities that countries or empires are selling and sending to other countries. The opposite, what countries receive, is called an import. So, Greeks would EXport olive oil, for example, and for the countries buying it, olive oil was an IMport.

**Feudalism:** Feudalism is a system of government and economics where the ruler grants land and self-government to landowners, who then owe military service and (probably) taxes to the central government.

**Gladiator:** Gladiators were men who trained to fight against either other gladiators or wild animals. These fights would happen in arenas in front of huge crowds!

**Legalism:** A system of legalism puts the focus on rules and laws, rather than trusting humans to be naturally moral.

**Legions:** In Ancient Rome, legions were units of soldiers.

**Loess:** Loess is a sediment that is distinctive for two reasons. First, its color is a unique yellow-gray; and second, loess soils make for some of the most fertile soils in the world!

**Mariners:** A mariner is a sailor or seaman who can take on any number or responsibilities aboard a ship.

**Mosaic:** Mosaics are pictures made from many smaller colored pieces of glass, marble, or stone.

**Nirvana:** In Buddhism, the central goal is to reach nirvana, which is a state of perfect happiness free from suffering.

**Oligarchy:** Oligarchy is the opposite of democracy. It's when just a small group of people have authority over a country or group.

**Oral Tradition:** Oral tradition is the collection of history, culture, and mythology passed down by word of mouth, rather than through written documentation.

**Patricians:** Patricians are upper-class landowners. Early on in the Roman Republic, much of the ruling power was in the hands of patricians, rather than held by all the other folks, or plebeians.

**Peninsula:** A peninsula is a landmass that is surrounded on THREE sides by water but is still connected to the mainland. It's almost an island, but not quite! Some peninsulas you might recognize are Italy, Florida, and Baja California.

**Plateau:** A plateau is an area of highly elevated level ground.

**Reincarnation:** Reincarnation is the belief that a soul can come back to life in a different body or being, even after it dies in one body.

**Republic:** A republic is a form of democratic government in which people vote for officials to represent them.

**Tragedy:** You might know the word tragedy to mean something very sad, and that's one use! Tragedy can also describe a play that deals with intense or sad events, has an unhappy ending, or whose plot follows a character's downfall.

**Tyrant:** A tyrant is a powerful, cruel, and oppressive leader.

# NOTES

# 3 POST-CLASSICAL HISTORY

The Post-Classical period, roughly 600 to 1450 CE, was a time of huge change in the world. Powerful empires came and went, and people grew more and more connected through trade. But do people only exchange products as they trade? What other kinds of things might get shared? Hint: some of them you can't see or touch.

# THE GROWTH OF CHRISTIANITY

In order to understand the history of Europe, the Age of Exploration (coming soon!), colonization, and important aspects of Western culture, you need to understand Christianity. We will explore here the beginnings of Christianity and how it spread. Going forward in future chapters, we will see the extent of the church's influence over hundreds of years and into our own time.

## ANCIENT JUDEA IN THE FIRST CENTURY CE

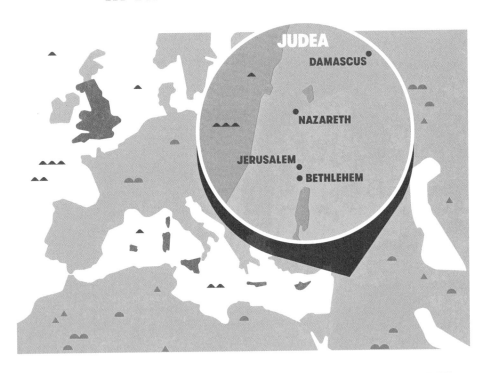

## THE BEGINNING OF CHRISTIANITY

Let's travel back to the beginning of the Roman Empire, during the reign of Augustus.

The Romans had allowed the Jews to keep to their faith as subjects of the Roman Empire, so they lived a fairly peaceful existence during Roman times, mainly gathered in an area then known as Judea, which today we call Israel.

The Jews carried on there, keeping to themselves as they always had, worshipping their one God, and upholding the laws and rituals of their tradition.

## JESUS OF NAZARETH

Jesus, the son of a Jewish carpenter, was born sometime between the years 6 and 4 BCE. Jesus was Jewish in all respects. He was brought up to worship one God and follow Jewish laws, just like his Hebrew ancestors.

At around the age of thirty, he began traveling and preaching. News spread quickly about some big ideas he was introducing, which some people thought were dangerous. Jesus offered people salvation through faith alone. They didn't have to do certain things to know God, they had to believe in the power of love and mercy. He asked people to approach each other with forgiveness.

*ou have heard that it was said, 'Love your neighbor and hate your enemy.' But I tell you, love your enemies and pray for those who persecute you, that you may be children of your Father in heaven.*

—Matthew 5:43-44

Do you think it is a good thing for people to love their enemies? Why do you think Jesus asked people to do something that seems to be the opposite of what people might naturally do?

_____

_____

_____

_____

_____

_____

_____

_____

_____

People who were suffering found great comfort in Jesus's preaching. Many stories from the New Testament of the Bible describe times when he healed sick people with just the miracle of a blessing. Jesus valued and gave dignity to the poor, preaching that "the meek shall inherit the earth." His message and the story of his life have come to be known as the "Gospel," derived from the Old English word godspel [god=good; spel=news or story].

> **Gospel:** The Gospel is generally used as a term to refer to Jesus's message and the story of his life. It's taken from an Old English word, "godspel," meaning good news.

## A CONTROVERSIAL CLAIM

There is one thing Jesus said that got him in a lot of trouble with some powerful people:

"I and the Father are one." People interpreted these words in all kinds of ways. Jesus's followers understood (and still understand) this to mean that Jesus was God, in a human form. They wrote about him as the Son of God.

*or God so loved the world that he gave his one and only Son, that whoever believes in him shall not perish but have eternal life.*

—John 3:16

You can imagine that this did not sit well with many of his fellow Jews, whose religion taught them that God was non-physical, almighty, even unknowable, and thus NOT to be confused with a mortal human being.

## PONTIUS PILATE STEPS IN

Another person who had trouble with this concept was a Roman official by the name of Pontius Pilate. He figured that Jesus's words meant that Jesus was highly ambitious, wanted to be king of the Jews, and would launch a rebellion against the Romans. Also, many followers of Jesus had refused to take part in the custom of scattering incense before images of the emperor, who, by the way, considered himself to be a god as well.

*The Roman Colosseum as it appears today*

## THE BIRTH OF CHRISTIANITY

And so, as the sad story goes, Jesus was sentenced by Pontius Pilate to death by crucifixion. The Romans had many ways of publicly executing people. Sometimes they burned people alive or they unleashed wild animals on them in a stadium called the Colosseum, where many kinds of gruesome events took place.

**Crucifixion:** Crucifixion was a Roman form of punishment where a criminal was nailed to a large wooden cross and left to die.

**Colosseum:** The Colosseum was an enormous amphitheater from Roman times. It was an entertainment venue that featured gladiator battles, animal fights, and even naval battle reenactments. Much of the Colosseum is still intact today!

The very worst form of capital punishment was crucifixion, reserved for the worst of criminals, at least those who were not Roman citizens. Crucified people were nailed through their hands and feet to an elevated, human-sized cross, and left there to slowly die.

The fact that a man who told people "love your enemies" was nailed to a cross brought Jesus even more followers after his death. He and many of his disciples became martyrs (people who suffered pain or death because of their beliefs), which evoked in people feelings of compassion and devotion.

Add to this the resurrection: Jesus is said to have risen from the dead three days after he died on the

The crucifix is an important symbol of the Christian faith. Crucifixes appear in certain churches and in Christian art. You might have seen one on a necklace, too.

cross. News of this miracle traveled swiftly. More people began to believe that Jesus was divine, and that they themselves might have an afterlife if they followed Jesus. As the number of Christians grew, Roman officials grew more and more uneasy because this new faith seemed as powerful as they were—or maybe more powerful.

**Martyr:** A martyr is someone who sacrifices their own life or suffers pain for their belief or their cause.

**Resurrection:** Resurrection generally refers to when a person rises from the dead. In this chapter, you'll be learning specifically about the supposed resurrection of Jesus Christ and the impact it had on history.

## CHRISTIANS ARE PERSECUTED IN THE ROMAN EMPIRE

In 64 CE, a terrible fire destroyed much of Rome. The Emperor Nero blamed the Christians. He ordered them killed by many gruesome methods, while he continued to hold lavish parties.

For a couple hundred years, the Romans killed and tortured the Christians. Sometimes Christians were tattooed on their foreheads so that they could be identified. The Romans did not allow Christians to practice their religion or own certain businesses. They were often made to work in the mines. Christians could only meet and worship together in secret.

*Nero was a famously strange and cruel Roman emperor who constantly feared that someone was trying to kill him.*

Biblical scholars estimate that Jesus began with about twenty followers—including twelve main apostles. Within 300 years of his death, over 3 million people were followers of Jesus. One hundred years later (400 CE), 30 million people identified as Christian, about half of the population of the Roman Empire, stretching from Europe to the Middle East.

Let's pause a moment around this big fact that changed history forever. What are you wondering about? (Remember, no Internet, no airplanes. A camel for transport, if they were lucky.) How did this big change happen?

_____

_____

_____

_____

_____

_____

_____

**Gentile:** A gentile is anyone who isn't Jewish.

**New Testament:** The New Testament is the second part of the Christian Bible, following the Old Testament (creative names, right?). The New Testament includes the teachings of Jesus and his early followers.

**Missionaries:** Missionaries are people sent on religious missions to promote Christianity and convert others. Their job is to spread the Gospel (remember that word?!).

# HOW AND WHY CHRISTIANITY SPREAD

| | |
|---|---|
| People were receptive to Christ's message. It gave them hope and a sense of belonging. | • Anyone was welcome: rich or poor, Jewish or Gentile.<br><br>• With the decline of the Roman Empire, the number of poor people was rising.<br><br>• People were comforted by the belief of a reward in heaven. |
| People were amazed by the stories of miracles performed by Jesus. | • Jesus was said to have done things that no one could explain, including: healing the sick, raising the dead, walking on water, and turning water into wine.<br><br>• Christians believe these miracles took place due to people's faith and Jesus's divinity. |
| Jesus's disciple Paul spread the word. | • Paul had a vision and felt called upon to teach people about the Gospel.<br><br>• He wrote tons of letters, and perhaps half of the books of the New Testament, Christianity's most important sacred text.<br><br>• Roman roads helped Paul and other missionaries travel widely to spread Jesus's teachings. Paul traveled 10,000 miles over the course of thirty years. |
| Emperor Constantine ended all persecution of the Christians in 313 CE. | • Through the influence of his mother Constantine became Christian himself.<br><br>• Emperor Theodosius declared Christianity the official religion of the Roman Empire in 380 CE. |

# THE RISE OF ISLAM

About 600 years after Jesus was preaching in Galilee and Judea, a new religious leader came on the scene in Arabia (now known as Saudi Arabia). This man's name was Muhammad, and he founded a religion called Islam that is today practiced by about one-fourth of the world's population. It is remarkable how quickly Islam flourished in the Middle East and beyond. We'll see how it began quietly, but later spread widely by missionaries, and through battle and conquest.

## PRINCIPLES AND PRACTICES OF ISLAM

It is interesting that the word Islam means "surrender" in Arabic. The surrender called for in Islam is not a surrender to people or ideas. It is a surrender to the one and only God, or Allah. Like Judaism and Christianity, Islam proclaims the oneness of God with no compromise. Consider this quote from Islam's holy text, the Quran:

> "Allah. There is no god but He, the Living, the Self-subsisting, Eternal. No slumber can seize Him nor sleep. His are all things in the heavens and on earth."

—Surah Al-Baqara, 2-255

When you read these quotes, can you feel what Muslims, the followers of Islam, might feel about Allah? What words come to mind?

_____

_____

_____

_____

_____

For Muslims, the Quran is the holiest of holy books. They believe it was revealed directly to Muhammad; and, like all religious texts, it was passed down through an oral tradition for many years before being written down.

> **Quran:** The Quran is the Islamic sacred book, and it is believed to be the word of God as spoken to Muhammad.

## BUILDING ON EARLIER TRADITIONS

Muslims see their religion as linked to the traditions of Judaism and Christianity. They acknowledge Abraham, Moses, King David, and Jesus all as messengers of God, with Muhammad being the last in the line of prophets. However, Muslims do not consider Muhammad to be divine.

In fact, Muhammad is rarely represented in any Islamic art. Islamic art is typically formed of geometric or floral patterns. If you visit a mosque (an Islamic house of worship) you can find beautiful calligraphy, wood carvings, architectural designs, ornamental carpets and tile mosaics—but no idols or human representations.

## THE STORY OF MUHAMMAD

Muhammad was born around 570 CE in the bustling city of Mecca. He belonged to a powerful family, but his life was not easy. Muhammad was adopted by his uncle, who brought him on trade excursions where Muhammad was exposed to many cultures and belief systems.

Muhammad became a successful merchant himself, and was well liked and trusted by those who met him. He was curious about people's faiths and enjoyed talking with Christians, Jews, and others about their beliefs and practices.

## FIVE PILLARS OF ISLAM

- Faith. Above all, Muslims have faith in their one God, whom they call Allah.

- Prayer. Muslims pray facing Mecca five times a day.

- Charity. Muslim typically give 2.5% of their wealth to the needy.

- Fasting. Muslims fast from sunrise to sunset during the month of Ramadan.

- Pilgrimage. At least once in their lives, Muslims travel to Mecca to visit the place where they believe Allah revealed his teaching to Muhammad. This is called the *hajj*.

When he was twenty-five, Muhammad won the favor of a wealthy widow named Khadija, fifteen years older than he was. She proposed to him and he accepted. Khadija was the first to believe in Muhammad as a prophet and she became the love of his life. During Muhammad's time, the area of Arabia was not unified. Some people were settled but many were nomadic Bedouins who formed tribes and fought among themselves.

Being people of the desert, they often fought over water. They made their own laws, often based on revenge and protection of their own, which also gave rise to lots of conflict. Most people worshipped many gods, and merchants made a living from selling figurines of idols in cities where commerce thrived.

Bedouins: The Bedouins are a nomadic and tribal people. Muhammad encountered many Bedouins in Arabia during his time, but there are still many Bedouins living today in the Middle East.

Idol: An idol is a figurine or image meant to represent a god.

*To this day, the Kabaa is considered by Muslims to be the holiest place on Earth.*

## MUHAMMAD'S HOME CITY, MECCA

The largest of these cities was Mecca, Muhammad's hometown, where a very important building called the Kabaa housed a stone that was said to have been placed there by Abraham. During the early days of Muhammad's life, however, the Kabaa was a place of business, and it was controlled by Muhammad's own tribe, the Quraysh.

According to Islamic tradition, Muhammad received the word of God when he was about forty years old while meditating in a cave. He was confused and disturbed by these messages, so he didn't share them with very many people.

When he did begin to preach about the oneness of Allah, guess who did not like it one bit? You got it—the merchants. And the most powerful merchants were his own people. They knew their businesses would fail if people listened to Muhammad. Why would people buy idols if they believed in one god, a god they couldn't see? The Meccan merchants wanted Muhammad and his followers dead. So, the Muslims fled to a neighboring town called Medina where Muhammad developed a community of followers and became both a religious and political leader.

A Bedouin caravan

## MUHAMMAD RETURNS TO MECCA

In 630, Muhammad returned to Mecca with 10,000 of his followers. He could have destroyed the place and everyone in it, but he peacefully took over the city, and booted out the idol merchants. He made Mecca the religious center of Islam, and it remains as the center today.

Muhammad worked to unite the various tribes under Islam. After his death, disputes arose over who should succeed him, which led to a split into two factions of Islam: Sunni and Shi'ite. After some rocky times, the Muslims managed to hold it together, but the split in Islam still exists today.

## MUSLIM CONQUESTS

Then the hugely successful conquests began. The Quran tells of miraculous victories, even when the Muslims were far outnumbered. Muslim armies, led first by Muhammad and later by other leaders called caliphs, pushed forward and acquired enormous amounts of territory. Amazingly, all this happened within about a hundred years.

 Let's pause here and think about how and why a religion (and a government, too) could catch on so fast. Pull on your prior knowledge boots. We've read about dynasties rising and falling in ancient China. We've seen how the Romans took over, and how the Greeks finally fell. Some of those patterns repeat themselves with the rise of Islam, along with some new factors.

What are some of the factors that these religions and governments have in common? Let's take a look at some big ideas we can name about the rise and fall of empires.

# REVIEW: SOME BIG REASONS
# WHY EMPIRES RISE AND FALL

| | |
|---|---|
| A lack of unity can pave the way for unity. | People want to be secure, so they unite around a strong power when the current government starts to crumble. The Muslims were able to unify areas where the Byzantine Empire was weak, or where tribes of people were warring. |
| People follow powerful leaders and tend to trust those who rule with tolerance. | Muhammad, like Pericles (or Julius Caesar, or Jesus, or Buddha), attracted people through his example and the power of his personal message. Although the Muslims conquered many cultures, they allowed them to hold to their own religions and ways of life. (This was also true of the Romans.) |
| People respond to ideas that give them hope or power. | Islam does not have a priestly class or a hierarchy of power. It is accessible to anyone regardless of their wealth, social status, race, or gender. This meant that all people could embrace it directly, and they did. (Remember how Jesus's message appealed to the poor?) |
| Conflict uses up energy and resources, making an area ripe for a takeover. | The Byzantine and Persian armies were embroiled in conflicts so the Muslims were able to sweep in and defeat them both. (Remember how the Romans became vulnerable to invasion because the empire got so large? They were defending far-reaching borders and could not fend off the northern invaders.) |
| Unshakable commitment brings strength, extraordinary courage, and sacrifice. | Remember how the Greeks fought off the Persians because they were fighting for their beloved culture? The Muslims believed in Allah above all, and their tradition proclaimed that it was glorious to die in battle. They went into battle with full-on commitment and passion. |

# THE BYZANTINE EMPIRE

Remember how we said the Roman Empire fell in 476 CE? Well, actually it didn't—at least not all of it. As you recall, the Roman Empire got so huge that the rulers had trouble managing it and defending it. So in 286 CE, Emperor Diocletian divided the empire into east and west. And then in 330, Emperor Constantine moved the capital of the eastern part way east—to a city called Byzantium that had been fought over by the Greeks and Persians for centuries.

## THE ROMAN EMPIRE, AROUND 400 CE

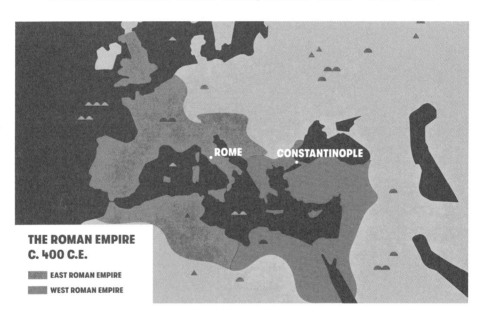

THE ROMAN EMPIRE
C. 400 C.E.

■ EAST ROMAN EMPIRE
■ WEST ROMAN EMPIRE

## A CITY NAMED CONSTANTINOPLE

This move by Constantine was pure genius. Not only was the city of Byzantium a crossroads of trade, it was also surrounded by water on three sides (a peninsula). Later, the Byzantines built a mighty wall to seal off the rest of the city, so the place was virtually unconquerable.

# BYZANTIUM IS RENAMED

Constantine renamed the city after himself (as emperors will do), and over the next hundred years or so Constantinople became more and more prosperous while Rome declined. Even after the western areas of the Roman Empire were taken over by Germanic tribes, the eastern parts flourished for about one thousand years. Yes, one thousand years! That's longer than any other European empire.

Today Constantinople is called Istanbul, and it is in modern-day Turkey. It is still a thriving city. The Byzantines didn't think of themselves as part of a new or separate empire. Historians only decided to call them that many years later. The Byzantines considered themselves to be Romans. And yet, they spoke Greek! So, Byzantine culture became a melting pot of Greek, Roman, Persian, Christian, and other influences. Christianity was extremely important in Byzantine life and art.

In fact, Christianity was declared the state religion and became firmly established during the reigns of the ninety-four emperors who ruled during the empire's long history. The spread of Christianity into Eastern Europe and Russia is largely due to the influence of the Byzantines.

# ARGUMENTS OVER ART

One type of Christian art started to cause trouble. Monks had begun to create paintings of Jesus and other saints to inspire people to connect personally to these religious figures. Their paintings, called icons (from the Greek word *eikon*, meaning "image"), often showed Jesus or Mary or a saint looking straight ahead with a golden halo behind their heads.

Some people would pray to these images. But officials in the church (including the Pope in Rome) wanted this to stop. They felt everyone should strictly abide by God's instruction to Moses not to pray to "graven images" but only one, invisible God. (Remember?) Others thought the art helped people to experience faith and wonder.

A Byzantine icon of the Virgin Mary holding the baby Jesus

This dispute went on for some 350 years. Lots of artwork was destroyed; actual battles broke out. Then finally, in 1054, as the Byzantine Empire was beginning to fall, the Christian church divided into two groups: Eastern (Greek) Orthodox and Roman Catholic. This was the first division of the Christian church.

| ICONOPHILES "We love icons!" (some monks, artists, and common folk) | ICONOCLASTS "Icons must GO!" (led by Emperor Leo III) |
| --- | --- |
| Praying to icons of Jesus and the saints make us feel closer to them. | The Old Testament says we are not allowed to pray to a "graven image." |
| Jesus was a real person and should be shown as a person. | Worshipping a picture is like worshipping an idol. |
| Making beautiful portraits of Jesus, and other saints, is a way to glorify them. | Jesus was God and you can't make a picture of God. By emphasizing his body you are taking away his spiritual (unseen) nature. |

"Phil" means love (from Greek).

Today an iconoclast is a person who goes against tradition.

# A BYZANTINE GOLDEN AGE

Like the other empires we've studied, the Byzantines had their own golden age with many accomplishments, and it took place mainly during the time of the emperor Justinian, from 527 to 565 CE. Justinian himself is famous for having "codified" Roman law, meaning he organized it and made it clearer. Justinian's legal ideas made their way into Western Europe and had a lasting impact on both European and international law. He also had over thirty churches constructed, the most magnificent being the Hagia Sophia, which you can go and visit.

*Built as a church by the emperor Justinian, the Hagia Sophia was converted into a mosque after the Ottoman conquest of Byzantium in 1453.*

*"The church is singularly full of light and sunshine; you would declare that the place is not lighted by the sun from without, but that the rays are produced within itself, such an abundance of light is poured into this church..."*

—Procopius (c. 500–c. after 565), a Byzantine scholar, on the Hagia Sophia

Theodora, the daughter of a bear trainer for the circus, came from a common family. She rose up through the social ranks and eventually met Justinian in 533. At that time, royal persons were not allowed to marry common people, so Justinian changed the law and married her.

## JUSTINIAN AND THEODORA

Emperor Justinian did not always have an easy time. Luckily, he had a very intelligent and confident wife. As we know, it was extremely rare for a woman to have power during this time, but Theodora ruled with Justinian as an equal.

## A POWERFUL EMPRESS

As empress, Theodora sponsored her own projects, made decisions with Justinian, and fought for the rights of women and oppressed religious groups. When Justinian faced a violent rebellion, Justinian and his advisers thought of escaping. But Theodora insisted they stay and crush the rebellion, even if they ended up dying. In a famous speech, she said, ". . . for one who has been an emperor it is unendurable to be a fugitive."

Let's look at the situation from Theodora's point of view. She's saying that a person who has been an emperor just can't take being a fugitive (a person on the run). Why do you think she sees it this way? What do you think it would feel like to be a "fugitive" after being a king or queen?

_____

_____

_____

_____

_____

_____

_____

_____

_____

_____

Justinian and Theodora stayed, the rebellion was stopped, and they retained their power. In this way, Theodora, the daughter of an animal trainer, changed history.

# EARLY AFRICAN CIVILIZATIONS

So, now we turn our full attention to the continent of Africa. Africa is enormous. It's the second-largest continent in the world! When you approach a new subject, your brain has to get ready. That's the way our brains work—new knowledge hooks onto knowledge already in our brains.

So, let's start with the shape of Africa. If you've ever looked at a world map, this shape might be familiar. Africa presently contains fifty-four countries. OK, that's overwhelming—not good for the brain (another scientific fact). So, another way to make learning easier is to break things up. Let's break apart Africa into four pieces using the good old compass, which tells us what is north, south, east, and west.

## ANCIENT AFRICAN CULTURES

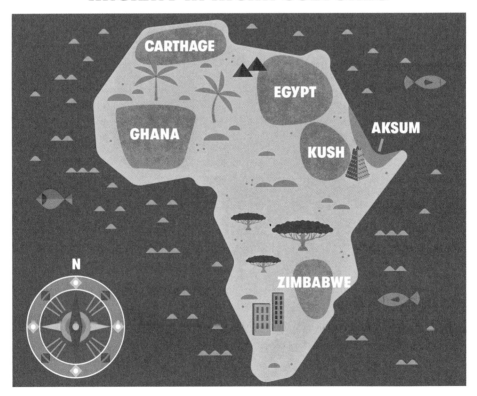

## WHY HAS THE HISTORY OF AFRICA BEEN OVERLOOKED?

Even back in ancient times, Europeans have dominated the writing of history. European writers valued the European explorers and colonizers above the indigenous cultures of Africa. African civilizations had rich oral traditions for remembering their history, but few Europeans could speak these languages or understand the history that had been handed down, and most just didn't value it. Over the last fifty or so years, historians have begun to uncover the truth about the accomplishments of African civilizations.

# NORTH AFRICA

We looked at Egypt, the best-known African civilization, in Chapter 1. Egypt seems to get all the attention for Africa in textbooks, but there were many other great civilizations that people are often surprised to learn about. When ancient Egypt was starting to wind down, the other big power up north was Carthage (814 BCE to 146 BCE).

## CARTHAGE

Poised on a point jutting out into the Mediterranean Sea, Carthage controlled most of the African land surrounding the western Mediterranean, as well as the region we now call Spain, and the islands of Sicily and Sardinia.

Carthage had a strong navy and wealth from hundreds of years of successful trading. It was a force to be reckoned with, even for the Romans. Three wars with Rome, called the Punic Wars, dragged on for decades because the Romans wanted to own Carthage and its turf badly. One of the greatest war stories of all time stars a fierce Carthaginian general named Hannibal.

# HANNIBAL, A CARTHAGINIAN GENERAL

Hannibal was so determined to defeat Rome that he took the battle to Rome itself. First, he had to get his troops across two huge mountain ranges, the Pyrenees and the Alps. The Romans never suspected anyone would try such a thing. But off Hannibal went, on a 1,000-mile journey, with ninety-thousand soldiers, twelve-thousand men on horseback, and thirty-seven elephants.

Only about half of the men made it across the Alps (and less than half of the elephants), but Hannibal and his army, still relentless, hung around Italy for another fifteen years. They fought and fought until the Romans gradually wore them down. In 203 BCE Hannibal retreated back to Carthage. In 146 BCE Rome launched its final attack and destroyed Carthage once and for all.

## HANNIBAL'S MARCH: FROM CARTHAGE ACROSS THE PYRENEES AND THE ALPS

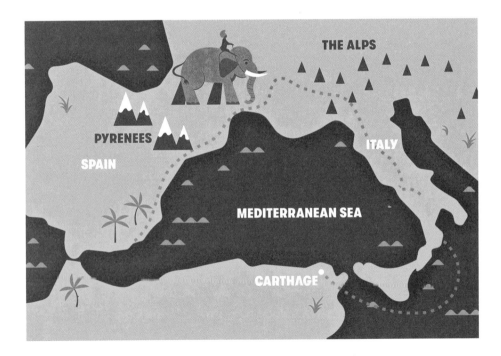

# EAST AFRICA

Before we dig into details about the grand Kingdom of Aksum, let's see what the Greek historian Herodotus (see p. 78) had to say about it. While you read, see if you can imagine what he saw.

> *"There gold is obtained in great plenty, huge elephants abound, with wild trees of all sorts, and ebony; and the men are taller, handsomer, and longer lived than anywhere else. The Ethiopians were clothed in the skins of leopards and lions, and had long bows made of the stem of the palm-leaf, not less than four cubits in length."*

— *The Histories*, Book III, c. 430 BCE

Now read it again (yes, do it! Rereading is a must for analyzing primary sources). Maybe read it out loud. What kind of feeling do you get from his words?

_____

_____

_____

_____

_____

_____

_____

_____

At its height (200–500 CE), the Kingdom of Aksum was a wondrous place, and it stands to reason that it would be. Aksum was located at the base of the Red Sea and served as a gateway for the huge amounts of trade going on between Europe and Asia. Today, we know this area as the countries of Ethiopia and Eritrea.

# AN ADVANCED EMPIRE

Many people don't know this, but Aksum was just as important and developed as other empires of the time. The people of Aksum created their own alphabet and money system. The powerful King Ezana, ruling from 303 to 350 CE, conquered many kingdoms along the Red Sea, including the rival kingdom of Kush.

Like the emperor Constantine in Rome, Ezana converted to Christianity and made it the official religion of his empire. Today about 60 percent of Ethiopians still identify as Christian. Aksum is known for its tall granite towers (called stelae) that look like large pencils pointing up from the earth to mark the tombs of King Ezana and others. Ezana's stela is 79 feet tall and carved with false doors at the bottom and windows going all the way up.

*The stela of King Ezana*

**Stelae:** Stelae are stone slabs that served as monuments. They might have inscriptions or images carved into them, and they have often been erected at tombs as grave stones.

People of all cultures and products from all over the world passed through Aksum. And many of the most precious products came from the African continent itself. Today we might not think these materials are valuable, or even know what they are. Here's a partial list of the riches Africa offered the world:

# RICHES OF AFRICA

| WHAT IS IT? | WHERE DID IT COME FROM? | WHY DID PEOPLE WANT IT? |
|---|---|---|
| **GOLD** | West Africa—Ghana and later Mali | To make jewelry, luxury goods, coins, clothing decoration, illuminated artwork, and calligraphy; does not tarnish or decay. |
| **SALT** | Northwestern Sahara Desert | Preserve meat, season food |
| **IVORY**—elephant and sometimes hippo tusks | Elephants—mainly in the north | Soft, so artisans could carve it into small statues and use it to decorate jewelry, knife handles, furniture; symbol of wealth |
| **EBONY**—rare and expensive black wood from certain evergreen trees | West Africa | Rare, hard wood, very durable, used to decorate same items as ivory |
| **FRANKINCENSE**—dried sap from Boswellia trees | Eastern Africa (horn) | Used for incense in religious ceremonies and for healing—was as valuable as gold |

# WEST AFRICA

The swap of gold for salt kept people traveling the Sahara Desert, from northern regions where salt abounded, down to the gold centers in the west, and back again.

## GHANA

One of the first civilizations to take hold in West Africa was Ghana (different from present-day Ghana, which is south of the Sahara). This community, located where the Niger and Senegal rivers meet, grew rich from the gold trade and attracted many Muslim merchants who made their homes there.

In 1050, Muslims from the north came down, wanting to spread their own version of Islam, and Ghana became governed by them. But the northerners could not sustain control over such a distance, so about 200 years later Ghana was taken over by the neighboring empire of Mali.

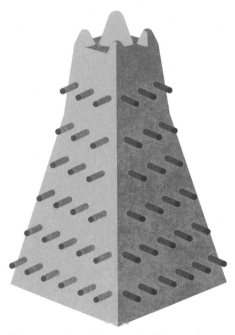

The tower of the Djinguereber Mosque in Timbuktu, Mali, built in 1327 as a spiritual and learning center. The mosque is still in operation today.

## MALI

Mali got richer and richer, and so did its kings (or Mansas). Mansa Musa, ruling from 1312 to 1337, is thought to be the richest person who ever lived! After becoming a Muslim, Mansa Musa set out on a *hajj*, which you remember is a pilgrimage to the holy city of Mecca required of all Muslims who are able to do it.

Even though the journey to Mecca was 4,800 miles, Mansa Musa did it, and he became world famous for it! He brought with him thousands of camels and people, and enough gold to give lots of it away.

## TIMBUKTU BECOMES A WORLD CITY

When people in Muslim cities saw the riches of Mansa Musa and his devotion to Islam, they wanted to go to Mali. Upon Mansa Musa's return to Mali, the city of Timbuktu grew to become a major center of learning, art, and architecture for the Muslim world.

# SOUTH AFRICA

Southern Africa also had wealthy trading centers. The city of Great Zimbabwe, within the Kingdom of Zimbabwe, controlled the trade of gold, ivory, copper, and cattle in the area. Zimbabwe, in Bantu (the ancient language of the region), means "big stone houses."

*The stone walls of Great Zimbabwe (called the "Great Enclosure," were constructed without the use of mud or mortar to hold them together.*

Great Zimbabwe is famous for the beautifully smooth stone walls and buildings that were constructed so skillfully that mud or cement was not needed to hold them together. Some of the granite walls were over 36 feet high. This was a great accomplishment for builders in the twelfth century.

However, European explorers who visited in the 1800s looked down on native African people and did not think it was even possible that the Bantu people could build such amazing structures.

They thought that Portuguese travelers built them, or maybe the Chinese or the Persians. These were prejudiced theories, not facts. In 1905, a British archaeologist, David Randall-MacIver, found evidence that proved that Great Zimbabwe was indeed constructed by the Bantu people.

What lessons does Great Zimbabwe teach us about the telling of history, the power of prejudice, and the importance of evidence? What if Randall-MacIver had not made these discoveries?

# IMPERIAL CHINA AND ITS DYNASTIES

*"The empire, long divided, must unite; long united, must divide. Thus it has ever been."*

—Luo Guanzhong, *Romance of the Three Kingdoms*

This simple quote, from a Chinese historian writing during the 1300s, describes the pattern of China's very long history. Over a couple thousand years, ruling families gained power for long periods of time, but eventually gave way to a new ruling family, or dynasty.

We left off in Chapter 2 as the Han dynasty was coming to a close.

As you recall, the Han had stabilized China. It was a time of wealth, growth, and advancement. But eventually the Han did fall, and from there a period of disunity followed for about 400 years. A new series of dynasties took hold again around 600 CE.

Let's zero in on the Tang and Song dynasties, two high points of progress and cultural achievement.

## THE TANG DYNASTY, 618–907

The Tang dynasty was a great time to be alive in China. The Tang ruled a huge territory, the arts were flourishing, and China was trading with countries all over the world. Thousands of people from foreign lands lived right inside of Chinese cities and brought with them ideas, goods, and new delights.

The religions of Christianity and Buddhism made their way into China and got established right alongside China's traditional religions of Confucianism and Taoism. No one minded. They intermingled ideas, and got along fine.

The Tang government was strong and stable, founded on ideas from the Han dynasty. As we've seen, when people are fed and live in peace, new ideas and advancements result. The Tang people could turn their attention to living well, not just surviving. Knowledge expanded, and a number of extremely important inventions came to be.

The Empress Wu declared herself to be empress in 690, but had already been in power for several decades. Has she been judged unfairly because she was a woman?

## THE INVENTION OF GUNPOWDER

Gunpowder was invented, first just for fun (fireworks), but then for use in weapons. This changed the nature of war in the whole world forever. The Chinese also invented block printing, which meant more books could be printed more easily. More books increased literacy and education, giving more people a chance at passing the exams that led to better jobs (again, a Han idea).

## EMPRESS WU

During the Tang dynasty, China was ruled by the first and only female monarch in its three thousand year history. Her name was Wu Zetian, or Empress Wu, and she came to power in 690, after the death of her husband, Emperor Gaozong. Empress Wu was extremely important to the success of the Tang dynasty, but she has often been portrayed as cruel and oppressive.

Empress Wu had plenty of enemies, partly because followers of Confucianism (basically the state religion) thought it was a very bad idea for women to be leaders. Many historians don't believe everything written about Empress Wu because so much of it was written by her critics. Some people also argue that Empress Wu should not be judged harshly because male emperors of the time did the very same things that she did to retain power.

## EMPRESS WU: HEROINE OR VILLAIN?

| HEROINE | VILLAIN |
| --- | --- |
| Strengthened the central government | Maintained a secret police force that informed her of any threats |
| Extended Chinese empire into Central Asia | Ordered people (even family members) killed and tortured if she found out they were not loyal |
| Gave land to the peasants | |
| Built canals and roads | |
| Raised the status of women (which was pretty low in Chinese culture) by having biographies of notable women published | |

Was Empress Wu a hero(ine) or a villain? Do you think historians of her time told the truth? How can we figure out whether a source of information is reliable?

_____

_____

_____

_____

_____

_____

## AMAZING ART

The artistic achievements of the Tang dynasty were stunning, and grew
only more stunning during the Song dynasty as artists continued to refine
their techniques.

Toward the end of the Tang dynasty, when life got harder, people wanted to retreat into nature for peace and comfort. Buddhist ideas were seeping into the culture, which put a higher value on the serenity of spirit than on worldly affairs. So artists started to create landscape paintings that portrayed the tranquility of nature, often of a mountain and water scene, usually with no people present at all. In the Song dynasty, about fifty years later, landscape paintings became even more spiritual, showing distant shadowy mountains, painted with misty, muted colors.

## MORE THAN JUST PAINTING

Tang artists also invented porcelain, a very beautiful and durable kind of pottery. The fine china used today (that's why it's called china!) is still made from methods developed over a thousand years ago. Tang porcelain was often used to make colorful figurines (small statues) for tombs.

In the Song dynasty, as with the landscapes, artists used more muted colors and the shapes became smoother and simpler. Artisans discovered new ways to make porcelain vessels and easier ways to produce them. Soon, Chinese porcelain was being exported throughout the world as a luxury item.

## SOCIAL CLASSES

You might be wondering, did everyone in Tang and Song China enjoy these beautiful things? Sadly, no. Imperial China had a similar social structure to other civilizations we have studied, with royalty, scholars, and governmental officials at the top, and laborers, farmers, artisans, and slaves at the bottom. It was not impossible to move among levels, but it was difficult.

During the Song dynasty, people basically split into three levels: the gentry (folks from families with land, money, and influence) at the top, the peasants in the middle (poorer folks who lived off the land, had few luxuries, and wanted to be gentry), and the merchants (people who sold goods, bred animals, or loaned money) at the bottom.

# SOCIAL HIERARCHY IN THE TANG AND SONG DYNASTIES

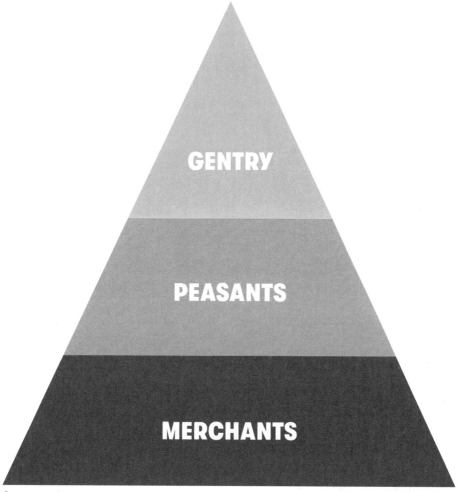

GENTRY

PEASANTS

MERCHANTS

*Some merchants became rich, but they had lower status than peasants because their riches came from the work of others. But if they became rich enough, they could buy land and become gentry!*

# THE EUROPEAN MIDDLE AGES

We'll now look at the continent of Europe during the time span that begins with the fall of the Western Roman Empire and ends with the dawning of the Italian Renaissance. This in-between space in Western Europe is called the Middle Ages. You have probably seen pictures of castles and knights from this time, making it seem like a fairy tale. Sorry, but the Middle Ages were no fairy tale. For the most part, medieval times were a bummer. War, disease, famine—it's all here.

Historians divide the Middle Ages into three sections: the early, high, and late. We will examine one period at a time, in all its horror and (here and there) some glory.

> **Famine:** A famine is when there is an extreme shortage of food.

# EARLY MIDDLE AGES, 476–1000

Great advances were going on in other parts of the world, but Western Europe just couldn't get it together after the fall of Rome. After 476, Western Europe was all chopped up into random territories.

## POWER TO THE CHURCH

The Catholic Church held most of the power, now that Roman government was gone. Many Germanic tribes (Huns, Goths, Vandals, Bulgars, Alani, Suebi, and Franks, to name a few), continued to fight among themselves. They were nomadic (look it up if you don't remember the meaning), self-governing (sort of), and, from a Roman point of view, barbaric (see sidebar, "What Is a Barbarian?").

## WHAT IS A BARBARIAN?

The term "barbarian" was first used by the Greeks to mean any person who did not belong to Greek culture. Then Romans used the term to refer to anyone who was not part of the Roman civilization. "Barbarian" came to be a name for a person who was uncivilized, uncultured, wild, and probably violent. Historians have learned to not use this word much anymore, but you will still see it, especially in primary sources. When you do, put on your binoculars and remember it's coming from a certain point of view.

## THE FRANKS

The Franks were the biggest tribe. Led by their king, named Charles Martel, they stopped the Muslim armies from invading Europe. But Charles Martel's grandson Charlemagne (aka Charles the Great) became the real hero of the Middle Ages, at least for the church and for the people of Western Europe. He was named "Emperor of the Holy Roman Empire" by the Pope in 800, which angered the rulers of the Byzantine Empire in the east.

As you recall, the Byzantines considered themselves to be the leaders of the Roman Empire. So, Charlemagne's leadership further separated the Christian world along east and west. On the other hand, Charlemagne unified the separate tribes of Western Europe, created an efficient government, furthered education, and spread Christianity into eastern and northern Europe.

# A WHO'S WHO OF EUROPEAN FEUDALISM

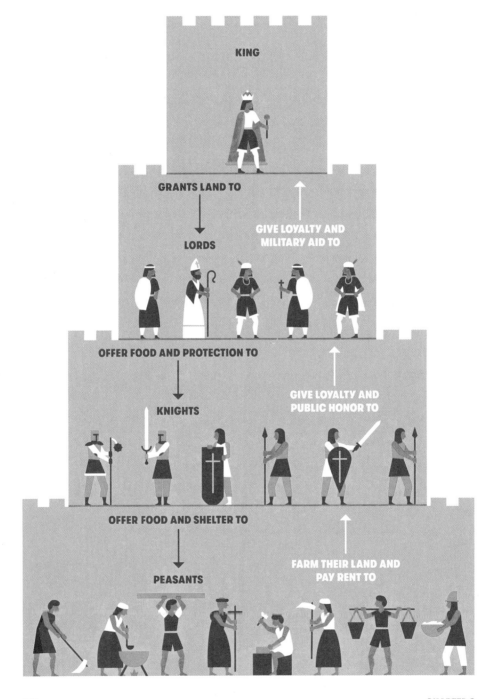

KING

GRANTS LAND TO

GIVE LOYALTY AND MILITARY AID TO

LORDS

OFFER FOOD AND PROTECTION TO

GIVE LOYALTY AND PUBLIC HONOR TO

KNIGHTS

OFFER FOOD AND SHELTER TO

FARM THEIR LAND AND PAY RENT TO

PEASANTS

# FEUDALISM DEVELOPS

Charlemagne is sometimes called the father of feudalism. As you remember from our study of ancient China, feudalism was a social system that centers around levels of power and land ownership.

Feudalism developed in Europe due to the constant fighting going on among small kingdoms. Powerful lords (nobles who held land) gave land and promises of protection to peasants (or serfs) in exchange for their loyalty and military services (and taxes, too). The peasants, farmers, and serfs farmed the land and gave a portion of the harvest to their lords.

 How is this hierarchy similar to and different from the other hierarchies we have studied in ancient Egypt and Imperial China?

_____

_____

_____

_____

_____

# HOME AND FORTRESS: THE CASTLE

More than ten thousand castles still dot the countryside of Western Europe and serve as enchanting reminders of feudal times. Kings and lords of medieval times built castles to protect themselves and their kingdoms from invaders. Built on high ground, castles had high walls, heavily protected gates, look-out towers, and few windows, all for protection. Some also were surrounded by a moat or ditch that encircled the castle complex and sometimes was filled with water.

# THE VIKING AGE

After Charlemagne's death in 814, things started to fall apart again, as often happens with the loss of a strong leader. His empire was divided between his three sons, who, of course, fought with one another. Things went further downhill as the relentless Vikings continued their raids.

## EXPERT SAILORS FROM THE NORTH

The Vikings came from the north, what we know today as Scandinavia—the countries of Sweden, Norway, Finland, and Denmark. They would sail down the Atlantic coast of Europe in expertly designed ships, traveling hundreds of miles into the Mediterranean Sea.

They first raided, then later traded, with communities near the coasts of present-day France and Britain. Often the Vikings would raid monasteries (communities where Catholic monks lived). They frequently killed people and ran off with whatever riches they could find.

## RAIDING MONASTERIES

The people of Britain and France feared the Vikings because their attacks were so fierce and sudden. Writings by monks a couple hundred years later describe the Vikings as bloodthirsty and uncivilized. Some scholars think the Vikings may have been especially harsh because of Charlemagne's attempts to convert people in Scandinavia to Christianity. Other scholars believe the accounts may have been exaggerated to show how uncivilized the Vikings were as non-Christian pagans.

We do know that the Vikings killed people, but it was for the loot, not for religious purposes. The Viking Age in Europe spanned hundreds of years, from 793 to 1066. Some Vikings eventually established communities in France and England, integrated into the cultures, and became Christian.

**Moat:** A moat is a defensive water-filled ditch surrounding a castle. It could only be crossed when the castle would lower a drawbridge, allowing safe passage without having to take a deep dive into the water!

# HIGH MIDDLE AGES, 1000–1300

Beginning in about the year 1000, things started to improve in medieval Europe. The Holy Roman Empire was still a weak and fragmented government, but invasions by tribes and the Vikings had begun to subside and people felt safe. The climate grew warmer, which allowed for better farming and a larger food supply. We know from our study in Chapter 1 that plentiful food allows the population to grow.

## THE RISE OF THE MERCHANT CLASS

Trade also increased. All kinds of luxuries were passing through Europe on their way to the other side of the world. Large cities like Milan and Venice began to develop, where things were bought, sold, and manufactured.

A huge change was taking place during the High Middle Ages. Now people could become big shots through their skill and their wealth—not just their rank or their allegiance to a lord or king. By the end of the High Middle Ages, feudalism was phasing out and a merchant class was phasing in.

## WILLIAM THE CONQUEROR TAKES OVER ENGLAND

But there were still kings, the church and, yes, conflict. One king of great importance during the High Middle Ages was William the Conqueror. You can guess what he did, right? He came from France, but decided he should rule England, too. So William led the Norman Conquest of England in 1066, employing all means necessary to conquer the Anglo-Saxon army. After six years, he secured his power and set about unifying the Anglo-Saxons and the Normans, including their languages, which created the beginnings of the English language.

## THE DOMESDAY BOOK

William also redistributed land to his supporters. To do this huge job, he first took stock of who owned what land and what it was worth. All this information was compiled in a record called the Domesday Book, which has been extremely important to historians who study this time period.

## THE CRUSADES AND THEIR IMPACT

The Europeans also exported conflict, mainly because of the spread of Islam. The Pope called on knights to go to Jerusalem and win it back for the Christians.

Though this exact conversation probably never happened, imagine what a Crusader and a Muslim warrior might say to each other at the time:

Our pope, the holy leader of Christians, has sent us to take back our holy land of Jerusalem! Jesus our savior preached here, and was resurrected here!

Your new Turk government is not allowing Christians to worship freely! And you've hogged our land from Roman times!

You have no claim to this holy city. It is OUR holy land. Muhammad ascended to heaven here!

We won this land fair and square in many battles. We must defend our right to stay in Jerusalem and spread the righteous word of Muhammad!

**CRUSADER**

**MUSLIM WARRIOR**

Do you think the Christians and Turks could ever understand each other? What could have been a solution to their fight over Jerusalem, which was (and is) so important to all three great religions? (By the way, people are still fighting over Jerusalem!)

_____

_____

_____

_____

_____

_____

The first crusade was successful but the seven that came after were not. Over the course of about two hundred years, the Muslims won again and again. Knights traveled hundreds of miles to engage in bloody battles that scarred the Muslim and Jewish communities they targeted. It might seem like a terrible waste of energy, money, and lives, but scholars point to some silver linings: cultural exchange and the growth of the European economy. Even as they clashed, cultures intersected.

Much like the cultural exchange of the Silk Road, travel over long distances for years and years brought a new influx of ideas, technology, and goods into Europe. The Crusades also sped up industry. War required more ships to be built, more supplies to be produced. Plus, the Crusades had to be paid for, and that stepped up systems for banking and taxation.

## THE MAGNA CARTA

In 1215, a bad thing brought a good thing for England, and even the world. The bad thing was a really, really bad king by the name of John. Historians agree that he was truly one of the worst kings ever. He starved people until they died, imprisoned his relatives, charged his barons extremely high taxes, and punished them if they couldn't pay. Eventually, the barons got fed up. They threatened civil war, and John had to negotiate.

# WRITING DOWN THE LAW

King John and his barons wrote down their agreements in a document known as the Magna Carta (meaning "Great Charter"). The charter declared that everyone must follow the law, even the king—a hugely important concept for that time (and ours!). Even though the Magna Carta did not establish peace, as was intended (civil war broke out), it paved the way for the British governing system of Parliament, still in use today, and inspired similar documents throughout human history, including the U.S. Constitution.

**Barons:** Barons were British nobility, but much lower in the social hierarchy than kings or queens. They pledged their loyalty to the king and were granted land in return.

**Parliament:** Parliament is the British legislature, which is a body of the people who write laws. It's pretty similar to the U.S. Congress!

 Who would be affected by this agreement? (Spoiler alert: When you get to the second and third words, you'll find some catches.)

*"No free man shall be seized or imprisoned, or stripped of his rights or possessions, or outlawed or exiled, or deprived of his standing in any other way... except by the lawful judgement of his equals or by the law of the land."*

—Magna Carta, 1215

Yes, so any FREE MAN had these protections. Serfs (the majority of the population) were not considered to be free. Most women were not protected by the Magna Carta either. Wealthy women (especially widows) of the noble classes derived some benefit, but women as a whole were subject to the notion of coverture.

## WHAT IS COVERTURE?

The legal doctrine of coverture states that when a woman gets married, all of her property, legal rights, and legal obligations are taken over by her husband. This law took hold in England during the Middle Ages and governed the lives of women in Europe for hundreds of years.

Women's rights activists of the nineteenth and twentieth centuries fought hard to get coverture laws abolished. Technically, they are a thing of the past, but the effects of coverture and similar customs are still experienced by women around the world. (See Chapter 8 for details!)

# LATE MIDDLE AGES, 1300–1453

What goes up must come down, and this is definitely true of the Middle Ages. Europe pretty much crashed after the relatively good times of the High Middle Ages. Climate changes brought on a famine that crippled the continent of Europe.

## THE GREAT FAMINE IN 1300S EUROPE: CAUSES

| | | | |
|---|---|---|---|
| **1** LOTS of rain (1315); cooler temperatures | **2** Farm-land floods | **3** Fewer crops | **4** Animals die from cold and rain |
| **5** Decrease in food supply; people (even the rich) don't have enough to eat; many starve | **6** People leave their farms, move to dirty, crowded cities (and starve there, too) | **7** By 1322, the Great Famine reduces population in Europe by 10–25 percent. | |

## THE HUNDRED YEARS WAR

As if starvation was not enough, the Late Middle Ages also saw the beginning of a long, long war known as the Hundred Years War. England and France had never really gotten along. They had been fighting over territory for years, and in 1337, they started fighting over who should be king of France.

Edward III, king of England, thought he should get to be the French king as well, through his family on his mother's side. The war was waged on again and off again for decades. It sounds unbelievable, but the person who gave the French army its greatest inspiration was a sixteen-year-old peasant girl named Joan of Arc.

## JOAN OF ARC

Joan said she had received a message from God when she was twelve, telling her to lead the French army in battle. When she was sixteen she set out and actually did it. The French won several battles under Joan's leadership, and later they won the war. Joan of Arc was captured by the English and burned at the stake when she was nineteen.

## THE BLACK DEATH

The worst, worst disaster in the Late Middle Ages came in the form of something very tiny: a bacterium called *Yersinia pestis*. This vicious and deadly germ was carried by fleas. Rats carrying the fleas would then crawl off ships at port and go into the cities.

Joan of Arc

Starting in about 1347, people in Western Europe became infected, and the disease, called the bubonic plague, spread very quickly around the world (remember people had moved to the cities). There was no cure, so some people tried to use witchcraft and magic to ward it off (which did not work). Many people thought God was punishing them because so many died so fast.

The plague caused people to develop lumps on their bodies and gruesome black spots on their skin. It was often called the "Black Death." There were so many deaths that bodies had to be piled in carts each day and buried in batches in giant graves. Here is how one historian in Florence described how bodies were buried:

> All the citizens did little else except to carry dead bodies to be buried [. . .] At every church they dug deep pits down to the water-table; and thus those who were poor who died during the night were bundled up quickly and thrown into the pit. In the morning when a large number of bodies were found in the pit, they took some earth and shovelled it down on top of them; and later others were placed on top of them and then another layer of earth, just as one makes lasagne with layers of pasta and cheese.

Over 25 million people in Europe died from the Black Death, or about half of the entire population.

> **Bubonic plague:** The bubonic plague was an extremely infectious and often fatal disease that got its name from one of its symptoms: buboes are painful and enlarged nodes.

# CHAPTER VOCABULARY

**Barons:** Barons were British nobility, but much lower in the social hierarchy than kings or queens. They pledged their loyalty to the king and were granted land in return.

**Bedouins:** The Bedouins are a nomadic and tribal people. Muhammad encountered many Bedouins in Arabia during his time, but there are still many Bedouins living today in the Middle East.

**Bubonic plague:** The bubonic plague was an extremely infectious and often fatal disease that got its name from one of its symptoms: buboes are painful and enlarged nodes.

**Caliphs:** Caliphs were leaders of Muslim communities during the times described in the Quran.

**Colosseum:** The Colosseum was an enormous amphitheater from Roman times. It was an entertainment venue that featured gladiator battles, animal fights, and even naval battle reenactments. Much of the Colosseum is still intact today!

**Convert:** Convert is both a noun and a verb. The verb means to join a new religion, and the noun refers to someone who has converted.

**Coverture:** Coverture is a legal principle stating that when a woman gets married, all of her property, legal rights, and legal obligations are taken over by her husband.

**Crucifixion:** Crucifixion was a Roman form of punishment where a criminal was nailed to a large wooden cross and left to die.

**Famine:** A famine is when there is an extreme shortage of food.

**Gentile:** A gentile is anyone who isn't Jewish.

**Gentry:** Gentry refers to people from families with land, money and influence.

**Gospel:** The Gospel is generally used as a term to refer to Jesus's message and the story of his life. It's taken from an Old English word, "godspel," meaning good news.

**Icon:** An icon is a painting of a Christian religious figure. They often show Jesus or Mary or a saint looking straight ahead with a golden halo behind their heads.

**Idol:** An idol is a figurine or image meant to represent a god.

**Lord:** Lords were nobles who held land under the feudal system.

**Martyr:** A martyr is someone who sacrifices their own life or suffers pain for their belief or their cause.

**Missionaries:** Missionaries are people sent on religious missions to promote Christianity and convert others. Their job is to spread the Gospel (remember that word?!).

**Moat:** A moat is a defensive water-filled ditch surrounding a castle. It could only be crossed when the castle would lower a drawbridge, allowing safe passage without having to take a deep dive into the water!

**Monastery:** Monasteries are communities where Catholic monks lived.

**Mosque:** A mosque is a Muslim house of worship.

**New Testament:** The New Testament is the second part of the Christian Bible, following the Old Testament (creative names, right?). The New Testament includes the teachings of Jesus and his early followers.

**Pagan:** Pagan is a term used to describe someone whose religious beliefs are at odds with any of the major world religions, most often Christianity.

**Parliament:** Parliament is the British legislature, which is a body of the people who write laws. It's pretty similar to the U.S. Congress!

**Quran:** The Quran is the Islamic sacred book, and it is believed to be the word of God as spoken to Muhammad.

**Resurrection:** Resurrection generally refers to when a person rises from the dead. In this chapter, you learned specifically about the supposed resurrection of Jesus Christ and the impact it had on history.

**Serf:** A serf is a peasant who worked on a lord's estate under the feudal system.

**Stelae:** Stelae are stone slabs that served as monuments. They might have inscriptions or images carved into them, and they have often been erected at tombs as grave stones.

# NOTES:

# 4 EARLY MODERN HISTORY

In Early Modern History, humans explore new lands and new ideas. Europeans grow in power as they take over new places and take on new ways of thinking. As the authority of the church diminishes, people dare to investigate the world for themselves. What do they discover? A ton.

## CHAPTER CONTENTS

# RENAISSANCE EUROPE

*Renaissance* is a French word that means rebirth. If you're wondering why Europe would need a rebirth, just think back to the hardships of the Middle Ages; namely famine, war, and a plague that wiped out half the population. The church held authority over almost everything. Most people lived as serfs and couldn't read or write. They relied on the church or their landlord to tell them what to do—and even what to think.

But a shift began during the fourteenth century. (What years would those be? Check back to Chapter 1 if you're not sure.) Economic changes brought about gradual shifts in social structures that paved the way for progress.

## WHAT LED TO THE RENAISSANCE?

| | | |
|---|---|---|
| The Silk Road and the Crusades increase production of goods. → | Cities (especially in Italy) thrive as gateways for trade. → | Artists and artisans organized into guilds, or associations, to support one another financially and artistically. ↓ |
| Some people get very rich. They have the time and money to focus on art and philosophy. | Authority of church and feudal lords declines. ← | A middle class of merchants and artisans develops. ← |

# HUMANISM

A wealthy group of businessmen, scholars, and a few priests in Florence, Italy, came to be known as humanists. They started to wonder if something wasn't missing from the medieval way of thinking. They believed in God and were devoted to Christianity, but they also believed in the potential of human beings. They thought back to the amazing art and philosophy of the Greeks and Romans, and longed to study it. Soon scholars were traveling Europe looking for classical texts, and artists in Florence started working in the style of the classical age.

## CLASSICAL GREECE AND ROME AS MODELS

Erasmus, a famous humanist philosopher and writer, said,

> *"I have turned my entire attention to Greek.*
> *The first thing I shall do, as soon as the money*
> *arrives, is to buy some Greek authors; after that,*
> *I shall buy clothes."*

The humanists wanted to both imitate and surpass the ancient Greeks and Romans. They thought that God gave humans creativity, intellect, and reason so that they could do amazing things. Their concept of the individual as powerful and wondrous inspired a flowering of inventions, artistic expression, literature, and architecture.

**Humanism:** A cultural movement of the Renaissance that put forth the belief that people had great potential to build up society. Humanists at this time largely returned to ancient Greek and Roman thought—hopefully you haven't forgotten those ancient societies yet!

**Renaissance:** The Renaissance period was a period of "rebirth" and new artistic expression and intellectual progress in Europe in the 1300s.

**Philosopher:** Philosophers study human thought and develop theories about knowledge and human existence.

FLORENCE

## WHY DID THE RENAISSANCE BEGIN IN FLORENCE?

The short answer is money. Florence was a center for banking and textile production, and home to a very wealthy family called the Medicis. Lorenzo Medici was both a businessman and a Humanist philosopher. He and his friend, Marsilio Ficino, a philosopher, studied the ideas of Plato and other Greek philosophers. They combined these ideas with Christian tenets to come up with a vision of how people could be their best and live the best life possible.

*"The contemplation of beauty causes the soul to grow wings."*

—Plato

# EXPLOSION OF ART, ARCHITECTURE, SCIENCE, AND LITERATURE

Lorenzo Medici could afford to commission art (pay artists to paint things at his request) from painters, sculptors, architects, and writers. All of these artists studied the classics, but they were also ready for something new and they achieved great things.

What's interesting about the Italian Renaissance, and perhaps different from our own time, is that art, science, and architecture intersected. For example, Michelangelo and Leonardo da Vinci, great artists of the time, were also scientists and inventors. They wanted to understand how the human body worked in order to paint or sculpt it accurately, so they studied anatomy. Some artists even cut open dead bodies to see the actual bones and muscles.

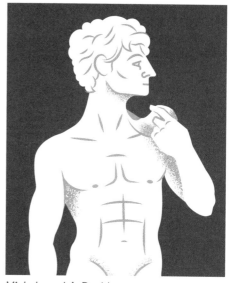
*Michelangelo's David*

## MICHELANGELO'S DAVID

Michelangelo's knowledge of the body helped him to create *David*, one of the greatest sculptures of all time (from the Bible story of David and Goliath). If you ever go see it in Florence, you will be amazed that anyone could carve something so beautiful, balanced, and life-like out of a slab of stone.

How do the changes in art during the Renaissance connect to the ideas of Humanism?

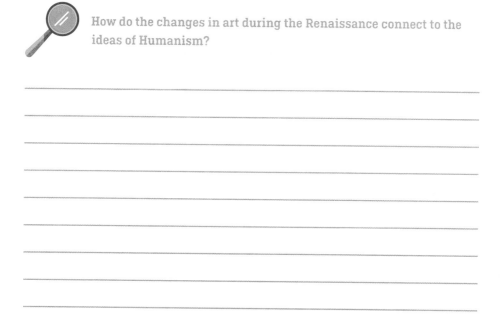

Architecture also advanced, as people were studying Greek laws of geometry and physics. If you walk around Florence, you can see how the buildings mimic those of ancient Greece and Rome in their proportions, columns, arches, and domes.

# BRUNELLESCHI'S DUOMO

The Duomo cathedral in Florence stands as a famous example of how Renaissance architects surpassed their ancient mentors. Brunelleschi designed the cathedral's dome in two layers to make it stronger and more balanced; these features allowed it to be very wide without collapsing. The Florentines liked to brag to the other city-states that they had constructed the largest brick dome in the world.

*The dome of the Florence Cathedral, called the Duomo, was the biggest in the world at the time. It was designed by Filippo Brunelleschi—who wasn't even trained as an architect!*

**Anatomy:** Anatomy is the study of the human body and all of its parts. A number of famous Renaissance painters became interested in studying human anatomy so their art would be perfect!

**Commission:** To commission work from someone is to pay them to create it.

**Physics:** Physics is the scientific study of matter and energy.

**Cathedral:** A cathedral is a large church that serves as the central church for the religious leadership.

# CHAPTER 4

## MONA LISA AND REALITY

Leonardo's masterpiece, the *Mona Lisa*, shows us two aspects of Renaissance art. (1) Mona Lisa is just a person, not a biblical figure, and (2) Leonardo uses color and shading to create a glow that looks like natural sunlight, and a 3D effect so that her image appears as real as a photograph. No one had been able to do this before the Renaissance.

## EDUCATION EXPANDS

As businesses and urban life advanced, more people needed to be educated. Bankers had to know math to keep track of money; merchants had to know how to read and write contracts; and foreign traders needed to understand other languages. The invention of the printing press quickly made more books available. Colleges and universities also began to spring up across Europe.

In the days of church-controlled education, monks learned to read and write in Latin only. When schools began to use Italian and other languages spoken by ordinary people, education became available more widely.

# THE PRINTING PRESS ROCKS EUROPE

**1** Books, mainly the Bible, are copied by hand by monks

(a few pages a day)

**2** Gutenberg invents the printing press in 1456

(prints 3,600 pages in one day)

**3** Many more books produced and distributed throughout Europe.

**4** More people learn to read and write.

- They no longer have to depend on the church for knowledge.

**5** People like Martin Luther and the Enlightenment philosophers begin to write their opinions.

**6** New ideas spread quickly through Europe and catch on:

- Reformation
- Enlightenment ideas
- Scientific knowledge

**7** Knowledge continues to grow, and governments, societies, and cultures change as a result.

Let's make a prediction. How do you think the invention of the printing press will change life in Europe? Will it strengthen or weaken the church?

_____

_____

_____

_____

As literacy spread throughout Europe, amazing writers came along in England, Spain, Germany, and France. You'll read many of the famous Renaissance writers in high school. In the meantime, you should know about William Shakespeare, considered to be one of the greatest writers of the English language.

## THE AMAZING SHAKESPEARE

People still study and perform Shakespeare's forty plays and 150 sonnets. His plays help us understand the history of his time, as well as the joys and troubles we all face today. People of Shakespeare's time flocked to theaters in London to watch performances of his plays. Someday you might read *Romeo and Juliet*, and when you fall in love, you'll know just what Shakespeare was talking about.

It's good to keep in mind that the Renaissance mainly affected the very wealthy and select artists, not the common folk of Europe (95 percent of the population) who still lived a basic feudal life. In fact, some historians think the Renaissance should not be considered its own thing, but more like a trend of the Late Middle Ages. Either way, there is agreement that it started something that led to big changes in European history.

**Sonnets:** Sonnets are a very specific form of poetry with strict rules for which lines have to rhyme and how many syllables each line should have. William Shakespeare famously wrote more than 150 sonnets!

# THE AGE OF EXPLORATION AND THE DAWN OF COLONIALISM

History has shown us that when human beings want something *really* badly, they will go to almost any lengths to get it. They will do heroic, amazingly intelligent things, and they will also do horrible, despicable things. As our journey continues now, we will see how the Age of Exploration brought out the best and worst in a group of adventurers who dared to sail all over the world. And it all started with people wanting stuff.

## FINDING A SEA ROUTE TO ASIA

From the Middle Ages right on through the Renaissance, Europeans wanted spices really badly. Sometimes they used spices to preserve meat, but mainly they wanted spices because they were yummy, and fancy, and could sometimes improve people's health.

Wealthy people would pay high prices for cinnamon, nutmeg, cloves, pepper, and saffron. In fact, some spices were worth more than gold! So, European merchants wanted to get spices and other luxury goods, like fine Chinese porcelain, as fast and as cheaply as they could. If they succeeded, they were guaranteed to be rich!

## A GEOGRAPHY PROBLEM

But nearly all of the condiments and luxury goods Europeans loved came from Asia (especially India and Indonesia). Merchants had been trekking back and forth on land routes (the "Silk Road") for hundreds of years, but foot travel took a *LONG* time and it was expensive.

There was one shortcut through the Mediterranean Sea, but when Constantinople fell to the Ottomans in 1453, that route was closed off. (During the Crusades, Europeans, who were mostly Christians, had learned not to mess with Muslims.) So the Europeans wanted to find their own direct maritime route to "the Indies." They knew they would have to make it around the enormous continent of Africa, and this would not be easy.

A caravel, a sleek and fast ship used by the Portuguese for exploration.

## PORTUGAL GOES FIRST

Prince Henry of Portugal led the way. Using his own money, he set up a school for navigation in 1418, and also invented a ship made just for exploring. The caravel was light and fast, and could sail near the shore in shallow water.

Maritime: Maritime means having to do with the sea. So, maritime trade might be exchanging goods by boat, and maritime routes are sea routes between places.

Navigation: Navigation is the process of figuring out where you are and how to get where you're going. The word is especially used when talking about travel by sea.

# PORTUGUESE EXPLORATION ROUTES, 1497–1502

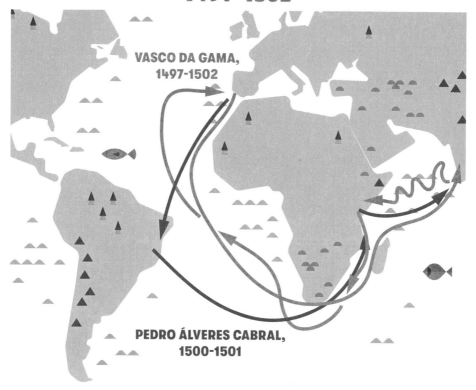

VASCO DA GAMA,
1497-1502

PEDRO ÁLVERES CABRAL,
1500-1501

## NEW (OLD) TECHNOLOGY MAKES NAVIGATION BETTER

Explorers also now had more accurate maps and a magnetic kind of compass called an astrolabe. This amazing instrument, invented by the ancient Greeks and perfected by the Arabs, allowed sailors to figure out their location by measuring the height of the sun or a star above the horizon.

# THE DAWN OF COLONIZATION

As the Portuguese explorers set out, they soon discovered off the coast several small islands, now known as Madeira and the Azores. They had an idea to set up sugar farms (plantations) to make some quick money. Madeira became a colony of Portugal, which means Madeira belonged to Portugal, and Portugal could use the land (and the people) for its own benefit—in this case, making money from growing sugar.

When the Portuguese needed people to work the land, they sailed over to Africa and bought some slaves. Planting, harvesting, and processing the sugar was extremely hard work. So when the Portuguese plantation owners had worked the first batch of slaves to death, they would return to Africa for a new batch of slaves. It's horrible, but it's true.

> **Plantations:** Plantations are large farms that grow a specific crop like sugar or tobacco. They often relied on the unpaid labor of enslaved people.
>
> **Colony:** A colony is a piece of land that another nation claims as its own, often using the people and land for its benefit. The process of *colonization* (founding new colonies) was often very violent.

Colonization became a pattern repeated around the world. It goes like this:

# HOW COLONIZATION HAPPENS

European explorers arrive and decide they own the place.

Europeans try to own the people there, too. Often, they force the people to convert to Christianity.

Europeans try to force native people to work for them to produce what they want and/or find gold.

Indigenous people get conquered.

- Sometimes they do as they are told because they think these new people are magical.
- Sometimes they fight back, but their weapons are not as powerful.
- Sometimes they aren't united and so the Europeans get support from a tribe's enemies.
- In the Americas and the Caribbean, native people get wiped out by diseases the Europeans are carrying.

Europeans need labor so they replace the natives with slaves from Africa.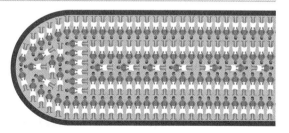

Europeans get rich from the crops and goods produced by free labor in the colony.

Europeans go back for more slaves.

Let's focus in on number 4 to get at the heart how Europeans conquered native people. Which forces do you think were most important? How do you think the world would be different today if native people had not experienced this violence?

_____

_____

_____

_____

_____

Portuguese explorers ventured further and further down the west coast of Africa. They set up colonies in West Africa, and an explorer named Vasco da Gama did finally make it around the southern tip of Africa. Only half of his crew survived the trip. Despite the dangers, exploring had become the thing to do in Portugal and there were many voyages.

## CHRISTOPHER COLUMBUS

Soon the king and queen of Spain grew jealous of Portugal's glory (not to mention its profits) and wanted a piece of the action. This was perfect timing for Christopher Columbus.

As a boy growing up in Genoa, a port city in what's now Italy, Columbus had dreamed of discovering a new route to the "Indies," finding gold, and spreading Christianity. But Columbus thought, "What if I went west across the Atlantic, instead of south and east? What if I wrapped around the world, and came up on the "Indies" from the other side?" It was not entirely a crazy plan—he had done some calculations—but the Portuguese royals said no.

## A CASE OF MISTAKEN IDENTITY

He then went to King Ferdinand and Queen Isabella of Spain and they decided to back him. Columbus and his crew embarked on the journey in 1492 with three ships. After several weeks at sea, they bumped into the Caribbean islands, thinking they had reached India.

# COLUMBUS'S FIRST VOYAGE
## TO THE AMERICAS

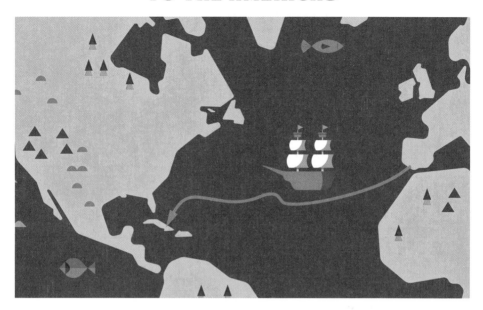

Columbus set about looking for gold on those islands, even though there wasn't much to be had. He and his crew treated the Indigenous people brutally.

## A VIOLENT CONQUEST

Unfortunately, this was common during the Age of Exploration. European conquerors scared people into submission using violence, and some very scary weapons. With the attitude of "I now own this place and I should own you," the Spaniards' cruelty went unchecked. They slaughtered men, women, and children alike, and cut off people's hands if they did not bring them enough gold. They shipped 500 of the Taino tribe to Europe as slaves. Only about half survived the voyage.

Even though Columbus changed history by crossing the Atlantic Ocean and "discovering" the New World, it was not a happy history for all.

## THE TREATY OF TORDESILLAS

Portugal and Spain started to compete for lands to colonize. In 1494, the
two powers came to an agreement, called the Treaty of Tordesillas. They
actually divided the whole world between the two of them, right down the
middle of the Atlantic Ocean, as shown below.

## EFFECTS OF TREATY OF TORDESILLAS, 1494

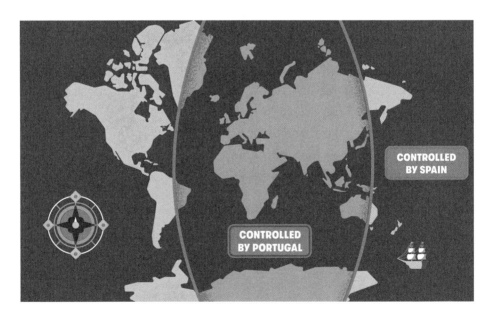

Have you ever wondered why Brazilians today speak Portuguese as their first language? Study this map and you'll have the answer.

# FRANCE AND ENGLAND ENTER THE PICTURE

The French and English did not get into the act until much later and pretty much ignored the treaty. By the way, nobody asked the people living in these places if any of this was okay. European explorers kept sailing on into the 1500s. The first person to conceive of sailing around the entire world was Ferdinand Magellan. He himself did not survive the long and dangerous voyage, and only 18 out of his 250 crew members made it back. Most of what we know about Magellan's voyage comes from the journal of an Italian passenger named Antonio Pigafetta. According to Pigafetta, things were pretty horrible, and this was the general state of things on voyages.

We were three months and twenty days without getting any kind of fresh food. We ate biscuit, which was no longer biscuit, but powder of biscuits swarming with worms. We drank yellow water that had been putrid (unpleasant or repulsive) for many days. But of all misfortunes the following was the worst. The gums of both the lower and upper teeth of some of our men swelled, so that they could not eat under any circumstances and therefore died.

*Journal of Antonio Pigafetta*

# SPANISH CONQUESTS AND THE FALL OF INDIGENOUS CULTURES

Spanish conquests into Central and South America started to heat up when word got out that there might be gold in those regions. Francisco Pizarro and Hernán Cortés went crazy for that gold. They sailed to the Americas (Pizarro in 1510; Cortés in 1519) and killed people by the thousands in order to get the gold. Remember the highly advanced cities of the Aztecs in Mexico and the Incas in Peru (pp. 61-63)? Gone. The Spaniards, along with their native allies, managed to destroy these civilizations through sheer force, and some trickery.

But *the* deadliest force in the downfall of these impressive people in the Americas was disease. The Europeans did not know it, but they were carrying some germs the Native Americans had never encountered. This meant that their bodies could not fight off the diseases. The illnesses of smallpox, measles, and whooping cough were so powerful that they killed 100 million, or 90 percent, of the indigenous people in the Americas. It was one of the worst tragedies in human history.

# THE PROTESTANT REFORMATION

Let's get your brain ready for the Protestant Reformation. You'll need to pull on your boots and circle back to these ideas from earlier chapters:

• Corruption in the Catholic Church, including indulgences

• Early Christian ideas on the power of faith

• Invention of the printing press

• Let's also look at the word *Reformation*, and break down an unfamiliar word into familiar ones: re (again) + form (shape) = reshape. When someone wants reform it means they want a change, a re-shaping of something to improve it.

*A heretic is burned at the stake.*

During the Middle Ages and even into the Renaissance, the Catholic Church in Europe controlled almost everything in a person's life. And if you didn't like what the church said, you'd better watch out. Heretics (people who didn't agree with the church) were sometimes burned at the stake.

## THE INQUISITION

The church got obsessed with rooting out its enemies. In 1478, it set up a special office called the Tribunal of the Holy Office of the Inquisition. The job of this holy office was to find, question, and torture anyone suspected of being a heretic. If they did not confess (and often even if they did) they were killed. The Inquisition did its worst work in Spain, where many Jews and Muslims suffered. Thirty-two thousand people were murdered during the Spanish Inquisition, which lasted about two hundred years. It was a dark time.

# CHURCH CORRUPTION

Even if they were not full-on abusive, many church officials got greedy and dishonest from having so much power. Some priests behaved like con men, selling people trinkets (little charms) for good luck—such as fake splinters from Jesus's cross or a so-called toe or finger from a saint. Yes, really.

Church officials also got rich from selling pieces of paper called indulgences that supposedly got people into heaven faster. Some priests even claimed that a pricey indulgence could erase sins the person had committed. So, people who were already poor often gave half their wages to church authorities who were already rich.

 You might be thinking—how lame! How could people fall for this? Good question! How *could* they? Take a minute to consider it. If you think for yourself on this, it will give you a clue to how people lived and thought at this time—and why they were stuck.

**Heretic:** A heretic is someone who didn't agree with the church. We might have religious freedoms now, but in the 1400s, heretics were often burned at the stake for their beliefs.

**Indulgences:** During the height of the church's power, indulgences were something you could buy that would essentially grant you forgiveness for a sin you had committed.

# MARTIN LUTHER SPEAKS OUT

In 1517, a monk living in Germany named Martin Luther got fed up. He believed only faith could "save" a person (keep a person from suffering in Hell), not a piece of paper from a priest. Martin Luther was aggressive and outspoken, and some say obnoxious at times. He wrote down ninety-five reasons why these indulgences were wrong and, according to legend, nailed it to the church door.

 Luther's ninety-five reasons existed. But did the nailing to the church door really happen? There is actually no record of it, but it makes a good story.

Martin Luther nails his 95 theses to the door of the Castle Church in Wittenberg on October 31, 1517.

Because of the speedy printing press, copies of Martin Luther's 95 Theses got handed out all over Europe and more people got fed up. The church told Luther to simmer down but he refused. In fact, he went on the attack even more.

## PROCLAMATIONS OF MARTIN LUTHER:

- People didn't need priests to tell them what the Bible means or how to behave correctly.

- A person's faith, not their actions (which can never be perfect), will bring them salvation.

- All the religious knowledge that people need is in the Bible.

- Anyone can understand the Bible, not just priests.

- We need to form a "priesthood of all believers."

Martin Luther translated the Bible from Latin into German, so that anyone could read it. People followed him and they formed a new "Lutheran" church. Later it was named the Protestant church because they were protesting the authority of the Catholic pope and the priests.

Martin Luther's religious protests also fueled social protests. The common people of Germany were definitely fed up. For hundreds of years they had lived under a feudal system that cost them high taxes and gave them next to nothing to live on. They were inspired by Martin Luther, and so launched the Peasants' War in 1524 against the nobles.

It became a bloodbath, killing tens of thousands of people, and the peasants lost the struggle. Martin Luther may have disliked the pope's power over the church, but he did not mind at all that the nobles and landlords had power over the peasants. In fact, he denounced the Peasants' War and helped the nobles instead of the common folk.

Protestant: The Protestant movement broke off from the Catholic Church, saying that the priests shouldn't tell people how to behave. Protestants believe that faith will bring them salvation.

Protest: To protest something is to speak up against it. Protests have taken many forms throughout history and in today's current events—see if you can brainstorm any modern protest movements to help understand this term!

## MARTIN LUTHER'S ANTISEMITISM

Historians agree that Martin Luther was *the* person to bring about the Reformation, and his courage was extraordinary. However, he had a stubborn and cruel side to him. Martin Luther disrespected those who disagreed with him, especially Jewish people. He wanted Jews to convert to Protestant Christianity.

When they did not, he said they should be chased out of Christian lands and their synagogues burned. Martin Luther wrote horrible things about Jews that were later used to blame them for all sorts of things. Martin Luther was not the first to mistreat Jews, but he did put in motion hatred and violence that others imitated long after his death.

 Was Martin Luther more helpful or more harmful to history?

## MARTIN LUTHER'S EFFECT ON HISTORY

| HELPFUL | HARMFUL |
|---|---|
| Exposed dishonesty in the church | Persecuted Jewish people, effectively giving his followers permission to commit similar abuses |
| Got rid of meaningless rituals | |
| Allowed clergy to marry | Did not support the Peasants' War |
| Believed in people, not authority | Thought he had all the answers |
| Allowed Christians to form lots of different churches with different approaches | Weakened the church by dividing it |

# THE SCIENTIFIC REVOLUTION

Right now, as you sit and read this book, you know certain things for sure. You know the roof over your head will (most likely!) not collapse. You know that if you start to feel sick, your parents can take you to a doctor and the doctor can give you medicine to help you feel better. You know that we live on the planet Earth.

And if you wanted to learn more about our solar system, you could go on the Internet and find *tons* of information—like how close Earth is to the Sun, and what other planets are orbiting the Sun along with the Earth, and how long a star lives. Huge amounts of knowledge are just part of our daily life, and our scientific knowledge keeps on expanding.

But it was not always this way. As you remember, during the Middle Ages, the Catholic Church was in charge of everything. There was really no such thing as a scientist. But during the Renaissance a few people got curious about some big questions, like "Why does an apple fall from a tree to the ground instead of going up?" People wondered how the human body worked, and how the planets were arranged in space. They didn't want a priest to simply tell them what to believe, they wanted to know for sure, and they were willing to do the work to prove their findings.

This was a brave step.

Church authorities did not believe a regular person could know more than what the church had taught for hundreds of years. We can also guess that deep down many people were afraid of a reality they knew nothing about.

## THE SCIENTIFIC METHOD

The thinkers of the Scientific Revolution had to use their own curiosity to begin their quests for knowledge. They had to work hard to measure things in nature precisely. They had to watch very carefully and take notes about what they observed. Then, they had to come up with some guesses about why things happened as they did, and test out those guesses to see if they held true.

We now call this process the Scientific Method. It's just what we do.

# A WHO'S WHO OF THE SCIENTIFIC REVOLUTION IN EUROPE

The European Scientific Revolution lasted from 1543 to around 1687. Many scientists made breakthroughs at this time. But here we will focus on the all-star geniuses, the big names who completely changed the way people understood the world. Without these people, we would not even know how to do an experiment—which means we wouldn't know how to discover anything new, which means. . . well, we would all be pretty clueless.

> **Revolution:** A revolution is an overthrow of a government or social order. One example is the Scientific Revolution, when scientists completely shifted our understanding of the world. A revolution could also be a violent uprising or war, like the American or French Revolutions (we'll learn about those soon!).

 "First" does not mean the first scientists ever. As we've seen, people in ancient cultures had been studying the world and how it worked for thousands of years. What's special about these European scientists is that they changed the way Europeans thought about things, and they paved the way for still more progress.

*Galileo and his telescope*

## NICOLAUS COPERNICUS ROCKS THE WORLD

Until Nicolaus Copernicus came along, everyone in Europe believed that the Earth was at the center of the universe and the Sun, stars, and all the other planets orbited around Earth. This idea was first posed by a man named Ptolemy who lived in ancient Greece. The Catholic Church liked Ptolemy's theory because it put humans at the center of the universe.

But the theory never made sense to Copernicus. It was complicated, and the math did not add up right. (Copernicus was also a mathematician—oh, and a doctor, artist, lawyer, governor, and an economist—super smart). A classic overachiever.

## MAKING OBSERVATIONS AND USING MATH

In 1523, Copernicus built his own observatory and watched the skies for years and made calculations. In 1542, a year before he died, Copernicus published one of the most important scientific books of all time, *Revolution of Celestial Spheres*. In this book he proved (with math) that the Greeks had it wrong.

Copernicus realized that the Sun was actually at the center of the solar system and the planets (including the Earth, which is just another planet) revolve around the Sun. It took hundreds of years for Copernicus's theory to be accepted by the church.

## GALILEO GALILEI TAKES THE HIT FOR COPERNICUS

Galileo Galilei was an Italian physicist, astronomer, mathematician, and engineer. He is known for inventing the telescope, but he didn't actually invent it. A Dutch scientist invented the first telescope, but Galileo improved on it greatly. In fact, Galileo's telescope was so powerful he was able to see the moons of Jupiter, irregular spots on the sun, and the rings of Saturn.

Living about a hundred years after Copernicus, Galileo saw the wisdom of Copernicus's theory, and he proved it even more fully. The Catholic Church went after Galileo much more than it did Copernicus (maybe because Copernicus had died soon after he published his book!).

The church had always taught people that God had set up the heavens to be perfect, with our planet at the center of things, and certainly no ugly spots on the sun. Galileo stood his ground that his theory was reasonable and that it did not disrespect God. In 1615, he wrote:

> *"I do not feel obliged to believe that the same God who has endowed us with sense, reason, and intellect has intended us to forgo their use."*

 In essence, Galileo is saying "God gave us a brain, so he must want us to use it." Let's think back to our introduction to Humanism. How does this quote align with the values of the Humanist movement? What problems does it present for the authority of the church?

_____

_____

_____

_____

_____

**Astronomer:** An astronomer is a scientist who studies space, planets, and the universe. These scientists do everything from naming planets to learning how the world works, like discovering that Earth rotates around the Sun and not the other way around!

**Intellect:** A person's intellect is their ability to reason and think critically.

## THE CHURCH FORCES GALILEO TO TAKE IT BACK

In 1633 the church made Galileo "recant," or take back the scientific claims he had made. For the last nine years of his life, he was sentenced to life imprisonment (in his house, because he was old). Galileo is called the Father of Modern Science because he laid the foundation of the scientific method. When you do any experiment, you are following the steps laid out by Galileo about 400 years ago.

# SCIENTIFIC METHOD

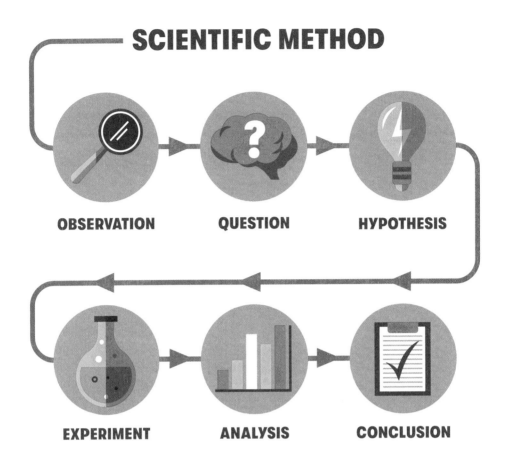

OBSERVATION     QUESTION     HYPOTHESIS

EXPERIMENT     ANALYSIS     CONCLUSION

# GRAVITY: THE FORCE THAT MOVES THE UNIVERSE

## SIR ISAAC NEWTON LAYS DOWN THE LAW

What goes up must come down. But why? That's the kind of thing Sir Isaac Newton thought about in England during the 1600s. Newton was a brilliant mathematician, just like those who had gone before him. He worked for twenty years to understand the orbit of planets and why things moved as they did on Earth.

In 1687, he published *Mathematical Principles of Natural Philosophy*, in which he showed that objects in the universe move according to mathematical "laws," or patterns. Newton said there is one single force, gravity, that governs the movement of everything—from objects in space to apples falling from trees. It's also what keeps you seated in a chair while you read this, as opposed to floating around up by the ceiling.

Newton also invented calculus, an advanced form of math you might take in high school or college. Some of Newton's theories have been questioned in the last hundred years, but many of the laws he identified are so solid they are still used in engineering and all the branches of science.

*Sir Isaac Newton finds enlightenment*

## "If I have seen further than others, it is by standing upon the shoulders of giants."

—Sir Isaac Newton

Newton's quote above is crucial to understanding the Scientific Revolution. Try your hand at unpacking some of his metaphors: What do you think Newton means by "seeing further" than others? Who are the "giants" he is talking about? What does he really mean by "standing on the shoulders"? Extra points if you can put this quote in your own words!

_____

_____

_____

_____

_____

_____

_____

Dozens of other genius scientists made big discoveries during this time. Here's a quick glance at some of them. If you are into science, the people listed on the next page are worth checking out.

**Elliptical:** An elliptical shape is an elongated circle, like this:

**Alchemy:** Alchemy was an early form of science that was mostly concerned with transforming matter. In other words, alchemy was all about trying to turn stones into gold!

# A FEW MORE IMPORTANT SCIENTISTS

| SCIENTIST | KNOWN FOR |
|---|---|
| **JOHANNES KEPLER** 1571–1630 | German astronomer. Built on Copernicus's theory. Proved that the orbits of the planets were not perfectly circular, but elliptical. |
| **FRANCIS BACON** 1561–1626 | English philosopher. Further refined and promoted the Scientific Method. |
| **ROBERT BOYLE** 1627–1691 | Applied scientific method and mathematics to the study of chemistry, rather than magic or alchemy. |
| **ANTONIE VAN LEEUWENHOEK** 1632–1723 | Dutch businessman and scientist. Discovered bacteria. |
| **TYCHO BRAHE** 1546–1601 | Danish astronomer. Further defined positions of the stars, moon, and planets. |
| **WILLIAM HARVEY** 1578–1657 | English physician. Described blood circulation in the human body. |
| **MARIA MARGARETHA KIRCH** 1670–1720 | German astronomer. First woman to discover a comet. |

# THE AGE OF ENLIGHTENMENT

People did not always think the way we do now. For example, if your friend says he can run faster than you, you would not necessarily believe him. You would want some proof. Before the Age of Enlightenment people believed mainly in magic and God, and forces they couldn't see. They depended on priests to interpret events. They did not believe they could do much to make things better for themselves.

So, we have to get into the heads of people back then to realize what a huge shift took place. Writers and thinkers during the Enlightenment wanted to enlighten (light up or awaken) people's minds—and they pretty much did. It was like Europe's big *aha*. The attitude of "I'll believe it when I see it and I'll decide for myself" came about (in Europe, at least) during this time we will call the Age of Enlightenment (1685–1815).

 Be careful with the dates we're giving you here of this age and that age. It's not like people said on January 1, 1685, "Oh, it's now the Age of Enlightenment, let's think by using our senses and our reasoning abilities." All change was gradual in any of these ages. People started to write down some new ideas, other people read them and talked about them. They expressed them to people in power who usually rejected them first, but slowly the ideas seeped into the culture.

As with any new phase of human history, it happened because of what went before. The Renaissance, the Age of Exploration, even the Middle Ages contributed to the Enlightenment movement, but none more than the advances in science we just read about.

## TIME FOR QUESTIONING

Once people started to question assumptions about the physical world, they started to also question assumptions about their social world, power relationships, and government.

The philosopher John Locke

# JOHN LOCKE

John Locke, one big thinker, wondered, "Is it really OK for kings and landlords to treat peasants like dirt? Don't all people have rights to happiness and property?" Well, he didn't actually put it that way. Here's a quote directly from Locke:

*"Being all equal and independent, no one ought to harm another in his life, health, liberty, or possessions."*

— John Locke, 1690

Flip back to our discussion of the Magna Carta on page 183. How is Locke's idea similar to and different from those in the Magna Carta?

_____

_____

_____

_____

_____

_____

_____

_____

_____

_____

We are lucky that people like Locke started to ask this and write about these questions. Locke's ideas shaped our own government and how we enjoy these rights.

# VOLTAIRE

A writer named Voltaire tested the limits of saying what he thought. He wrote books and pamphlets with ideas in them that shocked people. His most famous and most shocking book was his adventure novel *Candide*, in which he made fun of everyone, including the Catholic Church, the French government, and his own fellow philosophers. (Voltaire's outspokenness against the government landed him in jail for a year.)

Voltaire believed that human reason was all important and more reliable for making a better world than church or government authority. He was also a proponent of animal rights and freedom of religion. Voltaire was one of the first to insist that people have a right to say what they think, even if others don't agree with it.

The spirit of revolt was now spreading through Europe. People were discovering that they mattered as individuals, that they could question authority, think for themselves, seek out the truth, and take action to make a better world. The world was ripe for even more conflict, and even more progress.

**Monarchs:** Monarchs are people who rule over a kingdom or empire, such as kings, queens, or emperors.

**Social contract:** A social contract is an agreement among the people of a society to be governed and to cooperate for the good of all. It can be written or unwritten.

# OTHER KEY ENLIGHTENMENT THINKERS

| | |
|---|---|
| **JEAN-JACQUES ROUSSEAU** | Rousseau believed that people were basically good. He thought government was only good if it had a social contract with the people. In other words, the people agreed to be governed by it and it was for the good of all. This flew in the face of old ideas that monarchs governed through the will of God. |
| **MARY WOLLSTONECRAFT** | Wollstonecraft wrote a daring essay in 1792 called "A Vindication of the Rights of Woman," calling for women to have the same rights as men. She argued for women to be educated in order to fully participate in society and democracy. She was one of the first women to make a living as a writer. |
| **ADAM SMITH** | Smith put forth ideas about economics that are still relevant today. He believed in a free market, with no government control, that would regulate itself. |
| **DENIS DIDEROT** | Diderot gathered essays from over a hundred authors for a twenty-eight volume book called *Encyclopedia* (1751). The church tried to keep the book from being published and threatened to punish anyone who read it. But after twenty-five years of hard work, *Encyclopedia* got printed, translated into many languages, and distributed throughout Europe and the Americas. |

# CHAPTER VOCABULARY

**Alchemy:** Alchemy was an early form of science that was mostly concerned with transforming matter. In other words, alchemy was all about trying to turn stones into gold!

**Anatomy:** Anatomy is the study of the human body and all of its parts. A number of famous Renaissance painters became interested in studying human anatomy so their art would be perfect!

**Astronomer:** An astronomer is a scientist who studies space, planets, and the universe. These scientists do everything from naming planets to learning how the world works, like discovering that Earth rotates around the Sun and not the other way around!

**Cathedral:** A cathedral is a large church that serves as the central church for the religious leadership.

**Colony:** A colony is piece of land that another nation claims as its own, often using the people and land for its benefit. The process of colonization (founding new colonies) was often very violent.

**Elliptical:** An elliptical shape is an elongated circle.

**Guild:** Guilds were associations that artists and artisans organized to support each other financially and artistically.

**Heretic:** A heretic is someone who didn't agree with the church. We might have religious freedoms now, but in the 1400s, heretics were often burned at the stake for their beliefs.

**Humanism:** Humanism was a cultural movement of the Renaissance that put forth the belief that people had great potential to build up society. Humanists at this time largely returned to ancient Greek and Roman thought—hopefully you haven't forgotten those ancient societies yet!

**Indulgences:** During the height of the church's power, indulgences were something you could buy that would essentially grant you forgiveness for a sin you had committed.

**Intellect:** A person's intellect is their ability to reason and think critically.

**Maritime:** Maritime means having to do with the sea. So, maritime trade might be exchanging goods by boat, and maritime routes are sea routes between places.

**Monarchs:** Monarchs are people who rule over a kingdom or empire, such as kings, queens, or emperors.

**Navigation:** Navigation is the process of figuring out where you are and how to get where you're going. The word is especially used when talking about travel by sea.

**Philosopher:** Philosophers study human thought and develop theories about knowledge and human existence.

**Plantations:** Plantations are large farms that grow a specific crop like sugar or tobacco. They often relied on the unpaid labor of enslaved people.

**Physics:** Physics is the scientific study of matter and energy.

**Protest:** To protest something is to speak up against it. Protests have taken many forms throughout history and in today's current events.

**Protestant:** The Protestant movement broke off from the Catholic Church, saying that the priests shouldn't tell people how to behave. Protestants believe that faith will bring them salvation.

**Renaissance:** The Renaissance period was a period of "rebirth" and new artistic expression and intellectual progress in Europe in the 1300s.

**Revolution:** A revolution is an overthrow of a government or social order. One example is the Scientific Revolution, when scientists completely shifted our understanding of the world. A revolution could also be a violent uprising or war, like the American or French Revolutions.

**Social contract:** A social contract is an agreement among the people of a society to be governed and to cooperate for the good of all. It can be written or unwritten.

**Sonnets:** Sonnets are a very specific form of poetry with strict rules for which lines have to rhyme and how many syllables each line should have. William Shakespeare famously wrote more than 150 sonnets!

# NOTES

# 5 LATE MODERN HISTORY I

In Late Modern History, you'll find inspiring movements for social change, stemming from the Enlightenment, alongside one of the most shameful (and profitable) human industries ever: the slave trade. You'll see how European empires take full advantage of modern technology to extend their reach around the globe. Will greed or social reform win out?

# REVOLUTIONS

By now, we've seen that history is essentially a story of how things change. When a change is REALLY big, and human life is never again the same, we call it a revolution. A revolution might bring in a new form of government, new ideas, a new way of life, or all of these.

Many revolutions are violent and sudden, and they happen when people are completely fed up with having no power, or money—or food. Other revolutions can be gradual, taking place over many years. No matter how long a change takes, if it's big enough, we call it a revolution. Let's review a few of the revolutions we've studied so far.

## HUMANITY'S REVOLUTIONS THROUGH 1800

| NAME | DATE | WHAT CHANGED |
|---|---|---|
| **NEOLITHIC REVOLUTION** | New Stone Age, 8000–3000 BCE | Humans learned how to farm and began to live a settled life instead of a nomadic life. They invented more refined tools and started to produce a surplus of food. |
| **SCIENTIFIC REVOLUTION** | 1543–1687 CE | Authority of knowledge moved from the church to science and the direct observation of the world. |
| **THE ENLIGHTENMENT** | Late 1600s into 1700s | As scientific knowledge and literacy spread, people started to value reason and fairness more than religious authority, a belief known as "Humanism." They wanted to make the world a better place for everyone. |

# THE INDUSTRIAL REVOLUTION

The Industrial Revolution (1760–1840) had its roots in prior revolutions and advances. We'll see how food surpluses (which first happened in the Neolithic Revolution), inventions (from the Scientific Revolution), and the quest for progress (Enlightenment) culminated in a whole new way of life on this planet.

> **Industrial:** Industrial means something has to do with manufacturing, factories, trade, or technology.

*Before the Industrial Revolution, most people scratched out a living on the land.*

To imagine the world before the Industrial Revolution, think *Little House on the Prairie*. People lived off the land. They grew their own food, built their own homes, wove their own cloth, and made their own clothes. There were no cars, no highways, no planes, no computers, and no phones. People stayed close to home because it was hard to get around, and most everyone spent all day, every day, working to survive.

# A STEP-BY-STEP GUIDE TO THE INDUSTRIAL REVOLUTION

**1** Big landowners buy up smaller farms to produce more food faster and make more money.

**2** More food means more babies are born (and survive) and the population goes way up.

 More coal is needed to run the steam engines AND steam engines are used in coal mining. Lots and lots of coal mining happens in Britain. Many kinds of factories pop up.

People invent new kinds of transportation that run on steam power, including train locomotives and freighters. This is the beginning of our whizzing around the world.

So how did we get to where we are today, whizzing around the world, shopping in malls, going on vacations, and having technology at our fingertips? It's safe to say it is ALL due to the Industrial Revolution. And here's how it went down:

**3**

Extra food allows people to start to invent things instead of being farmers. They make simple machines, like spinning and weaving tools, that produce cloth much faster.

→

**4**

Machines get bigger and better. Factories replace homes as the places where things are made. Former farmers move to cities to be **laborers** in factories that make yarn and thread or weave cloth.

**5**

In the 1760s, James Watt improves the steam engine, which uses **coal** to produce energy.

←

**8**

People who own factories get very rich—a new social class develops called the **bourgeoisie**. Working people stay poor.

→

**9**

Cities grow, get overcrowded and dirty. Long work hours, dangerous factory conditions, and disease make life hard for the poor.

Labor/laborer: Labor is another word for work, but it often implies hard physical work (such as coal mining!). Laborers are the people doing that labor.

Coal: Coal is a black rock that miners dig up so it can be burned for energy. During and after the Industrial Revolution, coal was the main energy source for many places in the world.

Bourgeoisie: The bourgeoisie are a social class who own most of society's wealth. That means these are the guys running the factories but not the actual factory workers!

Child labor: Child labor refers to the practice of exploiting young kids (sometimes as young as six years old!) and having them work, often in unfair conditions.

## WHY DID THE INDUSTRIAL REVOLUTION HAPPEN IN BRITAIN?

Historians don't completely agree about why the Industrial Revolution first happened in Britain, but here are some main factors:

• Clothing manufacturing started in Britain because cotton and wool were plentiful. Wool came from the sheep of England, and lots of cotton came from English colonies in the Americas and India. With a steady stream of resources, manufacturing companies could produce lots of cloth and then sell it back to the colonies.

• Britain had lots of coal and iron resources.

• Britain had developed a stable government and could support growth.

• People were already getting rich there from trade overseas (including the slave trade). Wealthy folks had extra money to invest in mines, factories, and railroads.

Some people hated the factories. Not only were factories dangerous, they took away the art of people making things by hand.

Some people got so mad about this that they barged into factories and started destroying the machines. They called themselves Luddites, after Ned Ludd, who supposedly was the first person to protest against the machine age by breaking stuff. (But. . . no one knows if he really existed.) To this day, anyone who doesn't like the way the world is so techy is called a "Luddite."

## WAS THE INDUSTRIAL REVOLUTION A GOOD THING OR A BAD THING?

| PROS | CONS |
|------|------|
| • Lots of jobs were created—and more people could earn a living. | • People lived in dirty, crowded cities. |
| • Better and faster ways of making things came about—lots of cool inventions. | • Food shortages happened. |
| | • Disease spread. |
| • Mass production created more goods (like clothing), which gave more people access to goods. | • Child labor interfered with children's education and put them at risk. |
| • Workers joined together to fight for better conditions, and usually got them. | • Many factories were dangerous—people got hurt by accidents with machines. |
| • Railroads and big ships powered by steam allowed for much faster and easier travel. | • People worked long hours for not much money. |
| • International trade soared and produced great wealth. | • Industrialized countries got richer but non-industrialized ones got poorer. |
| • Today we have lots of stores full of products and ways to get around the whole world. | • Industrial power and technology allowed Europe and United States to develop more rapidly than other areas of the world and become dominant in trade. |
| | • Today we have big problems with pollution and climate change. |

If you had to argue whether the Industrial Revolution was good or bad, where would you come out? What would be your two strongest pieces of evidence? There's no right answer here. What matters is the strength of your evidence!

---
---
---
---
---

# THE AMERICAN AND FRENCH REVOLUTIONS

The American and French revolutions were not the gradual kind of revolutions. These two revolutions involved fighting and lots of passion. Both occurred right around the same time and they share certain things in common.

For starters, they both grew out of the ideas of the Enlightenment and ended with new governments and documents that completely changed history. In these important treatises below, the new leaders of the United States and France laid out their beliefs and their vision for new governments.

Even with small excerpts, you can get to the heart of documents if you read carefully enough. Make a list of the ideas you see repeated in the U.S. and French declarations.

---
---
---
---
---

# U.S. AND FRENCH DECLARATIONS OF INDEPENDENCE

| DECLARATION OF INDEPENDENCE 1776 | FRENCH DECLARATION OF THE RIGHTS OF MAN AND OF CITIZENS 1789 |
|---|---|
| "We hold these truths to be self-evident, that all men are created equal, that they are endowed by their Creator with certain unalienable Rights, that among these are Life, Liberty and the pursuit of Happiness." | • Men are born and remain free and equal in rights.<br><br>• These rights are liberty, property, security, and resistance to oppression. |

**INSPIRATION FROM ENLIGHTENMENT THINKERS**

*"All mankind…being all equal and independent, no one ought to harm another in his life, health, liberty or possessions."*
—John Locke

*"To become truly great, one has to stand with people, not above them."*
—Montesquieu

*"I believe in the equality of man; and I believe that religious duties consist in doing justice… My own mind is my own church."*
—Thomas Paine

**Self-evident:** Something that is so clearly true that you don't need proof.

**Unalienable:** Something that can't be taken away.

**Resistance:** The attempt to prevent something by arguing or fighting against it.

**Oppression:** The unfair use of power to control a person or people.

*The Battle of Lexington, 1775*

Now take those ideas from the documents and compare them to the Enlightenment quotes. Do you find many of the same ideas?

_____

_____

_____

_____

Thought so. That's what historians do, they look for connections.

But it wasn't only ideas that drove people to revolt. In both revolutions, people rose up because of injustice. Both the American colonists and the working people in France got sick and tired of being treated unfairly by the rulers who had power over them. They said, "Enough! We demand freedom and fairness!" Injustices looked different on each side of the Atlantic, but both led to forceful calls for change.

> **Revolt:** A revolt is a rebellion against something. It often can be quite violent—just wait until you read about guillotines!
>
> **Injustice:** Injustice is when something is unequal, unfair, and even morally wrong. Can you think of some modern injustices to help you understand this term?

# AMERICAN REVOLUTION

In America, injustice was coming from the fact that the thirteen colonies were. . . well, colonies. If you flip back to pages 208-209, you'll recall that the whole point of one country taking over an area and setting up a colony was to get something out of it—resources, labor, goods. So George III, the king of England at the time, saw the American colonies as a source of money for England (and they needed it). Here's how things came to a boiling point:

# EVENTS LEADING UP TO THE AMERICAN REVOLUTION

**1** England spends money defending the colonies in the French and Indian War

**2** King George of England wants to regain the money, so he makes the colonists buy special stamps and pay high taxes on sugar, molasses, wine, coffee, tea, and other imports.

**3** American colonists resent having to buy British goods AND pay taxes. Especially when they had no say in the matter.

**6** Tensions erupt in Boston when a crowd of colonists taunt British soldiers. The soldiers lose control and fire on the crowd, killing three Americans.

**5** American colonists boycott (refuse to buy) British goods.

**4** More and more, Americans think of themselves as separate from Britain and don't want to be controlled by a government far away.

**7** A group of colonists protest a tax on tea by dumping 92,000 pounds of English tea into Boston Harbor.

**8** King George cracks down. He outlaws public gatherings and sends more British soldiers over.

**9** First battle occurs.

*King Louis XVI and Marie Antoinette*

## FRENCH REVOLUTION

In France, it was also a king (Louis XVI and his queen, Marie Antoinette) doing the oppressing. Add to this a whole estate system that kept people down. It was a holdover from the feudal system and it divided people into three levels: clergy, nobles, and commoners (98 percent of the population).

## THE ESTATE SYSTEM

Guess who did all the work? Yep, common folk. Guess who paid the highest taxes? Common folk, again. Guess who had very little food and no say in government? Right again.

So you get the idea. These days, even though there are great differences in wealth, we can't imagine a government where common people have no voice, but that's because of these two revolutions! (And those Enlightenment thinkers, too!)

On July 14, 1789, people from the Third Estate (the commoners) stormed the Bastille prison in Paris. About 100 people were killed, including the king and queen, and the violence continued for years.

# THE REIGN OF TERROR

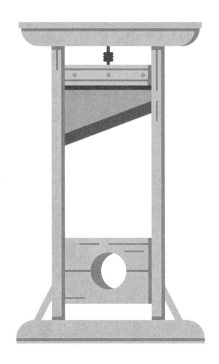

During a gruesome time known as the Reign of Terror (September 1793 to July 1794), 17,000 people were executed with a tool called the guillotine. This invention made killing people quick and easy: a super sharp blade would drop down from a tall frame to neatly chop off a person's head. Beheadings became quite the rage in revolutionary France, and children even had toy guillotines!

Guillotine: The guillotine is an invention that gained popularity during the French Revolution. It's a tool that made it easier and quicker to kill people, by dropping a huge blade onto them and beheading them. Ouch!

## A WORD FROM DR. GUILLOTINE

"You've got the wrong guy! I mean, name!"

Guillotines were first used in the Middle Ages. During the French Revolution, a doctor named Joseph Ignace Guillotine suggested using them, but only because he was against the death penalty and wanted to find a way to make executions painless.

The actual workings of the guillotine were developed by another French doctor and a German engineer. But the name Guillotine stuck and Joseph Guillotine was never OK with it.

# RESULTS AND NON-RESULTS OF THE REVOLUTIONS AT A GLANCE

| AMERICA | FRANCE |
|---|---|
| • Independence from England | • End of monarchy in France |
| • Formation of a new nation and government | • End of feudalism |
| • 30 percent of the population remained in slavery | • End of church authority to make laws |
| • Helped inspire the French Revolution | • New system of government |
| • Women could not vote | • Women could not vote |

Which do you think caused a bigger change?

_____

_____

_____

_____

_____

_____

_____

_____

_____

_____

_____

_____

_____

_____

# THE SLAVE TRADE AND ITS IMPACT

We've seen how the Enlightenment allowed a new social order to take shape in Europe. Common people moved from being subjects of a king to citizens of a nation. But many historians question whether the American Revolution was all that revolutionary.

In other words, did it really change the way society worked in colonial America?

The Declaration of Independence declared that all men were created equal and deserving of rights, and yet 30 percent of the population continued to endure a life of slavery, with no rights whatsoever. It took over a hundred years for American slaves to be set free, and even then they didn't have full rights.

## A TERRIBLE LEGACY

The story of slavery is one of the saddest, most horrifying aspects of human history. You're old enough now to face it, and face it you must to see how our society went wrong. You might find yourself in disbelief that people could be so cruel, and you'll probably be surprised at how much slavery affected history.

By the way, we won't be sugarcoating it either. So grab all your tools and get ready for a hard look at a difficult subject.

# THE BEGINNINGS OF THE SLAVE TRADE

Let's backtrack to the 1500s when Portuguese and Spanish merchants were trading with West African kings. Part of what they were trading was people. Most African states had their own systems of slavery well before

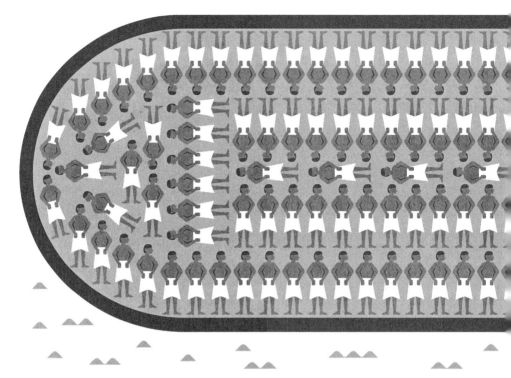

*Diagram showing the space allocated on a slave ship for a journey lasting between two and three months*

the Europeans arrived. When communities battled with another, the winning side would take prisoners of war who became enslaved laborers. Sometimes these slaves could own land. Sometimes they could work to attain rights. Also, criminals could be sentenced to slavery. So there was a ready supply of slaves that leaders in Africa traded for European goods.

## THE TRANSATLANTIC VOYAGE: SHIP OF MISERY

When European merchants loaded these people onto ships to take them across the Atlantic Ocean, the slaves experienced torturous conditions.

Often people were branded on their faces, or sometimes their ears were cut off to identify them as slaves. People were packed in like luggage, individuals getting four square feet, a space smaller than the bed you sleep in.

They had hardly any food or exercise. During a two or three-month voyage, they had to live with urine and feces all around them and many

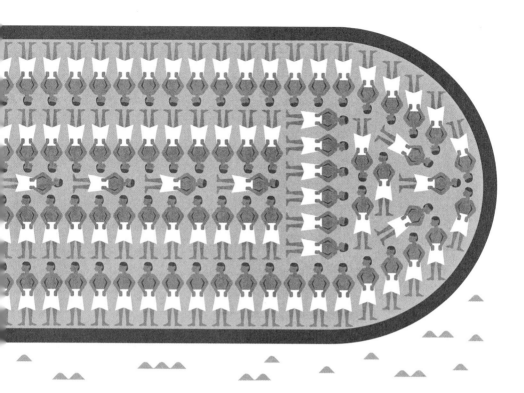

became sick and died. Some jumped overboard to avoid such suffering; others were thrown overboard if they did not cooperate.

It is estimated that about 30 percent of Africans who were transported across the Atlantic Ocean died on the way from the terrible conditions. Once they arrived (most of them in the Caribbean and Brazil) they were sold at auctions to plantation owners. Families were separated.

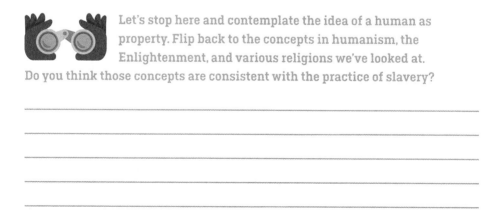

Let's stop here and contemplate the idea of a human as property. Flip back to the concepts in humanism, the Enlightenment, and various religions we've looked at. Do you think those concepts are consistent with the practice of slavery?

_____

_____

_____

_____

_____

Read this account by Olaudah Equiano, who was captured in what is now Nigeria at about the age of eleven. Equiano was transported in a slave ship across the Atlantic to the West Indies, where he was sold to a Royal Navy officer.

Many years later, Olaudah was one of the very few slaves who was able to buy his freedom.

> The stench of the hold while we were on the coast was so intolerably loathsome, that it was dangerous to remain there for any time. . . some of us had been permitted to stay on the deck for the fresh air. But now that the whole ship's cargo were confined together, it became absolutely pestilential. The closeness of the place and the heat of the climate, added to the number on the ship, which was so crowded that each had scarcely room to turn himself, almost suffocated us.

Olaudah Equiano

# THE SLAVE TRADE EXPLODES

By the late eighteenth century, African slave traders could hardly keep up with the demand for slaves in Brazil, the Caribbean, and the American colonies.

Landowners were developing sugar, cotton, and tobacco plantations at a rapid pace, and the owners needed someone to do all that work of clearing land, planting, and harvesting. (They assumed that people beneath them should have to do it for free.)

# WHY AFRICAN SLAVES?

Settlers might have preferred to use the people already there as slaves, but as you recall, most of the Native Americans had died from disease. Those surviving often escaped because they knew the lay of the land. But African slaves were immune to those diseases, arrived disoriented to a foreign land, and, of course, were already in shackles.

By the late 1600s the Portuguese, British, Spanish, French, Dutch, Danish, and Americans were all in on the slave trade and began to compete. The numbers of imported slaves rose and rose, peaking in the early 1800s.

## RISE AND FALL OF THE TRANSATLANTIC SLAVE TRADE

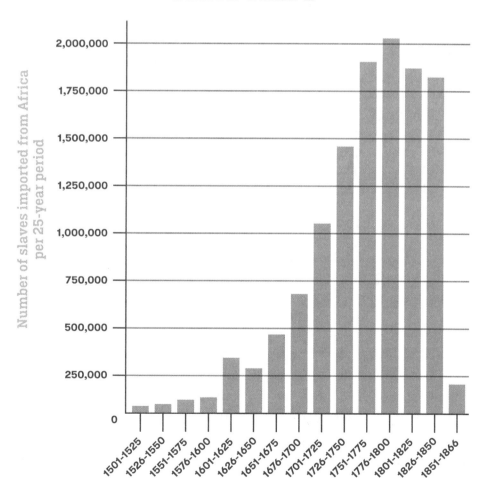

Europe and the United States derived huge wealth from the absolutely free labor that slavery provided. Take a look at the diagram below and you'll see how it worked.

> **Pestilential:** This means very, very unhealthy conditions where disease can spread easily.
>
> **Shackles:** Shackles are chains that are used to confine and imprison people.

# THE TRIANGULAR TRADE

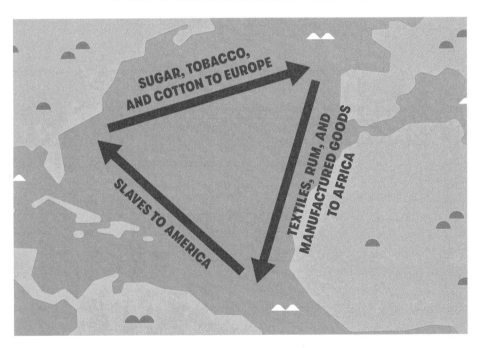

Slavery allowed for a steady supply of raw materials to flow into Europe. There, they were processed into products like fabric and rum. Those goods were then transported to Africa and traded for people, who were carried across the ocean to do the work of producing raw materials that then went back to Europe. And the cycle repeated. It was a fast and furious cycle, a huge, huge movement of people that caused major changes on three different continents.

# THE IMPACT OF SLAVERY ON...

| | |
|---|---|
| **AMERICA AND THE CARIBBEAN** | Slavery spurred rapid development. If not for slave labor, growth of the New World would have been slow at best. It is doubtful that the colonies could have ever developed enough wealth to separate from Britain. |
| **EUROPE** | Slavery paved the way for the Industrial Revolution. Absolutely free labor made for huge profits, which in turn could be reinvested. Materials flooding in from the Americas put English industry into high gear, and also created a huge appetite in Europe for luxury goods like sugar and tobacco. |
| **AFRICA** | The slave trade brought great loss and increased conflict. The relentless demand for slaves made capturing them the reason for war rather than a result from it. Also, the loss of 11 million people, mainly men, drained communities of manpower for sustaining their communities and made Africa more vulnerable to conquest by the Europeans. |
| **AFRICANS AND AFRICAN AMERICANS** | Twelve million people were torn out of their own culture, forced into strange and hostile environments, and treated as less than human. Racist attitudes took hold in the United States. Even after emancipation, African Americans struggled to regain their culture and secure the rights enjoyed by white Americans. |

 What are some of the present-day consequences of slavery in the United States? In other parts of the world?

_____

_____

_____

_____

_____

# THE AGE OF IMPERIALISM

When you hear the word imperialism, just remember to leave off the last part of the word (-alism), switch around the first I to an E and you'll have the word "empire."

Anything that's called imperial has to do with an empire, and (as you remember) an empire is born when a powerful nation gets even bigger by taking over and controlling other nations or states or communities.

Imperialism: Imperialism is when a larger or more powerful country extends its power by taking over smaller territories and countries and building huge empires.

When the Age of Imperialism kicked in (roughly 1760), empires became a thing—and mainly a British thing. In fact, the British Empire grew to be the largest empire of all time during this age.

## GREAT BRITAIN: MASTER EMPIRE BUILDERS

But how did a tiny country, the size of the state of Louisiana, end up controlling one quarter of the Earth's total land area? You actually already know the answer because you know about colonization, industrialization, and technology.

## ELEMENTS OF IMPERIALISM

| COLONIZATION | INDUSTRY | NEW TECHNOLOGY |
|---|---|---|
| Taking over and settling a new place provides the raw materials for making things. | Gets a good deal from free slave labor and raw materials from colonies<br><br>Products are made and sold back to the colonies<br><br>Industrial countries get richer | Steam power<br><br>Railroads<br><br>Ocean freighters<br><br>Telegraph<br><br>Weapons |
| European countries set up colonies in Asia, Africa, and the Americas | Imperial nations compete for territory so that their industries can keep growing | Technology allows Britain and other European powers to control far-away places (in a way the Romans could not) |

Imperialism of the eighteenth and nineteenth centuries did not usually involve sending people to live somewhere and take it over from the native people (as in the Americas in the 1600s).

## THE TOOLS OF EMPIRE

Instead, the "mother country" controlled the territory in economic and political ways. Often imperial nations governed their territories through local rulers already in place, keeping them in power in exchange for their loyalty and compliance. Imperialism involved economic control of areas outside the "mother country."

> **Raw materials:** Raw materials are the basic materials that something is made from.
>
> **Territory:** A territory is an area of land under the control of a government. As you're reading about different empires and imperial governments in this chapter, try to keep track of who controls which territories!

# BRITISH IMPERIALISM IN ASIA

By 1800, the little country of Britain was a mighty force, but it did not have a lot of natural resources. For its manufacturing, it needed materials like cotton, iron, and copper, so it set up colonies to get these materials from other places.

It also wanted people in other countries to buy its products. If they didn't want to, it had ways of making them do so (yes, weapons). Other European countries also wanted a piece of the imperial pie. So over the next hundred years European powers tried to grab up and dominate as much of the world as they could.

# FROM THE MOTHER COUNTRY TO THE COLONY AND BACK

| MOTHER COUNTRY | ITEM | COLONY |
|---|---|---|
| | ← Raw materials (like cotton) | |
| | → Manufactured goods | |
| | ← $$ from selling goods | |
| WANTS: raw materials for industry, more people to buy stuff, more territory | ← Taxes | |
| HAS: money, technology, transportation, weapons | ← People (enslaved laborers, soldiers) | |

How would a king explain this system? How would a colonist describe it? An Indigenous person?

_____

_____

_____

_____

_____

_____

_____

# THE EAST INDIA COMPANY

The East India Company was founded back in 1600 by a group of English traders who put up their own money and asked Queen Elizabeth I for a royal charter to get lots of Indian spices and luxury items for Britain.

## TOOLS FOR DOMINATION

Through the years this company grew to become one of the most powerful forces of British imperialism, responsible for half of Britain's trade. Equipped with ships, thousands of soldiers, guns, and slaves, the East India Company would forcibly take over territories, set itself up as the government (even though it was really a business), and charge the people taxes. Then they would buy English goods with the taxes. Pretty sweet setup for the Brits.

In India, they kicked out the Portuguese, Dutch, and French and eventually took over the whole subcontinent. At its height, the East India Company also controlled parts of China, the Middle East, and Southeast Asia. Eventually, the company got so corrupt the British government took control of it.

*An East India Trading Company ship*

## THE OPIUM WARS

The Brits and the East India Company had a problem with China. British people loved stuff from China—porcelain, silk, and tea especially. But Chinese people didn't need or want much from England.

## THE EAST INDIA COMPANY'S SOLUTION: SELLING DRUGS

So the East India Company decided to correct this imbalance by selling the Chinese opium made from flowers called poppies that grew in India. Opium is a highly addictive narcotic (drug). The British said to China, "You need to legalize opium and let us sell you other stuff too." The Qing emperor did not want a country of drug addicts, so he flat out refused.

And then the fighting began, called the Opium Wars, lasting from 1839-1860.

## FIGHTING ON TWO FRONTS

China also had a very bloody civil war raging. The East India Company blasted in with its warships, and eventually the Chinese had to give in. The English demanded that five ports be opened along the Chinese coast where they could sell things, including opium. They also took China's territory of Hong Kong and made the Chinese pay for the opium they had dumped into the ocean during the war. At the end of the nineteenth century, almost one-third of the Chinese population had become addicted to opium.

# SCRAMBLE FOR AFRICA

Ever since the Portuguese started a few colonies in Africa during the 1500s, Europe had its eye on Africa. It was huge and rich with resources. But for many years their attempts at conquering and colonizing inside of Africa failed.

As we know, technology has a way of removing obstacles. Here's how science and technology eventually allowed Europeans to get in, and eventually take over.

**Port:** A port is a place where many ships can dock and unload. Ports can really open up trade to an area, since so much of the world economy at this time happened through trade by sea!

# TECHNOLOGY AND COLONIZATION

| OBSTACLE FOR EUROPEANS IN COLONIZING AFRICA | KEY TECHNOLOGY | HOW TECHNOLOGY HELPED THE EUROPEANS |
| --- | --- | --- |
| Many Africans were immune to the disease of malaria, but Europeans weren't. Malaria killed people and horses who tried to infiltrate Africa. | Quinine, an anti-malaria drug, is discovered. Quinine is made from the bark of a special tree found in South America. | More Europeans survived excursions into Africa and more were willing to go. |
| Climate and terrain made it difficult for Europeans to access most of the African continent, and they needed horses and lots of equipment to get from the shore inland. Progress was slow and difficult. | Steam-powered engines were smaller than previous engines, but more powerful. This allowed for the development of smaller and sleeker ships. | Previously, European ships were only able to travel along coasts, but with these new steam ships, Europeans could travel on rivers into the heart of Africa. |
| African warriors could attack and drive out European settlers. | Advanced weapons like the muzzle-loading rifle allowed Europeans to more quickly and safely reload, as well as to fire shots rapidly. | Europeans could fend off attacks because their weapons were superior, and they had lots of them. |

Once getting a piece of Africa was possible, lots of European countries wanted in on the act. They started fighting over who got what.

# THE BERLIN CONFERENCE

In 1885, representatives from fourteen European countries and the United States met in Berlin, Germany, to divide the continent of Africa among themselves. No Africans were invited to the Berlin Conference. The borders drawn did not respect cultural differences or the history of societies there. Most of the national borders are still in effect today. Most historians agree that difficulties in Africa today have their roots in the results of the Berlin Conference.

## AFRICAN COLONIES AFTER THE BERLIN CONFERENCE OF 1884

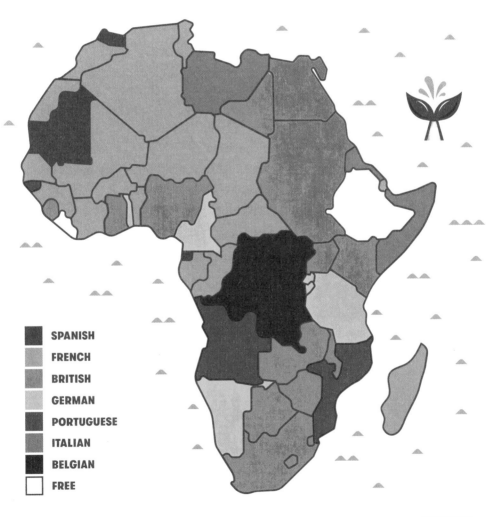

SPANISH
FRENCH
BRITISH
GERMAN
PORTUGUESE
ITALIAN
BELGIAN
FREE

# JAPAN AND THE MEIJI ERA

Wise people living on islands to the east of China were watching closely during the Opium Wars. They saw the humiliation that China suffered at the hands of the British. They also saw the British take over India, the Spanish taking over the Philippine Islands, the Dutch dominate Indonesia and the French eat up much of Southeast Asia.

"We could be next," they thought, and they were right.

## A TRADITION OF ISOLATION AND STRICT ORDER

These people were the Japanese and they had a long tradition of isolation. Their culture was agrarian, broken up into feudal farms with a strict social order, similar to that of Europe during the Middle Ages. They had an emperor, but he had very little power. Instead, a military government called the Tokugawa Shogunate had kept order for hundreds of years. Content in their traditional way of life, the Japanese wanted nothing to do with the West and closed themselves off.

Agrarian: When something is agrarian, that means it has to do with farms. An agrarian economy, for example, is one based on agriculture and farming for economic means.

Shogunate: The shogunate was Japan's military government that ruled for hundreds of years. The shogun was essentially a military dictator who answered only to the emperor.

*Meiji, the "boy emperor"*

# A BOY EMPEROR BRINGS VAST CHANGE

In 1853, along came Matthew Perry, a naval officer, who pretty much told the shogun ruler that the Japanese had to open themselves to trade with the West. The Japanese, being realistic, took one look at Perry's fleet of warships and signed some very unfair agreements. The people were disappointed that Shogun Tokugawa had sold out, and in 1867 he resigned.

## THE CHARTER OATH

Japan was ready for a change, which came in the form of a "boy emperor," only fifteen years old, named Meiji. Meiji and his government studied the West and used what they learned to modernize and unify Japan.

One of their first actions was to lay out their goals clearly in a document called the Charter Oath.

# THE CHARTER OATH OF THE MEIJI RESTORATION (1868)

1. Assemblies shall be widely established and all matters decided by public discussion.

2. All classes, high and low, shall unite in vigorously carrying out the administration of affairs of state.

3. The common people, no less than the civil and military officials, shall each be allowed to pursue his own calling so that there may be no discontent.

4. Evil customs of the past shall be broken off and everything based upon the just laws of Nature.

5. Knowledge shall be sought throughout the world so as to strengthen the foundations of imperial rule.

How are the ideas in this charter similar to and different from the excerpts we looked at from the American and French revolutions? Do you see any Enlightenment ideas hiding in here?

_____

_____

_____

_____

_____

_____

_____

They wanted nothing less than to be an imperial power in their own right. (Spoiler alert: they did it!) As one Japanese leader put it, "If we take initiative we will dominate, if we do not we will be dominated." (Shimazu Nariakira, 1809–1858)

*A ship in the Meiji-era Japanese navy*

Unified the government by restoring power to the emperor

Ratified a constitution with rights for people at all levels of society

Established a strong army and navy

**MEIJI RESTORATION, JAPAN'S EXTREME MAKEOVER**

Provided (and required) public education

Created their own industrial revolution—built railroads, steamships, telegraph lines, coal mines

Created a tax system

In the space of less than fifty years, Japan advanced from a traditional farming society into an advanced industrial nation.

It didn't happen through war or conquest. Governmental policies and declarations and actions brought on the change. It helped that a stable period preceded the Meiji regime, but Japanese leaders also knew what they were shooting for.

## TURNING OUTWARD

By 1912, when Meiji died, Japan had annexed neighboring territories of Korea, Taiwan, and Southern Manchuria, making it the most powerful imperial nation in East Asia.

> **Annex:** When one country annexes another territory, that means they are claiming that territory as a part of their country.

Thinking back to our first encounter with revolution and its definition, do you think the Meiji Restoration should be considered a revolution? Why or why not?

_____

_____

_____

_____

_____

_____

_____

_____

_____

_____

_____

_____

# DEMOCRACY AND THE BEGINNINGS OF SOCIAL CHANGE

The late 1800s was a period of stark contrasts. Factories churned out products, a few folks were getting wealthy, but most lived in crowded cities working for low pay, or they managed to eke out a living from agriculture outside of the big cities. Problems like poverty, slavery and its aftermath, women's oppression, child labor, and other social ills caused a lot of misery.

But here's the thing to remember about human beings by this time: they believed they could try to change things. They weren't like the people of the Middle Ages or before who pretty much did as they were told by the church or a king.

## THE WORD SPREADS

People were starting to hear about events where people rose up, and they knew that some governments were democratic, or allowed citizens to have a say in who ran a nation and what decisions they made.

# A TIME FOR REFORMS

By 1850, democracy had taken hold in several countries, and was on the way in others. But even established democracies were far from perfect. Women, former slaves, and people of the lower classes in Britain were excluded from full voting rights for many years.

Still even the *idea* of democracy—and, of course, all the problems—inspired people to fight for reforms. To reform something is to make it better, and usually that means fairer.

> **Reform:** To make something better, and usually more fair.

Sometimes people still had to demand to be heard, but many governments during this time either improved their democracies or took steps to pave the way for people to participate in government.

# CHANGES IN THE NINETEENTH CENTURY

Here is a glimpse at some pockets of change around the world that were popping up in the mid to late nineteenth century.

| UNITED STATES | RUSSIA |
|---|---|
| Trade unions for skilled workers were legalized in 1871.<br><br>The 1884 Reform Act gave the vote to poor farmers and laborers (at least those who were male and over twenty-five). | In 1861, Alexander II freed 23 million serfs from a feudal system that kept them controlled by "lords" or landowners. This allowed one-third of the population to seek other kinds of jobs and eventually led to Russia catching up with industrialization. |
| **OTTOMAN EMPIRE** | **MEXICO** |
| The Tanzimat (reorganization) period between 1839 and 1876 promised equality to non-Muslims, created a new code of law (based on laws in France), instituted public education, and set up local assemblies to give communities a voice in government. | During a time called La Reforma (1854–1876), the Mexican government drafted a constitution that reduced the power of the church, abolished slavery, and gave citizens rights, including freedom of speech and freedom of assembly. |

Representatives from Europe, the United States, and leading Muslim powers meet at the Brussels Anti-Slavery Conference (1889-90) to put an end to the international slave trade.

# WOMEN AND SOCIAL CHANGE

*"Now all we need is to continue to speak the truth fearlessly, and we shall add to our number those who will turn the scale to the side of equal and full justice in all things."*

—Lucy Stone, in a speech to the Congress of Women held at the World's Fair, Chicago, 1893

This quote not only gives you a sense of how passionate some of the reformers were, it also provides a big hint into who many of the reformers were: women. They couldn't vote, they didn't hold government positions, most didn't own businesses or even have advanced education, but many women worked for social change during Late Modern History, especially in the United States and Great Britain.

Women were among the first in the United States to join the abolitionist movement (to abolish slavery).

Later, as women entered the workforce in factories, working long hours under dangerous conditions, they joined in the movement for workers' rights. Women also called for prison reform and laws against child labor. They worked for better education for girls and women, and for newly freed slaves.

## THE TEMPERANCE MOVEMENT TAKES ROOT

Women were crucial to the movement to ban alcohol consumption, called the temperance movement (even though it didn't succeed).

**Abolition:** To abolish something is to permanently get rid of it, so abolitionist movements at this time were working to end slavery.

**Temperance movement:** A movement to ban the sale and consumption of alcohol, which many felt was at the root of social problems.

They felt that many men drank too much, which endangered the well-being of their wives and children. Women in favor of temperance wanted bars to shut down and laws changed so that women could escape marriages to hard drinking men.

*Temperance supporters fought against alcohol consumption*

## SENECA FALLS CONVENTION

In 1840, two women abolitionists from the United States traveled to London to attend the World Anti-Slavery Convention. When they arrived at the meetings, they were shocked to find that women were not permitted to speak, and even had to sit separately behind a partition. The two women, Elizabeth Cady Stanton and Lucretia Mott, had had enough. They decided it was time to organize the first ever U.S. conference on the rights of women.

The Seneca Falls Convention was held July 19 and 20 in 1848 in Seneca Falls, New York. About three hundred people gathered there (including some men) to name nineteen rights that had been denied to women and to call for change.

Mott and Stanton wrote a document called "The Declaration of Sentiments," which purposely used the language from the Declaration of Independence to show how women had been excluded from the rights and freedoms upon which the country had been founded. "We hold these truths to be self-evident; that all men *and women* are created equal," it began. They argued that "life, liberty and the pursuit of happiness" had been granted to all men but denied to all women.

Remember that the common law legally put all of a couple's property and decision-making in the hands of the husband. At the time, even single women could not own property (and yet they paid taxes).

Why do you think the authors of the Declaration of Sentiments decided to use the language of the Declaration of Independence instead of creating new language around women's rights?

_____

_____

_____

_____

_____

_____

_____

## FREDERICK DOUGLASS LENDS A HAND

*Frederick Douglass*

Some men attended the convention; among them was Frederick Douglass, an African American writer and lecturer, and leading voice of the abolitionist movement. Douglass ended up being extremely important to the women's convention. There was much debate about whether to include in the document a demand for women's voting rights.

Some people (including some women) argued that it was not yet time for such a shift. Some felt that women deserved other rights, but should remain in the home and not be part of public life. Both Douglass and Stanton made impassioned speeches, urging that woman suffrage be included.

At the end of the convention, by a close vote, a demand for woman suffrage was included in the document. This first step was important, but it took seventy more years for a law to be passed that allowed all women in the United States to vote in elections.

*Elizabeth Cady Stanton*

# WOMEN'S RIGHTS IN BRITAIN

Women in England also fought the long fight. During the early twentieth century, British women's rights activists drafted petitions, marched in protests, and even went on hunger strikes to call attention to their cause. In 1910, in an event known as Black Friday, three hundred suffragettes were arrested, assaulted, and beaten by police for marching on the Houses of Parliament. Eight years later, women in the United Kingdom finally achieved the right to vote.

# DEMOCRACY VERSUS IMPERIALISM

Progress was starting inside of some countries, but let's remember that imperialism was the main game between countries in Europe, Africa, and Asia.

## WHO GETS TO BE A CITIZEN?

So democratic "mother countries," such as Great Britain, were in control of people in their territories, and these people did not count as citizens and lacked many rights of the conquerors. Imperialism and colonialism were seen as noble missions by those who conquered and ruled other lands and restricted the freedoms of those who lived in those countries.

But as we've learned, history is all about who gets to tell the story.

If a democratic country controls other areas, and the people in those areas don't get to vote, do you think that country should still be called democratic? This question has been debated by politicians and historians throughout history, but see if you can state how imperialism and slavery created contradictions for democratic countries.

_____

_____

_____

_____

_____

_____

_____

_____

_____

_____

_____

_____

# CHAPTER VOCABULARY

**Abolition:** To abolish something is to permanently get rid of it, so abolitionist movements at this time were working to end slavery.

**Agrarian:** When something is agrarian, that means it has to do with farms. An agrarian economy, for example, is one based on agriculture and farming for economic means.

**Annex:** When one country annexes another territory, that means they are claiming that territory as a part of their country.

**Bourgeoisie:** The bourgeoisie are a social class who own most of society's wealth. That means these are the guys running the factories but not the actual factory workers!

**Charter:** A charter is a written grant (a bit like a field trip permission form) from a ruling power that defines the rights and privileges of another city, colony, or company.

**Child labor:** Child labor refers to the practice of exploiting young kids (sometimes as young as six years old!) and having them work, often in unfair conditions.

**Coal:** Coal is a black rock that miners dig up so it can be burned for energy. During and after the Industrial Revolution, coal was the main energy source for many places in the world.

**Declaration of Sentiments:** An 1848 document that echoed the language of the Declaration of Independence to protest women's inferior legal status and demand equality for women, including the right to vote.

**Guillotine:** The guillotine is an invention that gained popularity during the French Revolution. It's a tool that made it easier and quicker to kill people, by dropping a huge blade onto them and beheading them.

**Imperialism:** Imperialism is when a larger or more powerful country extends its power by taking over smaller territories and countries and building huge empires.

**Industrial:** Industrial means something has to do with manufacturing, factories, trade, or technology.

**Injustice:** Injustice is when something is unequal, unfair, and even morally wrong. Can you think of some modern injustices to help you understand this term?

**Labor/laborer:** Labor is another word for work, but it often implies hard physical work (such as coal mining!). Laborers are the people doing that labor.

**Malaria:** Malaria is a life-threatening disease that can be passed through mosquitoes to people.

**Monarchy:** A monarchy is a form of government with one supreme ruler, usually a king or queen.

**Oppression:** Oppression is cruel treatment to keep someone below you. It's usually used to describe groups of people, like women or people of color, experiencing unjust treatment in society.

**Pestilential:** This means very, very unhealthy conditions where disease can spread easily.

**Port:** A port is a place where many ships can dock and unload.

**Raw materials:** Raw materials are the basic materials that something is made from.

**Reform:** To make something better, and usually more fair.

**Resistance:** Resistance is fighting against something and refusing to go along with it.

**Revolt:** A revolt is a rebellion against something. It often can be quite violent.

**Self-evident:** When something is self-evident, that means it is so clearly true that you don't need proof.

**Shackles:** Shackles are chains that are used to confine and imprison people.

**Shogunate:** The shogunate was Japan's military government that ruled for hundreds of years. The shogun was essentially a military dictator who answered only to the emperor.

**Suffrage:** Suffrage is the right to vote. We may take our ability to vote in elections for granted now, but throughout history many groups have had to fight for their suffrage.

**Suffragette:** Supporters of voting rights for women in Great Britain were known as "suffragettes." In the United States, they were called "suffragists."

**Temperance movement:** A movement to ban the sale and consumption of alcohol, which many felt was at the root of social problems.

**Territory:** A territory is an area of land under the control of a government.

**Unalienable:** Unalienable is used to describe something that can't be taken away.

# NOTES

# 6 LATE MODERN HISTORY II

Get ready, you're about to see history repeat itself. You'll see how the Industrial Revolution accelerates and spreads, again affecting the balance of wealth and the technology of war. Unfortunately, you'll see a repeat of human cruelty, too, and the destructive power that the leaders of nations can have.

## CHAPTER CONTENTS

# THE GILDED AND MACHINE AGES

In 1898, George Washington Vanderbilt decided to build a nice little mansion for his family in Asheville, North Carolina (that's it on the previous spread). Actually, it was more of a castle. With 250 rooms, including forty-three bathrooms, this home is still the largest privately owned home in the United States.

Are you wondering how a family back in the 1800s got THAT RICH? Good job looking for causes. This section will answer that question—and why it matters, and how the world changed during the years the Vanderbilts were enjoying quiet evenings in front of their sixty-five fireplaces.

*Cornelius Vanderbilt*

You'll recall how when the people in Britain moved from working on farms to working in factories, the English economy shifted into high gear. The factory owners got rich, and the workers stayed poor, but lots of stuff got made. New technologies developed and, thanks to the steam engine, products could be shipped all over the world.

Later on, a similar process happened in the United States, but it was much, much bigger. Some historians call the period of 1870–1914 the Second Industrial Revolution. It's also called the Machine Age, and the Gilded Age (we'll get to that later), but the main thing to know is that this was a time in the United States when industry and technology sped up and huge profits poured in for a few businessmen.

> **Economy:** The economy of a country is their wealth, resources, production, and the system by which those are all managed. There are lots of different models for shaping an economy, and you'll see throughout history the tensions between countries advocating for different kinds of economies!

# INVENTIONS AND THEIR EFFECTS

The number of U.S. inventions over time:

| YEAR | 1790 | 1860 | 1890 |
|---|---|---|---|
| # OF INVENTIONS (PATENTS) | 276 | 60,000 | 450,000 |

You can see why this era is often called the Machine Age. People were busy inventing all kinds of machines. Several major inventions were key to the mega-trade and mega-profits of this era.

# EFFECTS OF
# THE MACHINE AGE

| MAJOR INVENTIONS (CAUSE) | EFFECT | BUSINESS EFFECT |
|---|---|---|
| Bessemer process for faster production of steel | 40,000 miles of railroad constructed across the United States<br><br>Goods could be shipped nationwide<br><br>Tall buildings could be constructed with steel | |
| Railway air brake | Made it safe for trains to go faster<br><br>More goods shipped faster | |
| Electric power | Electric power plants built, power lines laid<br><br>People could work longer hours, workspaces were safer (less risk of fire) | |
| Refrigeration | Fresh food could be shipped by railroad longer distances—more food available | |
| Telephone, typewriter, adding machine, cash register | Business could be done faster, in the moment, over distance | |

Notice how this chart shows that effects can then become causes of further effects. How do the effects in the middle column become causes of greater profits? Use your own reasoning to explain this. For example, how do you think that doing business faster over a longer distance led to more profits for companies?

_____

_____

_____

_____

_____

_____

Sounds great, doesn't it? Business was booming. Skyscrapers were popping up. New jobs were being created, and a middle class of office workers started to emerge. Men and women began working as secretaries, managers, and bookkeepers to keep businesses organized and profitable. They earned more than farmers and laborers. People began to seek education and training to get these new, plentiful jobs. All good, right? Until it wasn't.

## THE RISE OF PHILANTHROPISTS

A new, very small, ultra-rich class also came to be. These were large business owners who continued to build their empires and crowd out smaller businesses. Some wealthy people became philanthropists, meaning they had so much money they could give some away to the public and build, say, a whole university or hospital. Some of the billionaires' names might be familiar to you because they left behind businesses, universities, and museums that are still part of U.S. life today.

Philanthropists: A philanthropist is someone with lots of money who uses that money to help others.

| NAME | SOURCE OF WEALTH |
|------|------------------|
| Andrew Carnegie | Steel |
| J.P. Morgan | Banking |
| Henry Ford | Automobile manufacturing |
| John D. Rockefeller | Oil imports |
| Cornelius Vanderbilt | Railroads and shipping |

# ALL THAT GLITTERS IS NOT GOLD

Some of the richy-rich got greedy. Gobs of money gave them the power to influence people in government. Sometimes billionaires would donate money to help certain people get elected. Sometimes they actually bribed politicians to make decisions that benefited their businesses, giving them an unfair advantage. This is called corruption.

That's one reason why a famous writer of the time, Mark Twain, called these years the "Gilded Age." When something is gilded, it has a thin coating of gold, so it looks gold, but it's not truly gold. Inside it's made of something ordinary, like maybe plain old metal.

So underneath the glam, ugliness was lurking. The Vanderbilts may have had forty-three bathrooms (the flushable toilet was also invented during this time), but workers lived piled up in dank, dirty, overcrowded apartment houses called tenements.

Corruption: Corruption is when people in power use their position and behave dishonestly or commit fraud. Can you think of any modern examples?

# A RUSH OF IMMIGRANTS

Twelve million immigrants from Europe poured into U.S. cities looking for the wealth America seemed to promise. But factory workers got low wages because not much skill was required to operate machines. So, as life got more lavish for the wealthy, it got tougher for workers.

Finally, the workers came together and formed labor unions to demand better pay and better working conditions. If the company said no, they would strike until their demands were met. Today, unions still protect workers from unfair treatment by their employers, and just like in the Gilded Age, the gulf separating the rich and the poor has grown wider in recent decades.

*An urban tenement*

**Labor Unions:** When workers come together to bargain with their bosses as a collective, that's called a labor union. Unions exist in different trades and industries; there are teachers' unions, and unions for garment workers, and more!

**Strike:** When workers collectively decide to stop working, that is called a strike. It's a strategy to withhold labor in order to bargain with bosses for better conditions.

Some historians have been writing about present-day income inequality in the United States and comparing it to the Gilded Age. Have you heard the term "one percent?" It means that the richest 1 percent of people in the United States now own more wealth than all middle-class people put together. What do you think might happen if this trend continues?

_____

_____

_____

_____

_____

_____

_____

_____

_____

_____

_____

_____

_____

_____

_____

# THE UNITED STATES BECOMES AN IMPERIAL POWER

Remember how the British wanted to create more buyers (or markets) in the world for all their products? Now the United States took its turn to do the same. It needed money because things got very bad for the United States in 1893. Banks were in crisis, businesses were closing down, and people were losing their jobs. Here are the steps the United States took to launch its own empire:

## IMPERIALISM AND THE UNITED STATES, 1898–1946

**1.** The United States needs to get more trade going and it targets Asia

**2.** The United States needs to control some islands so that freighters can stop to refuel on the long trip to Asia

**4.** Spain gives the United States the Pacific island of Guam and the Caribbean island of Puerto Rico. The United States buys the Philippines from Spain.

**3.** The United States declares war on Spain and wins within four months. (1898)

**5.** The Filipinos rebel against the United States takeover. (1899-1902)

**6.** The United States puts down the Filipino rebellion and the Philippines become a United States territory until 1946.

# U.S. TERRITORIES FROM SPAIN, 1898

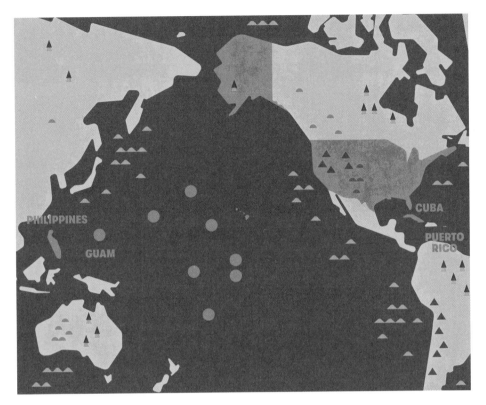

There was much debate in the U.S. about these moves. For a long time the United States had restrained itself from imperialism, but the acquisition of even these small islands was a game changer. Some people didn't like it, but it was too late.

# NATIONALISM AND WORLD WAR I

World War I, also called the Great War, was the biggest war yet. It sent a shock through the world about just how bad war could be.

## WHY DID IT HAPPEN?

At the close of the nineteenth century, life was changing quickly in Europe. Due to industrialization, people were moving from the countryside to cities. Thousands of the poor had left Europe to go to America. Laborers were striking, women were marching for their rights—the whole social order was in question and it made people uneasy.

### NATIONALISM TAKES ROOT

A new sense of separateness began to develop. People started to really get into being, say, French, or German. They began to care about their own country first and foremost, usually to the exclusion of other countries—or even to their harm. (That's called nationalism—remember this because it's going to be important from here out.)

Some countries started to not like each other very much. As imperialists, they were competing for territories. (Remember the "Scramble for Africa"?) And as industrialized countries, they were competing to be the biggest producer of goods.

### JUST BUSINESS: GERMANY CHALLENGES BRITAIN

In fact, Germany was starting to edge out Britain as a leader in industry, so those two countries were not getting along. They started to build up their militaries, too, making more ships and more weapons to try to have the strongest navy.

## THE DREYFUS AFFAIR

Alfred Dreyfus was a Jewish army captain who was accused and found guilty of selling French military secrets to the Germans in 1894. Dreyfus was sentenced to life in prison until evidence was revealed that proved his innocence.

"The Dreyfus Affair" is just one example of growing antisemitism (discrimination and violence against Jewish people) in Europe at this time.

## CHOOSING SIDES

All this arming up and competition made the nations of Europe not trust each other. They started to worry about getting attacked. So countries started to form alliances, like teams. Germany feared an attack from France and others, so it got Austria-Hungary on its team. Their team was called the Central Powers. Then other European countries piled on, taking one side or another, until two huge alliances formed, looking like this:

### POWERS IN EUROPE, PRE-WORLD WAR I

| ENTENTE POWERS (LATER CALLED THE ALLIED POWERS): | | CENTRAL POWERS: | |
|---|---|---|---|
| France | Italy | Germany | Bulgaria |
| Great Britain | Japan | Austria-Hungary | Ottoman Empire |
| Russia | United States | | |

**Nationalism:** The support and pride of your own country first and foremost above other nations or people.

Even though countries from around the world became involved in the war, most of the fighting took place in Europe. Take a look at this map to see how these alliances played out geographically:

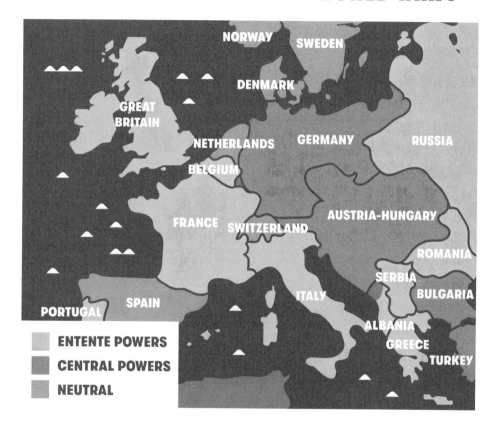

## CHOOSING TEAMS: EUROPEAN ALLIANCES IN WORLD WAR I

# ARCHDUKE FERDINAND OF AUSTRIA-HUNGARY IS ASSASSINATED

Historians are still debating all the reasons that war finally erupted, but most agree that the assassination of the Archduke of Austria-Hungary in 1914 got things started. Over the years, tension had built up between Austria-Hungary and Serbia. When Austria-Hungary, backed up by Germany, declared war on Serbia, Russia came to help the Serbians.

Then Germany declared war on Russia. France backed up Russia and Serbia, which made Germany declare war on France. So, then Germany marched into Belgium, which was supposed to be neutral, and that's when Great Britain entered the conflict. The United States stayed out of the whole mess for a couple years but finally entered in 1917.

Sound complicated? It is. You could study World War I for your whole life and still not master the political, economic, and military forces that made it such a catastrophe.

# A NEW KIND OF WAR

No one knew how deadly and how horrible World War I would turn out to be. New weapons technology brought more deaths than had ever occurred in a war. Machine guns fired a continuous stream of bullets that could mow down hundreds of soldiers in a matter of minutes. Poisonous gas choked, blinded, and burned the skin of soldiers. Zeppelins dropped bombs, and propeller airplanes mounted with machine guns fought it out in the sky. In total, 8.5 million soldiers died and 21 million were wounded.

**Assassination:** An assassination is a targeted and often politically motivated murder.

**Zeppelins:** During World War I and through the 1930s, the Germans used large cylindrical airships called zeppelins, first for bombing during wartime, and later for carrying passengers.

## TRENCH WARFARE: DANGER, DISEASE, AND STINK

Many World War I soldiers fought and lived in trenches, which were long ditches (which they also had to dig) where the troops hid until it was time to charge across a barren area called "no man's land." That's where most men died because they were easy targets for the other side.

They also died from the conditions in the trenches: freezing cold in winter and boiling hot in the summer. Often the trenches were muddy and smelly, too. Doctors on the battlefield tried to keep up with treating the wounded and taking away the dead, but sometimes bodies were left for days and began to decompose. Rotting bodies gave off a stench, which attracted rats, which brought lice and diseases such as trench fever and typhoid.

## A POET'S TAKE ON THE WAR

You'll get a feel for the experience of a soldier from this excerpt of a poem called "Dreamers" by Siegfried Sassoon, an English poet who served in the army during World War I:

> Soldiers are dreamers; when the guns begin
>
> They think of firelit homes, clean beds and wives.
>
> I see them in foul dug-outs, gnawed by rats,
>
> And in the ruined trenches, lashed with rain,
>
> Dreaming of things they did with balls and bats,
>
> And mocked by hopeless longing to regain
>
> Bank-holidays, and picture shows, and spats,
>
> And going to the office on the train.

**Trenches:** A trench is a long ditch that soldiers would hide in before charging into battle.

**Typhoid:** You may have heard the name Typhoid Mary, but it's more than a nickname! Typhoid is a highly infectious fever with severe symptoms. During this era, there was no vaccine to prevent it and catching it could often be a death sentence.

Why do you think the soldiers in Sassoon's poem become dreamers "when the guns begin"?

_____

_____

_____

_____

_____

_____

_____

_____

# HOW IT ALL ENDED

Even with the sacrifices of so many lives, not much ground was gained by either the Allied Powers or the Central Powers. The war dragged on for four years and was fought in two different locations: the East (Austria-Hungary, Germany, Russia, and Romania) and the West (mainly France and Belgium).

Some soldiers deserted or staged mutinies rather than continue the desperate fight. In March 1917 the Russians pulled out. They had their own violent revolution to deal with. Then the United States entered the conflict.

# ONE LAST PUSH FOR THE CENTRAL POWERS

With the Russians out of the way, the Central Powers could focus on the West, so they launched a huge offensive in Spring 1918. It was successful, and they gained about forty miles of territory in France, but such a move exhausted the German army. A few months later Bulgaria dropped out of the Central Power alliance.

The Germans tried to make one more push, but even more soldiers mutinied, and German citizens rose up against the war and their government. The kaiser stepped down and the new German government signed an agreement with the Allies to end the fighting.

# THE TREATY OF VERSAILLES

Months later, representatives from the countries of Europe met in Versailles, France, to figure out how to bring a lasting peace to Europe. Most historians agree that leaders from Britain and France wanted to punish Germany. They blamed Germany for starting the war and feared future invasions.

# A STEEP PRICE FOR DEFEAT

The Treaty of Versailles, signed June 28, 1919, made Germany pay back some of the expenses of the war, give back its territories, and strictly limited its military. The Germans deeply resented these actions, but had no choice but to sign—and they never got over it. Russia, Japan, and Italy were not happy with the deals they got either. And now you know one of the main causes of World War II.

**Mutiny:** Mutiny is the overthrow of authority figures, like commanders or officers.

**Kaiser:** The kaiser was the term for the German emperor. It's also a type of bread roll, but that's not what we're talking about in this chapter!

# THE INTERWAR PERIOD

Europe was not in great shape after World War I. So many deaths and so much destruction had taken a great toll. Cities needed rebuilding, veterans needed jobs, but the countries were also in debt from the war. Germany's economy was in the worst shape of all.

> **Veterans:** When soldiers finish their time in the armed forces, they become known as veterans.

Right after World War I, world leaders tried to prevent such a nightmare from ever happening again. They signed two treaties, promising not to be aggressive. Toward the end of the war, U.S. President Woodrow Wilson outlined "Fourteen Points" as a guide for preventing and resolving any future conflicts.

## THE LEAGUE OF NATIONS IS FORMED

Wilson also formed the League of Nations in 1920 to gather countries around a commitment to preserve peace. Interestingly, the United States never joined because Congress did not approve of membership—such is democracy. And as it turns out, none of this worked.

# UNREST IN THE EUROPEAN COLONIES

Effects from the Great War were also felt in the colonies of Britain and France. Soldiers from the colonies had been "mobilized" into the war on behalf of the imperial country. Many were injured or killed or mistreated, so people in the colonies started to want independence. A number of small wars and protests erupted in countries like Turkey, Egypt, India, Syria, Indochina, and Palestine. These rebellions were swiftly slapped down, but movements for independence would rise again.

## COLONIAL POWERS IN NORTH AFRICA AND THE MIDDLE EAST AFTER WORLD WAR I

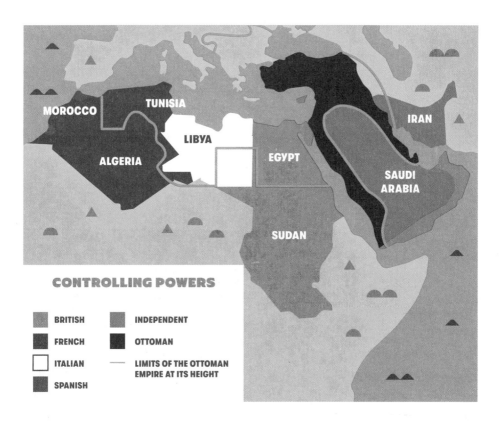

CONTROLLING POWERS

- ◼ BRITISH
- ◼ FRENCH
- ◻ ITALIAN
- ◼ SPANISH
- ◼ INDEPENDENT
- ◼ OTTOMAN
- — LIMITS OF THE OTTOMAN EMPIRE AT ITS HEIGHT

## SPANISH FLU

As if Europe did not have enough problems, a deadly flu pandemic began toward the end of the war and ripped through the world, killing at least 20 million people, twice as many as the war itself! It spread quickly because both soldiers and civilians were traveling more. Also, soldiers camped close together and germs spread quickly from one person to the next. The virus finally started to go away when people became more careful with keeping things clean and sick people were kept away from others so that germs could not spread.

 You may be thinking that the Spanish Flu started in Spain. Good guess, but it's not the case. It got the name Spanish Flu because you could only get accurate news about the pandemic in Spain. The Spanish were neutral in World War I and did not restrict the news that people got. The other countries hid information about the flu during the war so that people would not panic or lose hope.

**Pandemic:** A pandemic is the worldwide spread of a disease. In this chapter you'll learn about the Spanish Flu pandemic, which is one of many pandemics in world history. What other ones can you name?

**Civilians:** Civilians are members of a country who are not soldiers. You'll read in this chapter about how even regular civilians experienced the effects of wars.

# THE UNITED STATES PROSPERS

The United States was in much better shape than Europe after the war. They had come into the war late, so they had fewer losses. Plus, all the fighting took place in Europe, so destruction at home was not a problem.

*In the 1920s, products meant for leisure or for making housework easier became an important part of the U.S. economy for the first time. Advertising was introduced, and department stores became hugely popular.*

# THE BIRTH OF THE CONSUMER ECONOMY

U.S. factories shifted away from making weapons and into making household products that people now wanted, like refrigerators and vacuums. The automobile industry also took off.

Middle-class people got wealthier and enjoyed spending money. They now had conveniences like telephones and electricity in their homes. In major cities, people were having fun at parties, going to movies, listening to jazz, and dancing. Historians named this period the Roaring Twenties because the economy was growing fast and life was in high gear.

*"Flappers" were young women who wore their hair short, sported fashionable clothes, listened to jazz (then brand-new!), and embraced modern ideas of womanhood.*

## NEW ROLE FOR WOMEN

In the United States and certain cities of Europe, middle-class women started to enjoy more freedom. They had begun to work outside the home during the war and earn their own money. About 25 percent continued to work in offices, schools, and factories. Women's groups backed peace efforts and pressed for the right to vote, which they achieved for some women by 1920—most minority women had to wait several decades longer. In social life, many women tried on a new look with shorter skirts, make-up, and bobbed hair.

# THE GREAT DEPRESSION

But underneath this carefree time known as the Roaring Twenties, deep problems were brewing. Even though the rich were getting richer, 40 percent of the population was still living in poverty. Farmers needed new technology but were not able to sell their crops for as much money.

## DEBT AND INFLATION GET OUT OF CONTROL

People (and whole countries) were starting to pay for things with credit, which meant debts piled up that couldn't be paid. Inflation caused the prices of food and products to go up, while the value of paper money went down. In 1929, the Great Crash occurred in the United States, meaning stock market values dropped, banks started to close, and people scrambled to hang on to what money they had left.

# GET YOUR -ISMS STRAIGHT

| -ISM | WHAT IT IS |
|---|---|
| COMMUNISM | • Working people revolt and seize power from the bourgeoisie (the people who own big businesses). All property becomes property of the people, through their government.<br>• The most famous writer about communism and socialism was the German philosopher Karl Marx (1818–1883). |
| SOCIALISM | • The government provides education and healthcare and other social services.<br>• Some companies are owned by the state. |
| TOTALITARIANISM | • The state has complete control of the economy and society.<br>• All property belongs to the state. |
| FASCISM | • Extreme nationalism that encourages "us vs. them."<br>• Obsession with a "pure state" that excludes, and even kills, people thought to be outsiders.<br>• Leads to totalitarianism. |
| CAPITALISM | • Individuals and private companies own property, not the government.<br>• Free trade. Government does not control the economy. |

The effects of this economic disaster, known as the Great Depression, spread around the world, and people began to feel desperate. Many lost faith in democracy and looked to more extreme ideas for answers.

**Debt:** Debt is an obligation to pay someone money.

| | EXAMPLE |
|---|---|
| • When people get used to equality, they don't need the government any more. It goes away and everyone lives in peace and fairness. | Communism hasn't been achieved, but countries like Russia, China, and Cuba are still trying it. |
| • Everyone works for the government. The government gives people what it thinks they need. | So far, it has ended up looking something like totalitarianism. |
| • Elements of socialism can combine with a capitalist economy and a democratic government. | Democratic countries today like Sweden and Bolivia have elected socialist governments. |
| • Anyone who acts or speaks against the government is punished, imprisoned or killed. | North Korea today<br>China (1949–1976)<br>Soviet Union (1922–1992) |
| • Uses stories and people's anger to turn them against "others" and become loyal to a state, which holds complete power. Promotes traditional values. | Nazi Germany<br>Italy under Mussolini |
| • Modern capitalism does make some rules for business and has some socialist elements (like public education). | United States<br>Europe<br>Most modern economies |

Imagine you are living in Germany after World War I. You are feeling angry at the other European countries and the United States about the results of the Treaty of Versailles. You think Germany was treated unfairly and should stick up for itself. Which of these five -isms would appeal to you most?

_____

_____

_____

_____

_____

_____

_____

_____

_____

_____

# THE RUSSIAN REVOLUTION

(Technically there were two, but you can tackle that in high school!)

 We're jumping to a different region of the world, so we're also jumping out of chronological order. Pay attention to the years for each of these events to make sure you understand how they all fit together.

 To understand the Russian Revolution, it helps to think back to the French Revolution.

Remember how the feudal system had stuck around forever? And serfs got tired of having a miserable life? Well, a similar thing happened in Russia. The Russian landscape had medieval serfdom on one end and princes and landlords with enormous wealth on the other end. The Russian peasants and soldiers rose up against the tsar (Russian king) in 1917.

The revolutionaries, led by Vladimir Lenin, set up a government that was supposed to level the playing field and give the peasants and the workers more of a say in their lives and what they needed. But Lenin and his followers constantly feared that the tsar and those loyal to him, or even some of their own party, would try to take over.

*Vladimir Lenin*

## POWER LOVES MORE POWER

Lenin, and later Stalin who replaced him, turned to ruthless oppressive measures to retain power. There were two big waves of violence: the "Red Terror" in 1918, authorized by Lenin, and "the Great Purge" from 1936–1938, designed by Joseph

*Joseph Stalin*

Stalin. Stalin was determined to root out and execute or isolate anyone who could possibly interfere with his authority.

## THE MOSCOW TRIALS

Stalin set up fake trials called the Moscow Trials, where people confessed to being spies and traitors, and were then shot or sent off to forced labor camps called gulags. Later, historians discovered that these people had been interrogated and tortured into these "confessions."

Historians estimate that more than 750,000 people were executed after the trials. Over the course of Stalin's reign (1929–1953) 18 million people were sent to the labor camps, and over a million died there due to exhaustion, disease, or execution.

Was this what Karl Marx had in mind back in 1848? Hardly.

Check out the -isms chart. Which one fits best with Stalinist Russia?

_____

_____

_____

_____

_____

## THE SEEDS OF THE COLD WAR ARE PLANTED

Party leaders liked Marx's idea that the workers of the world would rise up to support them, so they made plans to expand and also promote communist revolutions around the world. Naturally, capitalist countries like the United States didn't like this at all. The U.S. government did everything it could to isolate Russia, and later the Soviet Union, which set up a whole new power dynamic internationally. More about that when we come to the Cold War.

# THE RISE OF FASCISM IN EUROPE

People in Italy were feeling crummy at the end of World War I. They did not get the land promised to them by the Allies, they were poor, and many did not have jobs. When they saw the Russian revolutionaries successfully kick out the tsar, some started to think that communism might be a better system. But other people were afraid of communism coming to Italy.

## MUSSOLINI AND ITALY

A journalist named Benito Mussolini came into power by promising to keep the communists out and "make Italy great again," like in the old days of the Roman Empire. He became the dictator of Italy. Mussolini protected his power with secret police who harassed or killed anyone who disagreed with his new fascist government.

# HITLER'S RISE

You have probably heard the name Adolf Hitler. More than any other individual, Hitler set off a chain of events that brought about a worldwide war.

He started out trying to copy Mussolini. One day in 1923, he stomped into a crowded bar in Munich where a rival was speaking, stood on a table, shot his pistol in the air, and proclaimed that his revolution had begun. He was immediately thrown in jail.

## *MEIN KAMPF*: AN ANTISEMITIC MANIFESTO

From his cell block, Hitler wrote a book titled *Mein Kampf* (My Struggle). This was a very dangerous book, and the bad news is it became a bestseller.

In this 720-page volume, Hitler told the German people (remember they were feeling like losers) that they were the greatest people on Earth and could become a "master Aryan race," if they "purified" the nation. He told them they had to get rid of or enslave all the people who had held them back, and here's who he listed: Romani people, communists, Slavs, gay people, disabled people, the mentally ill, and most of all, Jewish people.

Throughout history, antisemitic people had been blaming Jewish people for all kinds of things. Hitler picked up on this big time, and blamed Jewish people for all of Germany's trouble, including the loss of World War I.

# A WARPED MESSAGE FINDS AN AUDIENCE

It's hard to understand how so many people could believe what Hitler was saying, but they did believe it. And thousands followed him. Nobody checked to see if Hitler had his facts straight or if he was in his right mind.

Nobody even tried to stop him until he had started to carry out his plan. This brought on one of the greatest tragedies in the history of the human race. But we will come to that a little later.

# SPANISH CIVIL WAR

In 1931, the people of Spain elected a democratic leftist government that was partial to communism. But the rightists in Spain, led by an army general named Francisco Franco, hated communism. So Franco's nationalists began a civil war in 1936 to overthrow the leftist government. Each side got foreign support, depending on their politics.

> Leftist: Leftists are people who support left-wing politics, which typically advocate for social and economic equality. Leftists may be socialists, communists, liberals, populists, and more. On the other side of the spectrum are rightists, who oppose communism.

The Spanish Civil War was a very bloody conflict that killed half a million people. Franco ended up winning and stayed in power in Spain until he died in 1975. Heads up—we will see again and again how superpowers with opposing ideas compete for influence by entering into conflicts all over the world.

# NATIONALIST AND REPUBLICAN ZONES IN WORLD WAR II SPAIN

■ NATIONALIST ZONE (SUPPORTED BY MUSSOLINI AND HITLER)

■ REPUBLICAN ZONE (SUPPORTED BY THE SOVIET UNION AND OTHER
LEFTIST GOVERNMENTS)

# WORLD WAR II

You may have noticed how the history of the world can seem like the history of war. And if you've ever wondered which was the biggest, worst war EVER, World War II gets that prize hands down. It was literally fought around the entire globe. Whole cities were destroyed. An estimated 85 million people were killed, including 40 million civilians—more than any other war in history. World War II raged fiercely with new powerful machinery and tested the courage of leaders, soldiers, and citizens alike.

# WHY AND HOW IT BEGAN

The Treaty of Versailles turned out to be a bigger mistake than anyone could have guessed. The German people were angry and dejected. Even fifteen years after the war, people were poor and essentials were hard to get. Plus, the German government was still paying off its enormous debts from World War I.

## HITLER ON THE MOVE

More and more people started to listen to Adolf Hitler, who vowed revenge and promised glorification of the German people. In 1933, Hitler became Chancellor of Germany. Two things to remember about Hitler (that we know now): (1) He meant what he said about getting rid of the Jews and other "undesirables," and (2) He fully intended to carry out this vision worldwide.

## A SERIES OF GAMBLES

Here is how Hitler got his plan going and convinced other nations to play along. In 1938, he decided that Austria should really be part of Germany to keep all the Germans together. He got virtually no pushback from the international community. After taking over Austria, he went to the English, French, and Italian leaders and said "Could I just have part of Czechoslovakia? After all, Sudetenland is a big German area and they should be with us. I promise I won't take any more." So believing in compromise, Western leaders gave Hitler part of Czechoslovakia. The following year, Hitler moved in and took all of Czechoslovakia.

 Let's connect the dots here. Backtrack to the horrors of World War I, and the horrors of Hitler's ideas in *Mein Kampf*. What do you think Hitler is up to? Why do you think the leaders of other countries let him do this?

_____

_____

_____

Next, Hitler set his sights on Poland. He decided to make nice with Joseph Stalin (his arch enemy!) temporarily to get access to it because Poland lay between Germany and Russia. Stalin and Hitler agreed not to get into the mix if the other one got in a conflict. They also secretly agreed to split Poland between them.

Nine days later, the Germans invaded Poland. That got the Western democracies' attention. France and Britain promptly declared war on Germany. World War II had begun.

## THE TWO SIDES IN WORLD WAR II

| AXIS POWERS | ALLIES | |
|---|---|---|
| Germany | Great Britain | Belgium |
| Italy | France | Canada |
| Japan | United States | Australia |
| | Russia (after June 1941. Until then they had a nonaggression pact with Germany) | |

# BLITZKRIEGS BEGIN

The Germans kept right on hammering country after country with a strategy called blitzkrieg or "lightning war." People in Norway, Denmark, the Netherlands, Belgium, and finally France, hardly knew what hit them as bombs dropped out of nowhere and tanks barrelled through their cities. Great Britain was the next goal.

> **Blitzkrieg:** German for "lightning war," a blitzkrieg was a German war strategy that involved quickly entering into countries, dropping bomb after bomb, and bringing in tanks until the Germans had conquered the area.

## GERMAN TERRITORY GAINED

GERMAN TERRITORY GAINED

PRE-WAR GERMANY

# DUNKIRK

Once Paris fell to the Germans, thousands of British, French, and Belgian troops began to flee to the coast to retreat back across the English Channel to Britain. But German forces were fast approaching. The British had to act immediately to save soldiers from the French port of Dunkirk.

Regular naval vessels were too large to get near the shallow shoreline, so the British asked civilians to provide smaller boats, including private lifeboats, fishing boats, and yachts. For eight days, seven hundred "Little Ships of Dunkirk" and the British navy transported 338,000 soldiers from the beaches of France to safety in Great Britain.

*One of the "Little Ships of Dunkirk"*

## WINSTON CHURCHILL

Winston Churchill was one of the most prominent world leaders during World War II. After serving in the British army and in the government, he went on to be elected as prime minister of Great Britain in 1940. As Prime Minister, Churchill helped to inspire his country to persevere despite difficult circumstances, and he forged an alliance between Britain, the Soviet Union, and the United States. Churchill was known for his rousing speeches.

## BATTLE OF BRITAIN

Winston Churchill, prime minister of Great Britain, vowed that the British would "never surrender," and indeed they did not.

*Volunteers and the Royal Air Force managed to save London over nearly two consecutive months of nightly bombing in 1940.*

The Germans bombed London, between May and August 1940, for fifty-seven straight nights, but the citizens and the Royal Air Force held strong. Each night Londoners had to take shelter in their basements and in underground subway stations while bombs crashed above them. They covered their windows with black curtains so that German airplane pilots could not find their way. By the end of the three-and-a-half month-long battle, the courageous fire brigade had fought over 10,000 fires. Much of London was destroyed, but not all of it, and the Germans had been held off.

*They came just after dark, and somehow you could sense from the quick, bitter firing of the guns that there was to be no monkey business this night.*

*Shortly after the sirens wailed you could hear the Germans grinding overhead. In my room, with its black curtains drawn across the windows, you could feel the shake from the guns. You could hear the boom, crump, crump, crump, of heavy bombs at their work of tearing buildings apart.*

*About every two minutes a new wave of planes would be over. The motors seemed to grind rather than roar, and to have an angry pulsation, like a bee buzzing in blind fury.*

—Journalist Ernie Pyle describes a night raid on London in 1940

# CHAPTER 6

# MAJOR BATTLES OF WORLD WAR II (EUROPE)

| | |
|---|---|
| **THE BATTLE OF STALINGRAD**<br><br>**JULY 1942 TO FEBRUARY 1943**<br><br>**HITLER'S BIG MISTAKE** | What went wrong for the Germans:<br><br>• Hitler got obsessed with conquering the Russian city of Stalingrad and made bad decisions.<br><br>• Germany had to maintain two fronts: East and West. Too many troops were sent to Russia, which drained their strength in the West.<br><br>• Battle extended into winter. Five hundred thousand German soldiers died, often from starvation or the cold.<br><br>• The Germans had to surrender to the Russians, and they never fully recovered. |
| **D-DAY, INVASION OF NORMANDY**<br><br>**JUNE 6, 1944**<br><br>**THE ALLIES ARE VICTORIOUS** | What went right for the Allies:<br><br>• In a surprise attack, 150,000 American, British, and Canadian troops stormed the shores of Normandy, France.<br><br>• Allies bombed German railroads and bridges to slow down the German army.<br><br>• By liberating France from the Nazis, the Allies gained the upper hand in the war. |

| BATTLE OF THE BULGE | How it was the beginning of the end: |
|---|---|
| DECEMBER 1944 TO JANUARY 1945 | • The Allies advanced confidently into Belgium on their way to Germany |
| GERMANY'S LAST-DITCH EFFORT | • Germans tried to break through the Allies' line of defense (shaped like a "bulge" on the map) |
| | • The battle raged for over a month in the cold of December. The Germans surrendered on January 25, 1945. |
| | • The Allies kept up their bombing campaign on Germany, and Hitler began to lose support. |
| | • After several more German losses, the Russians closed in on Berlin. |
| | • Hitler and his wife committed suicide in their underground bunker and Germany surrendered. |

# THE WAR IN AFRICA

Although often overlooked, Africa's colonized people, strategic location, and raw materials all contributed greatly to the Allies' victory in World War II. Over 1 million Africans from British and French colonies served in the Allied forces around the world.

## BASE AT TAKORADI

In 1940, just as France was falling, Italy took the opportunity to invade Egypt and expand its hold on Africa beyond the colonies it already possessed. At this early stage of the war, the Allies were on the defensive so they scrambled to supply troops in Cairo with aircraft and other supplies.

## A VITAL LINK TO SUPPLY THE ALLIES IN NORTH AFRICA

Churchill set up a Royal Air Force base at Takoradi, a small city on the shore of a British colony then called the Gold Coast (now the country of Ghana). Crates of aircraft parts were shipped into Takoradi, assembled into fighter planes, and flown to Cairo to arm the Allies for a three-year battle for control of Northern Africa.

*Bauxite ore*

Without this trade route across three continents, and the work of the people of the Gold Coast, the Allies could not have amassed the airpower necessary to win the region. African colonies also continued to provide raw materials to their imperial countries, and now it mattered more than ever. Lots of rubber was needed for the manufacture of weapons and machinery and much of it came from Nigeria. Bauxite, a kind of rock used to make aluminum, came from the Gold Coast.

## CONTEST FOR NORTH AFRICA

The powerful machinery that drove World War II—tanks, aircraft, and war boats—could not run without oil. The British got most of their oil from the Middle East, so it was important to control sea routes for importing oil and other supplies. If the Germans got control, they would cut that lifeline and the Allies would be in trouble.

 Take a look at the map on the next page. Notice how the Suez Canal leads to the Red Sea, which gives access to the Middle East AND a shortcut to Asia.

## ROMMEL AND MONTGOMERY

The stakes were high in North Africa, and desert warfare wasn't exactly easy, so both sides sent in their best generals. The Germans sent Erwin Rommel, nicknamed the Desert Fox, to command the Afrika Korps. The British sent Bernard Montgomery ("Monty"), who led the 8th Army, fighters mainly from Australia, New Zealand, India, and South Africa.

# CONTESTED TERRITORY: NORTH AFRICA

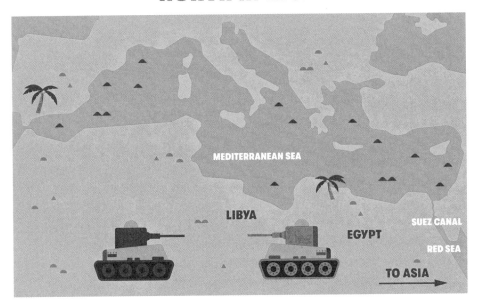

The Afrika Korps achieved a string of early wins through surprise attacks, but it was a close contest. The armies took turns outsmarting each other and trading victories in cities like Tobruk and Benghazi.

Finally, Montgomery's 8th army cut off German supply lines and pushed the Afrika Korps out of Libya and into Tunisia. In May 1943, when the Allies won the battle of El Alamein, it was all but over for the Germans. The victory at El Alamein gave the Allies power over a vital trade route, and a solid win when they needed it most.

# THE WAR IN ASIA

On December 7, 1941, the Japanese launched a surprise attack on U.S. warships docked in Pearl Harbor, Hawaii. No one saw it coming, and it got the United States hopping mad. More than 2,300 military personnel were killed in that one attack. The United States responded instantly by declaring war on Japan, thereby entering World War II.

# STRATEGIC PACIFIC ISLANDS

Remember those Pacific Islands that the United States had acquired back in the 1800s? Well, they were now Japanese territories because Japan had become an empire, too. The Americans and Australians fought hard to get those islands back, especially the Philippines. Located right on a trade route, the Philippines provided a place from which the Allies could control the flow of resources, including oil, from Indonesia.

The war in the Pacific was different from that in Europe or Africa. Most fighting took place on warships or in jungles on the islands. The Japanese were victorious up until 1942. But in June the Allies defeated Japan in the battles of the Coral Sea and Midway Island, and this turned the tide in favor of the Allies.

# THE JAPANESE MAINLAND

General Douglas MacArthur and his fleet of warships went on the offensive, moving closer and closer to Japan's mainland. When they got within range, the U.S. Navy bombed many cities and industries in Japan, but the Japanese would not surrender. In October 1944, General MacArthur succeeded in taking back the Philippines.

Even after Germany had surrendered in May of 1945, the Japanese continued fighting. The United States considered invading Japan, but military advisers told U.S. President Truman that the battles on the Japanese homeland would be very long and very deadly, killing as many as 1 million U.S. and Allied soldiers.

# THE FIRST NUCLEAR WEAPONS

There was also a brand-new weapon available. Scientists involved in the Manhattan Project had been secretly developing an atomic bomb, more powerful than anything the world had ever seen. President Truman made the decision to drop two atomic bombs on Japanese cities: Hiroshima and Nagasaki on August 6th and 9th, 1945. Many historians believe that the atomic bombings were unjustified, since Japan appeared to be on the brink of surrender anyway. The bombings killed 200,000 people, mostly civilians. And for years to come, survivors suffered from disease. On September 2, less than a month after they were dropped, Japan surrendered and World War II was officially over.

**Mainland:** The mainland of a country is the central landmass, rather than smaller offshore island or territories.

**Atomic bomb:** An atomic bomb is a powerful and extremely destructive nuclear weapon. To this day, only two atomic bombs have ever been used in war, when the United States dropped them on Japan during World War II.

*Churchill, Roosevelt, and Stalin: the leaders of the Big Three*

# THE YALTA CONFERENCE

**WHAT IT WAS:**

In February 1945, world leaders met at the Yalta Conference to figure out how to make Europe safe once the war was over.

**WHO MET: THE BIG THREE**

- Franklin Roosevelt (President of the United States)

- Winston Churchill (Prime Minister of the United Kingdom)

- Joseph Stalin (Premier of Soviet Union)

| WHAT DID ROOSEVELT AND CHURCHILL WANT? | WHAT'S YALTA? | WHAT DID STALIN WANT? |
|---|---|---|
| • Soviet help in the Pacific arena of the war<br><br>• Free elections in Eastern Europe<br><br>• Democratic governments in Eastern Europe (especially Poland) | A city in Russia where the conference took place. | • Influence in Europe<br><br>• A "buffer" of friendly countries in Eastern Europe (especially Poland) |
| **WHAT DID STALIN AGREE TO?** | **WHAT WOULD HAPPEN TO POLAND?** | **WHAT WOULD HAPPEN TO GERMANY?** |
| • Join the United Nations<br><br>• Help the United States defeat Japan (but they didn't end up needing help) | Neutral government | • Completely disarmed<br><br>• Divided up into four pieces governed by the United States, Soviet Union, France, and United Kingdom |

# THE U.S. HOME FRONT

Even though battles never occurred in the United States, World War II changed the way people lived. Citizens of the United States made an all-in effort for the war. But you'll see how some of the patriotism went too far, harming Japanese people and blurring the truth.

## RATIONING

During the war, many materials and foods were in short supply because they were needed overseas for the troops. Civilians in the United States could only buy a certain amount each month so that enough could be available for the war effort. People were given ration books with stamps in them that allowed them to obtain a certain amount of things like gasoline, tires, cars, coal, sugar, meat, and butter.

## VICTORY GARDENS

Americans helped the war effort by growing their own fruits and vegetables, even inside of cities. The government asked U.S. citizens to plant "Victory Gardens" and over 22 million responded, planting gardens in backyards, parks, and rooftops.

The famous Rosie the Riveter poster was created to inspire more women to enter the work force during World War II.

## WOMEN PITCH IN

U.S. industry was producing equipment for the war at an all-time high, but not enough men were available to run those factories. Women entered the workforce to keep the factories going. Often they performed tough physical and mechanical work usually done by men. Rosie the Riveter became a symbol of female power in making the United States strong.

# METAL SCRAP DRIVES

Lots of metal was needed to make the tanks, weapons, trucks, and airplanes needed for the war. Schools often held metal scrap drives, asking families to collect and donate tin cans, old appliances, and other metal that could be reused to create supplies for the troops.

*A monument now stands at the site of the Manzanar internment camp in California.*

# JAPANESE INTERNMENT CAMPS

After the attack on Pearl Harbor, many people, even the U.S. government, did not trust Japanese Americans. People assumed that someone who had come from Japan, even though they were now American citizens, might try to help the Japanese army invade the United States.

This irrational fear became so powerful that the government created camps for Japanese Americans that were like prison camps. Over 120,000 Japanese Americans, who had done nothing wrong, were forced to leave their jobs and their homes and go live in crowded, dirty camps under constant watch. It was a big mistake. Since then, the U.S. government has apologized and tried to make up for their mistake by paying Japanese American families for the hardship they suffered.

How do you think countries should take responsibility for the wrongs they've committed?

_____

_____

_____

_____

# U.S. PROPAGANDA

As we saw in Germany, propaganda is a powerful tool during wartime and the United States was not above using it. Some of it was fairly harmless. For example, a poster created by the government might glorify the U.S. soldier, or encourage citizens to support the war effort by planting a garden or collecting scrap metal.

These images were meant to make Americans feel proud and loyal to the cause of the war. But some U.S. propaganda was negative and racist. Artists portrayed Japanese people as evil or foolish—even sometimes as rats—while U.S. soldiers appeared only as heroes. Sadly, Americans formed attitudes toward the Japanese, which made the internment camps acceptable.

Think about the role of propaganda in shaping people's beliefs. Do you think propaganda is sometimes OK or never OK?

---

---

---

---

---

---

---

---

---

**Propaganda:** Propaganda is intentionally biased or misleading advertising to support a political view.

**Internment:** In this chapter, internment refers specifically to the rounding up of Japanese Americans who were confined and interned at government camps.

# THE HOLOCAUST

Many things about World War II are hard to understand. It's hard to understand how a person like Adolf Hitler could command the following of so many. It's hard to understand how Hitler and his followers could convince people to blame one group for everything that Germany suffered. And it's hard to understand how people could set up whole systems in order to imprison, enslave, and kill millions of women, men, and children just because they were Jewish.

## THE JEWISH EXPERIENCE

We can never fully know what victims of the Holocaust experienced, but we can read their stories and remember their suffering. Below are facts about the Holocaust that speak for themselves. Read them all carefully and bravely, and you will understand why nothing like this should be allowed to ever happen again. The Nazis first began their abuse of Jews in Germany by:

- Distributing propaganda against Jews

- Closing all businesses owned by Jews

- Taking away the licenses of Jewish professionals, like lawyers and doctors, so they could not work in their jobs

- Making Jewish people wear yellow stars on their clothes to identify themselves as Jews

- Forcing Jews to leave their homes and move into ghettos, which were small crowded neighborhoods that they couldn't leave; the Nazis gave the Jewish homes to Germans

- Burning books by Jewish authors

- Destroying stores owned by Jews

- Burning down synagogues where Jewish people worshipped

**Ghetto:** Ghettoes were enclosed districts or areas in cities where Jews were forced to live. Movement in and out of the ghetto was often restricted, and they were overcrowded and lacked resources.

**Synagogue:** Similar to a church for Christian communities, a synagogue is a Jewish house of worship. It may also serve as a Jewish community center.

# NAZI VIOLENCE

The Nazis created posters, pamphlets, and films to make people fear Jewish people. The Nazis continued their abuse of Jewish people in the countries they conquered by. . .

- Forcibly putting Jews and others on trains that took them to labor camps, prison camps, or extermination camps. The map shows where these places were located in Europe and how many there were.

- In the labor camps, prisoners were made to work like slaves and they were not fed enough. Many died from starvation or disease.

- Children were often separated from their parents.

- In the extermination camps, the Nazis told people they were going into showers but they were actually going into rooms filled with poisonous gas.

- Six million people were killed on purpose by the Nazis in these ways. In addition to Jews, the Nazis also imprisoned or killed:

    - Polish people
    - Romani/Roma people
    - Disabled people
    - Gay people
    - Jehovah's Witnesses

# NAZI DEATH CAMPS
# IN EUROPE AND AFRICA

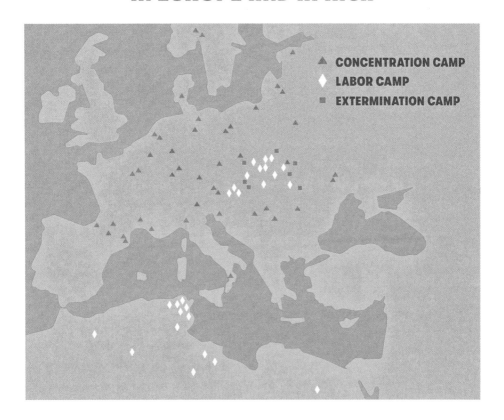

▲ CONCENTRATION CAMP
◆ LABOR CAMP
■ EXTERMINATION CAMP

# CHAPTER VOCABULARY

**Assassination:** An assassination is a targeted and often politically motivated murder.

**Atomic bomb:** An atomic bomb is a powerful and extremely destructive nuclear weapon. To this day, only two atomic bombs have ever been used in war, when the United States dropped them on Japan during World War II.

**Blitzkrieg:** German for "lightning war," a blitzkrieg was a German war strategy that involved quickly entering into countries, dropping bomb after bomb, and bringing in tanks until the Germans had conquered the area.

**Civilians:** Civilians are members of a country who are not soldiers. You read in this chapter about how even regular civilians experienced the effects of wars.

**Corruption:** Corruption is when people in power use their position and behave dishonestly or commit fraud.

**Debt:** Debt is an obligation to pay someone money.

**Economy:** The economy of a country is their wealth, resources, production, and the system by which those are all managed.

**Gilded:** When something is gilded, it has a shiny finish so that from the outside it looks fancy, even if underneath that gilded layer, it isn't. This is why we say not all that glitters is gold!

**Ghetto:** Ghettoes were enclosed districts or areas in cities where Jews were forced to live. Movement in and out of the ghetto was often restricted, and they were overcrowded and lacked resources.

**Internment:** In this chapter, internment refers specifically to the rounding up of Japanese Americans who were confined and interned at government camps.

**Kaiser:** The kaiser was the term for the German emperor. It's also a type of bread roll, but that's not what we're talking about in this chapter!

**Labor Unions:** When workers come together to bargain with their bosses as a collective, that's called a labor union. Unions exist in different trades and industries; there are teachers' unions, and unions for garment workers, and more!

**Leftist:** Leftists are people who support left-wing politics, which typically advocate for social and economic equality. Leftists may be socialists, communists, liberals, populists, and more. On the other side of the spectrum are rightists, who oppose communism.

**Mainland:** The mainland of a country is the central landmass, rather than smaller offshore island or territories.

**Mutiny:** Mutiny is the overthrow of authority figures, like commanders or officers.

**Nationalism:** Nationalism is the support and pride of your own country first and foremost above other nations or people.

**Pandemic:** A pandemic is the worldwide spread of a disease.

**Philanthropists:** A philanthropist is someone with lots of money who uses that money to help others.

**Propaganda:** Propaganda is intentionally biased or misleading advertising to support a political view.

**Strike:** When workers collectively decide to stop working, that is called a strike. It's a strategy to withhold labor in order to bargain with bosses for better conditions.

**Synagogue:** Similar to a church for Christian communities, a synagogue is a Jewish house of worship. It may also serve as a Jewish community center.

**Tenements:** A type of narrow, low-rise urban building that contained multiple dwellings. Often, tenements were dirty and overcrowded.

**Trenches:** A trench is a long ditch that soldiers would hide in before charging into battle.

**Typhoid:** Typhoid is a highly infectious fever with severe symptoms. During this era, there was no vaccine to prevent it and catching it could often be a death sentence.

**Veterans:** When soldiers finish their time in the armed forces, they become known as veterans.

**Zeppelins:** During World War I and through the 1930s, the Germans used large cylindrical airships called zeppelins, first for bombing during wartime, and later for carrying passengers.

# NOTES

•••• THE ••••
WORLD

# THE POSTWAR WORLD

After World War II, a new power struggle emerged in the world between the United States and the Soviet Union. The two powers competed for influence, land, and markets, and did everything they could to keep the other side down.

## CHAPTER CONTENTS

# THE COLD WAR

As we've seen with all wars, they create a gigantic mess. An international conflict like World War II created a *super-gigantic mess*. There was a lot to be done to put the world back in order:

- Cities in Europe and Japan were almost rubble and needed to be rebuilt.

- Borders of many countries needed to be redefined now that the Nazis had retreated.

- The Allies had to figure out what to do about Germany and how countries in Eastern Europe would rebuild their governments.

- Colonies around the world were again demanding independence and in some cases were waging war.

- Nazi war criminals needed to be brought to justice, and Jewish survivors and refugees needed to know they would be safe.

In the summer of 1945, leaders from the United States, the United Kingdom, and the Soviet Union met in Potsdam, Germany, to discuss the same end-of-war problems they tried to solve at Yalta five months earlier. But things were even more complicated this time.

## THE POTSDAM CONFERENCE

The powers that had been allies no longer had a common enemy because both Germany and Japan had surrendered. The leaders had different beliefs and opposing goals. Harry Truman, now the U.S. president, did not trust Stalin, the Soviet leader, one bit. The United Kingdom, exhausted by the war, was not the force it had been. The new prime minister, Clement Atlee, sided with the United States. Historians agree that the main result of the conference at Potsdam was tension and distrust between the world's two new great powers: the United States and the Soviet Union.

# CONFLICTING AGENDAS

As we know from the Yalta Conference, Stalin wanted to control the nearby Eastern European countries, so that Russia could have a buffer zone against any future invasion.

But Truman and Atlee wanted containment of the Soviet Union and its communist ideas, along with free elections in Eastern Europe. They feared that Stalin's brand of totalitarian communism would erase the people's freedom of speech and religion. (This is a good time to review the -isms cheat sheet in Chapter 6.)

Truman and Atlee were thinking of their own countries' bank accounts. Companies from the United States and Western Europe needed customers worldwide for the many goods they were churning out. If countries sided with the Soviets, they would buy Soviet products instead of products made in the United States or Western Europe.

> **Refugees:** Refugees are people who have to leave their country. They might be escaping war, political persecution, or natural disasters.
>
> **Buffer zone:** A neutral area whose purpose is to separate enemies. The Soviet Union controlled Eastern European countries in order to create a buffer zone against Western forces.
>
> **Containment:** Containment is a strategy that works to prevent the expansion of power or influence. In this chapter, you'll see how the United States worked toward the containment of the Soviet Union's power.

# DIVIDING UP GERMANY

The meeting at Potsdam ended with some agreements. Germany would be divided into East and West, with the capital city, Berlin, divided in two—East Berlin and West Berlin— within the territory of West Germany. Stalin did not keep his promise of allowing free elections in Eastern Europe. Instead, Europe became divided in two, like this:

# COUNTRIES FAVORING DEMOCRACY OR COMMUNISM

Notice how the two teams are competing for territory? Think about the U.S. policy of containment.

Which countries do you think the United States would most need to hold onto to keep the Soviet Union from getting bigger?

_____

_____

_____

_____

_____

_____

_____

_____

If you said Turkey and Greece, you're thinking like President Harry Truman did! In March 1947 he asked the U.S. Congress to give Turkey and Greece $400 million in aid—and the Truman Doctrine was born.

## THE TRUMAN DOCTRINE

The Truman Doctrine established that the United States would help out any countries who stayed away from communist influence.

From the map, it looks like another war is brewing, right? Sort of, but this "war" would be different. It would come to be called the Cold War because it never heated up to direct combat between the superpowers. This would be a long, tense, "cold" rivalry, with words and images used as weapons instead of guns.

*Arms manufacturers employed thousands of people.*

# NUCLEAR ARMS RACE

During the Cold War, the United States and the Soviet Union produced highly advanced weapons as fast as they could, but never actually used them on each other. Why? Think Hiroshima and Nagasaki. The new atomic bombs were so destructive they could wipe out a whole city, so no one dared use them.

But the strange part is, both sides kept making them. Over the course of 45 years, the two sides piled up a total of over 125,000 warheads.

## CONSTANT FEAR OF NUCLEAR WAR

The arms race built military strength on both sides, gave people jobs in armament factories, and made weapons companies very rich in the United States, but it also stirred up fear. During the Cold War, people lived with a constant worry that one side might flip the switch and unleash unthinkable destruction. Some families even built private fallout shelters stocked with supplies in their basements or yards. Schools conducted drills to train students to duck under their desks in case of attack.

**Combat:** Combat is conflict between armed forces. The Cold War is unique in that it was a "war" with no actual armed fighting like in previous wars.

**Warheads:** Warheads are the parts of missiles and other weapons that contain explosives.

**Arms race:** The global arms race was a scramble for countries to each be the nation with the most formidable weapons, generally nuclear weapons.

**Fallout shelters:** Fallout shelters are bunkers or buildings that are built to withstand nuclear explosions. During the Cold War, some people even built private fallout shelters in their basements or yards that they stocked with supplies.

Cold War propaganda

# PROPAGANDA

Both the United States and the Soviet Union used language and imagery to make the other side seem scary and evil.

In the United States, the "red threat" of communism was portrayed as an impending danger, spread by members of a global communist party who wanted to dominate the world.

# FINGER-POINTING AND A BLACKLIST

Even in government circles, people went around accusing people of being secret communists and they staged public hearings about it. Hundreds of people were found to be falsely accused of being communists, and they were "blacklisted" (marked for exclusion) and couldn't get jobs or home loans. These people were from all different organizations, including government agencies, universities, and Hollywood studios—and many of their lives were ruined as a result.

# THE SOVIET SIDE OF THE STORY

On the other side of the world, the Soviets painted the United States as an evil and greedy imperialist power that would eat up the world for its own profits.

Let's look at how two leaders used words to bolster their own side and put down the other. On March 5, 1946, Winston Churchill made his famous Iron Curtain speech that many historians say kicked off the Cold War. Here are some excerpts, along with some choice responses from Joseph Stalin.

## CHURCHILL AND STALIN ON THE COLD WAR

. . . an iron curtain has descended across the Continent.

I do not believe that Soviet Russia desires war. What they desire is the fruits of war and the indefinite* expansion of their power. . .

*indefinite= endless

**CHURCHILL**

Mr. Churchill now stands in the position of a **firebrand** of war.

Mr. Churchill wanders around the truth when he speaks of the growth of. . . communist parties in Eastern Europe. . . The growth. . . of communism cannot be considered accidental. It is a normal function.

**STALIN**

**Firebrand:** The literal definition of a firebrand is a piece of wood that is on fire, but it can also be used to describe someone who is passionate and outspoken about their cause, so much so that they incite action and might be seen as very radical!

The image of the iron curtain became a symbol of the Cold War. Think carefully about each word. What are the qualities of iron? What does a curtain do?

Why do you think Churchill chose this image to describe the Soviet presence in Europe?

_____

_____

_____

_____

_____

_____

_____

How do you think people in Europe and the United States felt, hearing that Soviet Russia desired "indefinite expansion."

_____

_____

_____

_____

_____

_____

_____

Think about the meanings of the word "firebrand." Why do you think Stalin uses this word to describe Churchill? What negative images does it create? How do you think he wants people in the Soviet Union to view Churchill and the West?

_____

_____

_____

_____

_____

# POSTWAR EUROPE

From 1948–1951, the United States gave $12 billion to Western European countries to help them rebuild. Most historians agree that the gift was half goodwill and half strategy to keep Western Europe loyal to the United States and out of the hands of the Soviets. The United States offered aid to the Soviet Union, but the Soviet Union refused to take it.

## THE MARSHALL PLAN

As a result of aid from the United States, the economies of Western European countries did recover fairly quickly. This, in turn, helped the U.S. economy because Europeans could now buy more U.S. goods. The Marshall Plan set in motion the U.S. policy of giving money to countries in trouble, which, in a limited form, continues to the present day.

> *The truth of the matter is that Europe's requirements for the next three or four years of foreign food and other essential products—principally from America—are so much greater than her present ability to pay that she must have substantial additional help or face economic, social, and political deterioration of a very grave character.*
>
> —George C. Marshall, Secretary of State, 1947–1949

# POSTWAR MIDDLE EAST

Some people think the idea for a Jewish state (Israel) resulted from World War II and the Holocaust, but that's not true. The Holocaust did make the formation of a Jewish state more urgent, but the process started many years earlier. Let's backtrack to get the whole story.

## ISRAEL BECOMES A COUNTRY

We've seen how even back to ancient times Jewish people had been mistreated or killed just for being Jewish. Antisemitism increased in Europe in the late 1890s (recall the Dreyfus Affair, Chapter 6). That's when some started to think a separate Jewish state in the area called Palestine—which included Jerusalem—would be a good idea.

But many disagreed, and kept disagreeing, and disagree to this day because Arab people were already living in Palestine. The time line below gives you a snapshot of a complicated and hotly debated process that led to the formation of the Jewish state of Israel.

# THE CREATION OF ISRAEL

| PRE-1917 | 1917 | 1922 |
|---|---|---|
| Palestine is part of the Ottoman Empire | The British issue the Balfour Declaration (the first official backing of Zionism.) | Collapse of the Ottoman Empire |

| 1922 | 1922–1935 | 1933–45 |
|---|---|---|
| League of Nations gives Palestine to Great Britain | More Jews move into Palestine; Jewish population rises from 10 percent to 27 percent | The Holocaust |

| 1947 | MAY 1948 | 1967 |
|---|---|---|
| United Nations proposes a plan to divide Palestine into two sections, a Jewish state, Israel and an Arab state, Palestine. Jerusalem, the capital, would be an international zone.<br><br>Arab leaders oppose the plan. They feel Arabs deserve more land because more of them lived there. | Israel declares independence and becomes a state.<br><br>Five Arab nations attack Israel. Israel wins and takes more territory. | The Six Day War<br><br>Israel is victorious against Egypt, Syria, Jordan, and Iraq, and doubles its territory to include the West Bank, Sinai peninsula, the Golan Heights, the Gaza Strip, and East Jerusalem. |

**Zionism/Zionist:** Zionism was originally a movement for the creation of a Jewish nation. Nowadays, it is a hotly contested belief!

# THE U.N. PARTITION PLAN

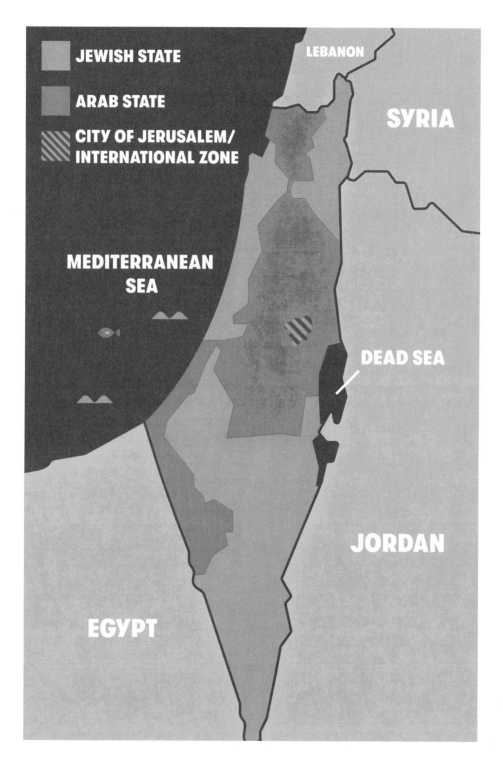

JEWISH STATE

ARAB STATE

CITY OF JERUSALEM/
INTERNATIONAL ZONE

LEBANON

SYRIA

MEDITERRANEAN
SEA

DEAD SEA

JORDAN

EGYPT

# BALFOUR DECLARATION: THE ISRAEL CONTROVERSY BEGINS

In 1917, the British issued a letter in support of a "national home for the Jewish people."

| WHO LIKED IT | WHO DIDN'T LIKE IT |
|---|---|
| **JEWISH PEOPLE:** Antisemitism was on the rise in Europe<br><br>Many Jews who wanted to return to their ancient home of Israel | **ARABS IN PALESTINE:** 750,000 of them lived in areas that were to become Israel |
| **GOVERNMENT OF GREAT BRITAIN:** Control of Palestine provided a foothold in the area, near Egypt and the Suez Canal, which kept the door open for oil imports | **ARAB STATES WHO HAD FOUGHT FOR THE ALLIES IN WORLD WAR I:** They were expecting to be granted self-government.<br><br>**OTTOMAN EMPIRE:** Didn't like it that Palestine would be under Great Britain's rule |
| **MILITARY LEADERS OF THE ALLIES DURING WORLD WAR I:** Wanted to gain support of Jewish people in neutral countries, especially Russia, to keep them from siding with the Soviets | **ANTI-ZIONISTS IN BRITISH PARLIAMENT AND ELSEWHERE:** Concerned that a Jewish state sponsored by Great Britain might actually increase antisemitism in certain parts of the world;<br><br>Jews from the United Kingdom might be favored because of Great Britain's control of Palestine |

Notice how very complex the Balfour controversy was! Read carefully and you'll find evidence of many ongoing global struggles we have studied so far: antisemitism, trade competition, military alliances, imperialism, colonization, and one more that figures largely during this time: anti-communism. But you knew that.

# POSTWAR ASIA

We saw how rebellions rose up in colonies just after World War I. Now, after World War II, those struggles continued and imperialist countries like England, France, and the United States knew they had to "walk the walk" on anti-imperialism. They could not easily say that Nazi imperialism had to be stopped, but British, French, and U.S. imperialism could go on as usual.

# INDEPENDENCE OF COLONIES

In Southeast Asia, many colonies asserted their independence just as the war was ending. Japan had surrendered and the United States helped rebuild their country as a representative democracy.

In other areas, too, newly independent countries had to choose what kind of economic system they wanted: communist or capitalist. The Soviet Union and the United States saw these new countries as places to gain more ground for their own ideas and their own power. The United States feared that if one country in an area went communist, others would follow and also become communist, like a line of dominoes.

## THE DOMINO THEORY

Historians point out that this line of thinking turned out to be wrong. At the time, it was very convincing, even to the U.S. President Eisenhower. This Domino Theory drove U.S. foreign policy decisions during the Cold War, including the decision to engage in grueling conflicts in Korea (1950–1953) and Vietnam (1954–1975).

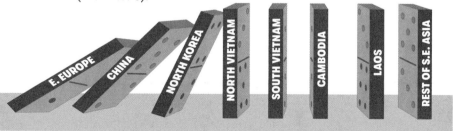

*The United States believed that if one country fell to communism, others would follow like dominoes.*

# COLONIES AND COLONIZERS PRE-1945

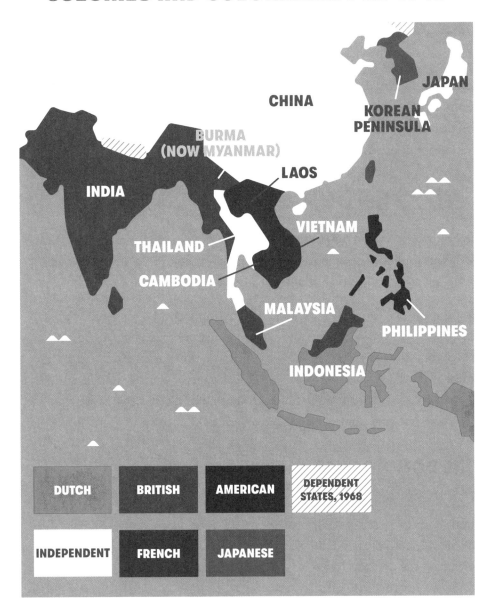

CHINA

JAPAN

KOREAN
PENINSULA

BURMA
(NOW MYANMAR)

LAOS

INDIA

VIETNAM

THAILAND

CAMBODIA

MALAYSIA

PHILIPPINES

INDONESIA

| DUTCH | BRITISH | AMERICAN | DEPENDENT STATES, 1968 |
|---|---|---|---|
| INDEPENDENT | FRENCH | JAPANESE | |

## INDIA

After 150 years as a British colony and many years of protest, India became independent in 1947. Nonviolent protests and boycotting tactics led by Mohandas Gandhi finally forced the British out of India.

# PAKISTAN

Hindus and Muslims did not get along in India, so a separate Muslim-only state called Pakistan was created in 1947, with east and west regions. India remained officially secular, but mainly Hindu.

## COMMUNISTS VS CAPITALISTS IN KOREA

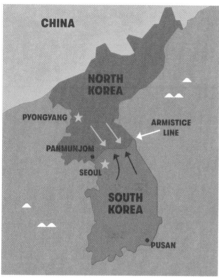

| | |
|---|---|
| **AREA OCCUPIED BY COMMUNIST FORCES** | **MOVEMENT OF COMMUNIST FORCES** |
| **AREA OCCUPIED BY U.N. FORCES** | **MOVEMENT OF U.N. FORCES** |
| | ★ CAPITAL |
| | ● OTHER CITY |

## KOREA

Korea was a unified colony of Japan until the end of World War I. When the Japanese surrendered, the Soviet Union and the United States decided (without asking the Koreans) that Korea should be divided in half to give both powers influence: North Korea and South Korea.

For some years, there was talk of trying to unify Korea again, but because of the Cold War, the two sides refused to compromise. Eventually the Korean War broke out (1950–1953), but it ended in a stalemate. To this day, Korea is separated into North and South.

**Boycotting:** A boycott is an economic protest tactic where people refuse to purchase specific goods or services for political reasons. For example, people might boycott a company if they disagree with its treatment of workers.

**Secular:** If something is secular, that means it is not religious, or does not observe religious traditions. A secular state is a country that isn't associated with a specific religion.

# VIETNAM GETS DIVIDED, TOO

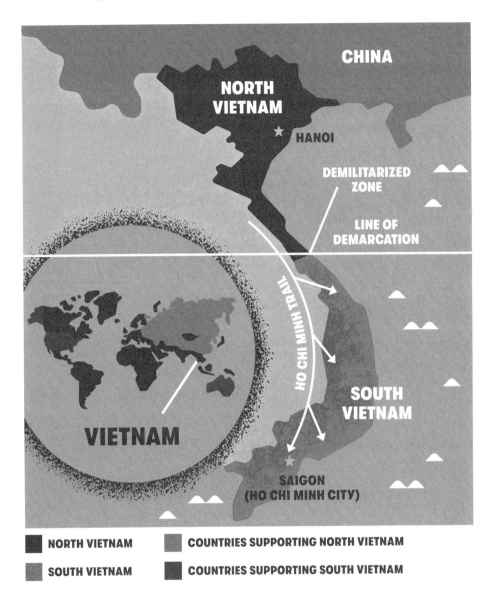

CHINA

NORTH VIETNAM

★ HANOI

DEMILITARIZED ZONE

LINE OF DEMARCATION

HO CHI MINH TRAIL

SOUTH VIETNAM

VIETNAM

★ SAIGON (HO CHI MINH CITY)

■ NORTH VIETNAM ■ COUNTRIES SUPPORTING NORTH VIETNAM

■ SOUTH VIETNAM ■ COUNTRIES SUPPORTING SOUTH VIETNAM

## VIETNAM

Before France began to colonize Vietnam in 1854 (part of what became "French Indochina"), Vietnam had struggled for centuries to remain independent of China. The French ruled Vietnam for nearly a century, until the country was occupied by the Japanese in 1940, in the early days of World War II.

As soon as the Japanese surrendered in September 1945, Ho Chi Minh, a communist revolutionary, declared Vietnam to be an independent communist state. The French then seized South Vietnam as non-communist. Twenty years of war followed, with foreign powers like the Soviet Union and China backing Ho Chi Minh, and the United States and France backing the non-communists.

# MEANWHILE IN CHINA...

After World War II, China underwent drastic change and some very rough times. As with much of Asia, foreign powers had their mitts all over China. Remember the humiliation of the Opium Wars (if you don't, see Chapter 5)? The Chinese continued to resent Western interference in their country. France, England, and the United States were supporting local warlords and China was one big fighting mess.

Mao Zedong

## COMMUNISTS GET THE UPPER HAND

Nationalism (look it up, people) was on the rise, and so was communism. For a short time, two groups joined forces against the warlords, even though they held opposite beliefs. But then the communists got the upper hand, largely through help from the Soviet Union. Eventually, a communist revolution swept through China and a famous leader named Mao Zedong began to run things.

## CHAIRMAN MAO

Mao had big dreams for China. He wanted China to have its own industrial revolution—and fast. He called his ambitious program the "Great Leap Forward," but it backfired into a disaster—a terrible famine that gripped China for years. Here's how it happened:

# THE GREAT LEAP FORWARD

Mao made any private business or farm illegal.

All farmers were required to join huge farms called **collectives**, run by the government.

Millions starved to death.

The government then took too much of the harvest away and there was not enough food left for the local people who had grown it.

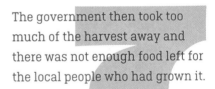

Collectives would keep some of the harvest but give the rest to the government to give out to other people.

For several years, the collectives were successful in feeding the Chinese population, which grew.

People were afraid to report the actual (low) amounts of harvest, so they lied and said they had huge harvests.

Mao pressured the collectives to produce even bigger harvests.

Mao also wanted China to become a leading producer of steel. Believe it or not, he made people try to make steel in their backyards! But they didn't know how or have the right materials. They spent their time and energy trying to make steel instead of growing food.

The horrible result of these and other policies was this: not enough food. Between 1959 and 1962, about 20 million people starved to death in China. It was one of the worst man-made disasters in human history.

**Collectives:** Collectives were huge farms run by the Chinese government.

## THE CULTURAL REVOLUTION

After the tragedy of the Great Famine, many people began to lose confidence in Mao and his brand of communism. Mao wanted to keep it going, of course, and also to root out his enemies, so he staged a new revolution in 1965, called the Cultural Revolution. In 1966, he closed all the schools and universities to stop any education in the "old ways." Schools did not re-open again until 1970.

## THE RED GUARD

Groups of teenagers and young adults took to the streets as part of a wild kind of army called the "Red Guard." Their goal was to erase anything related to the "four olds"—old customs, old culture, old habits, and old ideas.

Sometimes the Red Guard destroyed gravesites and monuments to former Chinese leaders. Often, they beat or killed teachers and professors. After a year, the chaos was so widespread and horrifying that the young revolutionaries had to be reined in.

To try to stem the violence of the Red Guard, Mao sent 17 million young people into the countryside to do hard labor on farms and learn from the peasants. He unleashed the army in cities to restore order, which brought on even more violence.

Between 500,000 and 2 million people died during the Cultural Revolution. It took many years for China to recover from the devastation of the Cultural Revolution.

*Red Guard teenagers*

# POSTWAR LATIN AMERICA

The Truman Doctrine and the Domino Theory led the United States to intervene often in the affairs of countries in Latin America. The United States gave arms, military training, and trade preference to Central and South American governments (even horrible ones) as long as they were anti-communist. Some governments friendly to the United States were ruled by cruel dictators who hogged money for themselves and kept their power through force.

## U.S. INVOLVEMENT IN LATIN AMERICA

■ COUPS WITH U.S. INVOLVEMENT
■ U.S. INVASION
■ UNITED STATES

▨ ATTEMPTED COUPS WITH U.S. INVOLVEMENT
▨ CLAIMS OF U.S. INVOLVEMENT IN REGIME CHANGE

Over time, the United States also secretly worked to bring down any leader who wanted to bring in socialist ideas. But the United States did not have its way with the nearby island of Cuba. The Cubans formed an alliance with the Soviet Union against the United States. Tension with Cuba and the Soviet Union led to even more U.S. intervention in Latin America.

## THE CUBAN MISSILE CRISIS

The Cold War conflict reached a peak in 1962 when the Soviet Union began to install missiles on the island of Cuba, just ninety miles from Florida. If fired, the missiles could reach parts of the United States within minutes.

U.S. President John F. Kennedy cut off all supplies to Cuba and called on the Soviet leader, Nikita Khrushchev, to remove the missiles. Khrushchev refused, and Kennedy considered invading Cuba, but the consequences of a nuclear war with the Soviet Union would be dire.

Finally, after seventeen days of tense negotiations between the two leaders, a compromise was reached. Khrushchev would remove the missiles if the United States promised to never invade Cuba, and also removed its missiles from Turkey and Italy, which were in striking range of Moscow.

# THE 1960S

Before we even get into what you need to know about the sixties, let's get your brain ready by pulling on your boots. Think about what you already know about the sixties. (New knowledge hooks onto old—scientists know this.) What comes to mind? Make your own list right now.

_____

_____

_____

_____

_____

If tie-dye is on your list of sixties stuff, that's a hint that this decade was a time of experimentation and "far-outness." If you thought of a peace sign, you know that peace was important to people (or some people) during the sixties. Maybe you already know that Martin Luther King, Jr lived (and died) during this time. Yes, the sixties was a time when people all over the world called loudly for peace and freedom, and the big movements for change were started by young people, mainly college students.

Caution! When you study any movement for change, especially those of the 1960s, be sure to avoid two common mistakes:

1. Don't assume that protests just suddenly started up one day. That's never the case. Small efforts always precede the big ones. If and when you study any of these movements closely, you'll uncover the people and events that paved the way.

2. Don't assume the goals of the movement got accomplished. Far from the truth, unfortunately. Plenty of people didn't want these changes, and still don't.

What's a movement? It's when a group of people says "It's time to get moving on changing things!" Once enough people get on board and start protesting and pressing for change without giving up, it gets to be called a social movement.

## SNCC AND SIT-INS IN THE UNITED STATES

The Student Nonviolent Coordinating Committee (SNCC) was a group of mostly African American students. They were the first to stage a nonviolent "sit-in" at a whites-only lunch counter in North Carolina. Similarly, the antiwar movement began with a group of students at the University of California who were protesting for free speech on their campus.

# CIVIL RIGHTS MOVEMENTS

After the lunch counter sit-ins, the U.S. civil rights movement gathered powerful momentum. African Americans, and others who supported them, called for an end to Jim Crow laws that made it difficult for Black Americans to vote, own property, or travel freely.

# FIGHTING JIM CROW LAWS

Jim Crow laws made Black children attend all-Black schools that were of poor quality. Trains, buses, waiting rooms, hospitals, and other public places were separated by race. A Black person could actually be arrested for riding on an all-white bus—and many were, as people began to board those buses in defiance.

All over the country, and especially in Washington, DC, people marched in huge peaceful protests against Jim Crow and racist practices. Riots broke out, as did brutal violence against African Americans by white supremacists and police.

> **Movement:** A social movement happens when people get together and push for change in society.
>
> **White supremacist:** Someone who believes that the white race is superior to all others is a white supremacist. Their beliefs are often expressed through violent attacks or discrimination.

*The United Farm Workers leader, César Chávez*

Starting in 1964, the U.S. government enacted laws to end segregation in schools and discrimination in public places and employment. Many white people resisted these changes, and fought back. The struggle for racial equality continues today, but laws passed in the 1960s still stand as important steps forward:

- The Civil Rights Act of 1964 made it illegal to discriminate against anyone on the basis of their race, color, religion, sex, or national origin.

- The Voting Rights Act of 1965 outlawed literacy tests and taxes that were used to keep African Americans from voting.

Other oppressed groups in the United States also protested for equal rights in the 1960s:

- In 1965, César Chávez, a Mexican American, formed the United Farm Workers union and went on strike to demand better pay and working conditions for farm workers.

- In 1969, Indigenous Americans occupied Alcatraz Island off of California, demanding that it be returned to the Native American tribe that had originally lived there. The protest was put down by government forces.

- In 1969, the Stonewall Riots broke out in New York City, which sparked the formation of the Gay Liberation Front, and the beginning of the global LGBTQ movement.

And across the world, civil rights movements like these were underway:

- In Northern Ireland, people began to organize and protest for the rights of Catholics who wanted Northern Ireland to be part of the Republic of Ireland and not the United Kingdom.

- "Prague Spring" occurred in Czechoslovakia in 1968, when the government began to promote human rights to create "socialism with a human face." (A Soviet invasion in the summer put a stop to this.)

- In 1968, human rights activists in the Soviet Union began publishing the *Chronicle of Human Events* to inform the world about how the Soviet government was sending people to prison, labor camps, or psychiatric hospitals just for their beliefs.

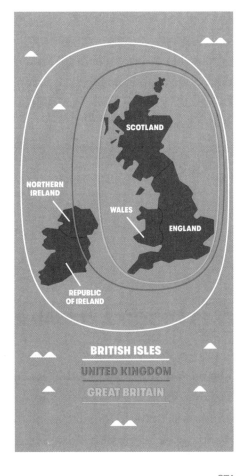

- In 1968, the anti-apartheid activist Steven Biko cofounded the all-Black South African Students' Organization (SASO), and became its first president the following year. Biko and SASO believed that Black South Africans should take control of their own destinies, and recognize their own self-worth, rather than relying on white support to end apartheid.

1968 was a year for student protests around the world. In Pakistan, Brazil, and Mexico, students marched in opposition to repressive dictatorships. In Poland, France, and Sweden students called for student voice in university decision-making. They took over university buildings, which led to arrests, imprisonment, and sometimes violence with police.

# THE ANTIWAR MOVEMENT

The Vietnam War (1954–1975) brought about huge protests as well. On television, people were seeing the horror of a war fought in jungles against hidden enemies, with land mines that could go off any time, and poisonous chemicals that killed and sickened both soldiers and civilians. Young people saw their friends get drafted into the U.S. military and never return from Vietnam.

**United Kingdom:** The United Kingdom is the official name for the nation made up of Great Britain and Northern Ireland.

**Draft:** The draft is when the government makes people (usually just men) join the armed forces. When someone "gets drafted," they are being called into military service.

## THE LARGEST ANTIWAR PROTEST IN U.S. HISTORY

In ten years, the Vietnam War killed over fifty-eight thousand U.S. soldiers, 1.35 million North and South Vietnamese soldiers, and 2 million Vietnamese civilians. People in the United States started to wonder why the United States was fighting for so long, so far away, with so little gain, and so many losses. Many also started to doubt the wisdom of the Truman

Doctrine and the Domino Theory, which had gotten the United States into the conflict to begin with.

On November 15, 1969, over half a million Americans joined in the largest antiwar protest in U.S. history. It took six more years for the United States to finally pull out of the Vietnam conflict.

# NEW SOCIAL PROGRAMS

In 1964, Lyndon B. Johnson was running for U.S. president after completing the term of John F. Kennedy, who was assassinated in 1963. On the campaign trail, he made a speech, promising that the United States would become a "great society" where. . .

> *". . . no child will go unfed, and no youngster will go unschooled. Where no man who wants work will fail to find it. Where no citizen will be barred from any door because of his birthplace or his color or his church. Where peace and security is common among neighbors and possible among nations."*

## THE WAR ON POVERTY

Johnson won the election and got to work on his promises, vowing to wage a "War on Poverty." It was a good thing, too, because 20 percent of Americans were living below the poverty line. During his presidency, spending to help the poor doubled, from $1 billion to $2 billion. Over two hundred laws and programs were enacted to improve public education, healthcare, public housing, and transportation.

By the time Johnson left office, the percentage of Americans living below the poverty line had been reduced to only 12 percent. Some programs were canceled by presidents who came after Johnson. But other programs still exist today, like Medicare and Medicaid, which provide free healthcare for elderly people, the disabled, and those living in poverty.

# THE WOMEN'S MOVEMENT

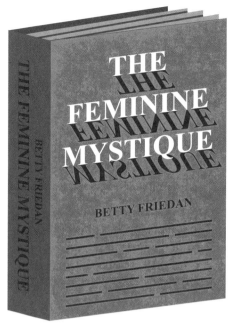

*Betty Friedan's 1963 book revived a movement.*

For most of the twentieth century, many middle-class women were stay-at-home moms. Even though the Seneca Falls Convention back in 1848 had begun the fight for equal rights, women of the 1960s still lacked many basic rights.

## WOMEN DENIED BASIC RIGHTS

A married woman could not get a credit card in her own name without getting her husband's permission. Married women working as teachers could be fired for becoming pregnant. People at that time assumed that women were happy to raise children and stay home, without careers or much education. A book called *The Feminine Mystique* gave everyone a wake-up call. The book's author, Betty Friedan, found out that many women were, in fact, pretty bored and frustrated just being home. They wanted to have challenging careers and satisfying lives outside the home, too.

## ACTIVISM LEADS TO NEW LAWS

The book was so popular that it inspired a second wave of the women's movement. Women demonstrated for equal opportunities, more access to education, and equal pay. In 1963, a law was passed that made it illegal to pay women less money for doing the same work as men. In 1966, the National Organization for Women was founded, which to this day continues to fight for women's rights.

# A GLOBAL IMPACT

The renewed fight for women's rights in the United States had a global impact as well, and women around the world joined the push for equal rights.

• 1966, India elected its first (and only) female prime minister, Indira Gandhi.

• 1967, the United Nations adopted a Declaration on the Elimination of Discrimination Against Women, which was essentially a global affirmation of women's rights.

• 1968 in Sweden, an organization called Group 8 was formed to fight for issues particularly relevant to women: expanded childcare and equal pay among them.

# THE YEAR OF AFRICA

The continent of Africa underwent drastic change in 1960. In the space of that one year, seventeen countries won independence: thirteen from France, and the others from the United Kingdom and Belgium.

As a result, people started calling it "the Year of Africa." In some ways, the Year of Africa really

began in 1958, when the first All African Peoples' Conference had been held in Accra, Ghana—the first conference of its kind to be held on African soil. At this conference, the leaders of African independence movements and delegates from already-independent African countries agreed to unite to promote independence, strengthen existing African states and governments, and fight control by colonial powers.

# PAN-AFRICANISM BRINGS RESULTS

This idea, called Pan-Africanism, had existed for many decades, but it was finally coming to fruition. On the map (next page), you can see how much of the continent of Africa was involved in independence movements during certain years.

The world now had to listen to Africa because it had more representatives in the United Nations. Africans around the world sought to unite through the Pan-African movement, which promoted African progress and celebrated the common heritage of Africans wherever they happened to live. Pan-Africanism and the Year of Africa also inspired African American activists of the U.S. civil rights movement.

# AFRICAN INDEPENDENCE MOVEMENTS, 1950–PRESENT

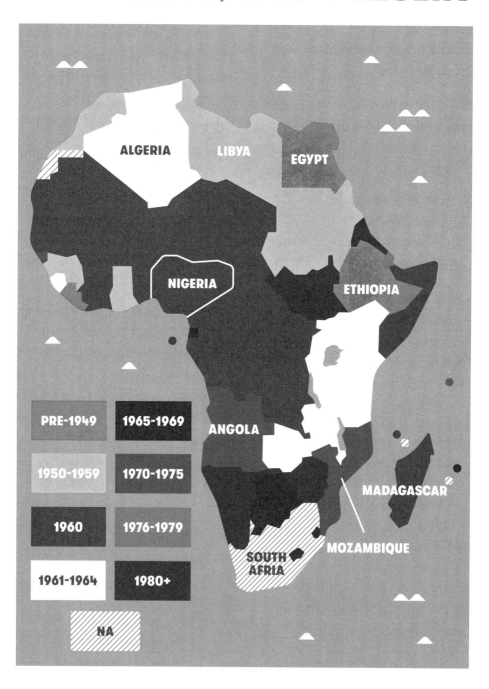

ALGERIA

LIBYA

EGYPT

NIGERIA

ETHIOPIA

ANGOLA

PRE-1949 | 1965-1969

1950-1959 | 1970-1975

1960 | 1976-1979

1961-1964 | 1980+

NA

MADAGASCAR

MOZAMBIQUE

SOUTH AFRICA

# THE FIGHT AGAINST APARTHEID IN SOUTH AFRICA

One African country was both incredibly oppressive and incredibly slow to change: South Africa. South Africa had (and continues to have) about four times as many Black people as white people. But for forty-two years, people of color lived under a racist system of laws called apartheid.

Apartheid laws were similar to the Jim Crow laws in the United States. They did what the word says: kept people "apart," and they kept Black people down—way down.

If you were Black in South Africa you could only live in areas called "homelands," very poor, crowded areas outside the cities, where people lived in shacks with no indoor plumbing. Many of these people labored in mines, almost like slaves.

Meanwhile, white people lived in big houses with modern luxuries. Apartheid laws prevented Black people from traveling to "white" areas, going to white schools, holding certain jobs, or even voting in national elections. If you were Black or brown you had to carry a "passbook" with you at all times, which listed information about you and where you lived. White police could stop you, demand to see your passbook, and kick you out of a white area and back to the homelands.

**Heritage:** A person's heritage is their ancestry or the background from which they come.

**Apartheid:** Apartheid was the South African policy of racial discrimination that lasted from 1948 until 1991. It was a system of laws designed to separate people by racial lines, with Black people at the bottom.

**Shacks:** A shack is a crudely built, temporary building, usually without comforts like bathrooms, kitchens, running water, and electricity.

## THE SHARPEVILLE MASSACRE

In the important year of 1960, as protests were breaking out all over Africa and the world, about five thousand Black South Africans refused to carry their passbooks and marched to the police station in a town called Sharpeville. The police opened fire on the crowd, killing sixty-nine protesters. The Sharpeville Massacre and other violence by police led to more protests and the imprisonment of thousands.

Artists and musicians got on board worldwide to call for an end to apartheid. "Free Nelson Mandela," released by the English band The Specials, became a top ten hit in 1984.

## NELSON MANDELA RISES

In 1964, a leader of the movement to fight apartheid, Nelson Mandela, was sentenced to life in prison.

Even from jail, Mandela continued to lead the fight against apartheid. In the 1980s, the world started to pay attention. Mandela became an international hero. He was finally released from prison in 1990, after twenty-seven years. And get this: In 1994, Nelson Mandela was elected the president of South Africa.

# CHAPTER VOCABULARY

**Apartheid:** Apartheid was the South African policy of racial discrimination that lasted from 1948 until 1991. It was a system of laws designed to separate people by racial lines, with Black people at the bottom.

**Arms Race:** The global arms race was a scramble for countries to each be the nation with the most formidable weapons, generally nuclear weapons.

**Boycotting:** A boycott is an economic protest tactic where people refuse to purchase specific goods or services for political reasons. For example, people might boycott a company if they disagree with its treatment of workers.

**Buffer zone:** A neutral area whose purpose is to separate enemies. The Soviet Union controlled Eastern European countries in order to create a buffer zone against Western forces.

**Collectives:** Collectives were huge farms run by the Chinese government.

**Combat:** Combat is conflict between armed forces. The Cold War is unique in that it was a "war" with no actual armed fighting like in previous wars.

**Containment:** Containment is a strategy that works to prevent the expansion of power or influence. In this chapter, you saw how the United States worked toward the containment of the Soviet Union's power.

**Draft:** The draft is when the government makes people (usually just men ) join the armed forces. When someone "gets drafted," they are being called into military service.

**Fallout shelters:** Fallout shelters are bunkers or buildings that are built to withstand nuclear explosions. During the Cold War, many people prepared fallout shelters as protective measures.

**Firebrand:** The literal definition of a firebrand is a piece of wood that is on fire, but it can also be used to describe someone who is passionate and outspoken about their cause, so much so that they incite action and might be seen as very radical!

**Heritage:** A person's heritage is their ancestry or the background from which they come.

**Refugees:** Refugees are people who have to leave their country. They might be escaping war, political persecution, or natural disasters.

**Secular:** If something is secular, that means it is not religious, or does not observe religious traditions. A secular state is a country that isn't associated with a specific religion.

**Shacks:** A shack is a crudely built, temporary building, usually without comforts like bathrooms, kitchens, running water, and electricity.

**United Kingdom:** The United Kingdom is the official name for the nation made up of Great Britain and Northern Ireland.

**Warheads:** Warheads are the parts of missiles and other weapons that contain explosives.

**White supremacist:** Someone who believes that the white race is superior to all others is a white supremacist. Their beliefs are often expressed through violent attacks or discrimination.

**Zionism/Zionist:** Zionism was originally a movement for the creation of a Jewish nation.

# NOTES

# 8 CHALLENGES TODAY

So, here we are, at the end of our story of the history of the world. Do you think we covered everything? Not even close. Will we now tie all of world history up in a nice bow for you? No way. History is never finished, and neither are its challenges. Let's see how history is unfolding right now. . .

79

By making it through this book (or even parts of it), you know that history is complicated. You know that human life keeps on changing. You've seen how the human race makes progress on some things, but slides backward on others.

Throughout these pages, you've watched new problems arise and others keep repeating. If you've paid attention and done some thinking, we think you are 100 percent set to survive middle school world history. In fact, you might know more than most adults.

## WHAT ABOUT NOW?

But what about the present? It counts, right? What's happening right now will become history. Let's think about that. Where does the present end and history begin? Should yesterday be considered history? A year ago? How about a minute ago? Technically, we could say a minute ago. One minute ago counts as the past, and communication is so fast now that we can find out about change by the minute. But our brains might explode if all of history were told in minutes!

## WHAT WILL OUR ERA BE CALLED?

Historians have done a nice thing for us by dividing history into eras or ages. For example, there's an era called Ancient History that we looked at, and one called Early Modern History, and Late Modern History and so on. (Historians love to argue about the exact beginnings and endings of such eras, but they agree on some basic divisions of time.)

So, how will historians describe this era that we're living in right now? What will they call it? What will we and people who come after us learn from it? We can't exactly know yet, but if we understand the challenges that face us right now, we can watch history unfold, and maybe even affect it.

**Era:** An era is a big chunk of time in history.

# THE DIGITAL AGE

Historians have already started describing our era as the Digital Age, brought on by the Digital Revolution. You now know a lot about revolutions, and this one's a biggie. Is it related to other revolutions? You bet. In fact, the Digital Revolution is sometimes called the Third Industrial Revolution.

## THE INDUSTRIAL REVOLUTIONS

| FIRST INDUSTRIAL REVOLUTION 1760–1840 | SECOND INDUSTRIAL REVOLUTION 1870–1914 | THIRD INDUSTRIAL REVOLUTION 1940–TODAY |
|---|---|---|
| Water and steam power allow machines to produce things quickly instead of people producing things slowly. | Electricity makes machines even more powerful. Production of goods gets even bigger and faster. Railroads and ships carry stuff farther and farther. | The whole world becomes connected by computers and the Internet. Communication and some trade happen instantly. Production of goods is increased. Artificial intelligence makes it possible for computers to "think" and replace humans in certain kinds of work. |

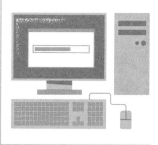

**Digital:** If something is digital, that means it has to do with computers and technology. This current era is often referred to as the Digital Age because computer technologies are a central force shaping modern history.

**Artificial Intelligence:** Artificial intelligence, or AI, allows computers to take on tasks that we normally think of as human: thinking, making decisions, understanding speech, and more.

The Digital Age has forever changed the way people live and the way the world works. Human beings have never had so much information coming at them so fast. It comes instantly, doesn't it? If you want to know what just happened in New York City today, or in your hometown, or in Cairo, Egypt, you can simply do a search on your phone, computer, or watch, and you'll know in a matter of seconds.

Forty years ago, you had to wait to read the news in the newspaper the next day. News had to be written down by a journalist, or broadcast by a reporter on the radio or TV before it could get to people. But now, if you have a device, you can get any news, straight up, right away. It might come as a 280-character tweet or a quick paragraph uploaded by a journalist onto multiple platforms.

 Remember how the printing press gave people direct access to the Bible in the 1400s? It brought down the authority of the Catholic Church to interpret Christianity and pretty much rule people's lives. How will the direct access offered by the Internet affect power relationships today?

_____

_____

_____

_____

Digital life comes with many benefits, but some risks as well. The great challenge for the digital generation (ahem. . . that's you) is to figure out how to get the benefits of the Internet, but safeguard the world against its dangers.

# PROS AND CONS OF THE INTERNET

| BENEFITS | DRAWBACKS |
|---|---|
| Information is directly available to everyone. You don't have to wait for a teacher or a journalist or a textbook to hand you information. | Not everyone in the world has full access to the Internet, so some people benefit a lot and others don't. |
| People can share their knowledge quickly. The world can learn more, much faster. | Not everything on the Internet is true. Sites like Wikipedia usually have quick ways that info gets corrected, but some websites and even some "people" online are fake. Sometimes people create false information. If it gets passed around, (and it does) it grows, and people get confused about what's true and what's not true. |
| On social media like Facebook, Twitter, and TikTok, people can share their opinions freely. | Some opinions are fine, but some can be really harmful, like racism. Cyberbullying can occur, too. There are some people who want to spread harmful ideas, and the Internet can make it pretty easy. |
| Social media helps people make friends (and have fun). 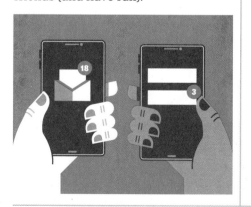 | Social media can be used to benefit some and not others. Some experts worry that, for many people, social media "friends" are replacing real-life friends.<br><br>The Internet also makes it easy for other people and companies to know more about you than you might want them to know. That's why privacy settings are so important. |

# SOCIAL MEDIA AND DEMOCRACY

All the above drawbacks combine into a challenge to democracy. Even though you can't vote yet, it's something to carefully consider right now. You learned in Chapter 4 about the Scientific Revolution, the Reformation, and the Enlightenment, which gave rise to the new concept (during those times) that people could think for themselves and could be trusted to have a say in how they were governed.

Right now, you may be wondering, what if people get swayed by tons of one-sided, or even false, information? What if they vote based on that information?

Well, lots of data suggest that it has already happened in elections in the United States and the United Kingdom. Social media amplified and spread true information—but also false information—at lightning speed, affecting the outcome of important elections.

It gets tricky because freedom of speech is so important in democracies. Historians of the present and future will be looking closely at the relationship between democracy and social media.

# CLIMATE CHANGE

There's no doubt that the state of our environment will shape history from here on out. Human beings have achieved amazing things during our three industrial revolutions. We've invented millions of machines, cars, planes— even ranch-flavored Doritos. We can produce tons and tons of stuff really fast, and get it all over the world. BUT—we did not do a great job of considering the impact on our planet.

# WHAT IS THE GREENHOUSE EFFECT?

The greenhouse effect is actually a beneficial process to keep the Earth's atmosphere warm, but it's gotten out of whack. Here's how it works.

The atmosphere (with its carbon dioxide and other gases), is supposed to trap heat, but because the carbon dioxide levels have gotten too high, too much heat is being trapped.

Why are these levels so high? From those three industrial revolutions! Our millions of machines mainly run on fossil fuels (coal, oil, gas), which create lots of carbon dioxide.

## SO WHAT'S THE BIG DEAL?

Rising temperatures on Earth are knocking nature off balance. Sea levels are rising because ice is melting in areas (like the North Pole) where it never melted before. Animal habitats are disappearing. Destructive storms come more often. Great cities, like Venice, Italy, are flooding more, and small coastal towns are being lost to the sea.

# THE GREENHOUSE EFFECT

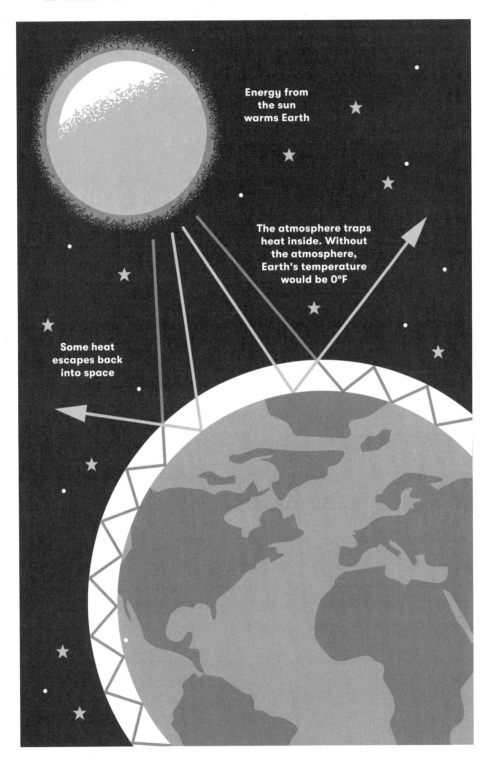

Energy from the sun warms Earth

The atmosphere traps heat inside. Without the atmosphere, Earth's temperature would be 0°F

Some heat escapes back into space

# THE NEED TO HEAL MOTHER EARTH

Scientists warn that if we don't change the way we live and reduce our carbon emissions, the human race could be in big trouble. World leaders have already come together to reach agreements and take action, but progress has been slow. In the meantime, grassroots activism, especially by young people, has gathered momentum.

Greta Thunberg

## A TEENAGER TAKES THE LEAD

In 2018, fifteen-year-old Greta Thunberg from Sweden made history by protesting outside of Swedish parliament rather than attending school. She inspired school climate strikes all over the world, and was invited to speak at the UN Climate Change Summit in New York in September 2019. "The eyes of all future generations are upon you," she told the world leaders at the United Nations. "And if you choose to fail us, I say—we will never forgive you."

> **Grassroots:** When activism or organizing is called grassroots, that means it's making change from the bottom up. It's often based in connecting with and organizing local community members.

Historians are likely to be writing for years to come about how, and if, world leaders can slow the destruction of the environment.

What do you think? Should governments implement changes to protect the environment or should it be left to individual choices?

_____

_____

_____

_____

_____

_____

_____

_____

_____

_____

# GLOBAL TRADE

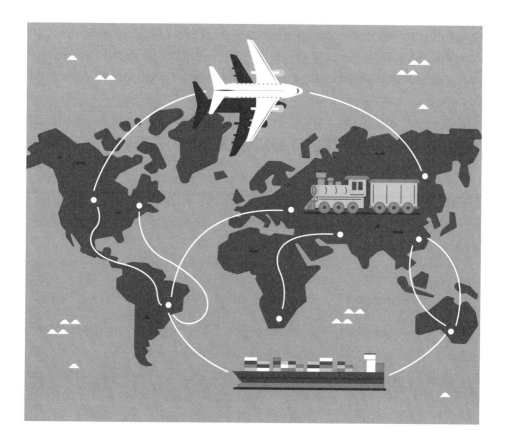

Ever since those first Portuguese sailors sought a route to Asia for valuable and yummy spices, people have traveled across continents to get what they want. When the Industrial Revolution took off, we saw how industrialized countries needed raw materials from places like the Americas, India, and Africa and so created colonies in those areas. We also saw how imperialist nations set up new markets for their goods in places like China. We've seen how history is often the story of how trade routes grew around the globe.

# THE GLOBAL SUPPLY CHAIN

So, let's think about our present, high-powered, technological age. Can you predict how trade and manufacturing are changing around the world?

Bigger, faster, and more complicated is right. These days, multinational companies engage in a process called the global supply chain. Any one of the stages of production or distribution can take place in any part of the world.

## YOUR WELL-TRAVELED T-SHIRT

Here's an example: Your T-shirt could be made from Texas cotton, which is made into fabric in China and sewn together in Bangladesh. The shirt travels back and forth across the Pacific Ocean until it finally reaches completion and ends up in a store in California.

Companies go to the trouble of shipping things around the world during the manufacturing process because it saves them money and that means a bigger profit.

Global supply chain: The global supply chain is the process by which many goods are made using materials and labor from around the world. Any one of the stages of production or distribution can take place in any part of the world.

Profit: Profit is the money made after expenses have been accounted for.

## WHERE ARE WORKERS IN THE CHAIN?

U.S. and European companies can pay workers in less-developed countries lower wages, so that saves on the cost of producing things. Sometimes, the taxes are lower in other countries, so they build factories there. Or, a company might have offices all over the world, with people doing things in different places.

A bank based in New York might send its customer service calls all the way to the Philippines, where workers there answer people's questions in real time.

## HOW NATIONS PROTECT THEIR INTERESTS

Countries sometimes try to protect their own industries from competition with other countries. For example, China, where workers don't get paid very much, likes to sell its products to Americans, but the United States wants people to buy things made by U.S. companies, which generally have to pay their workers more. So the U.S. government imposes tariffs to try to make trade fairer to the U.S. manufacturers and farmers.

It gets pretty complicated, but in the end, it's usually the consumer who pays the cost of the tariff! Historians will be watching how global trade plays out in the future. Countries build and break alliances based on trade, and struggle to arrive at fair agreements. Every person in the world is touched by the workings of the global supply chain because of the products that they use daily.

> **Tariffs: A tariff is a tax issued by a government on imports from other countries.**

# DISEASE

Our ever-expanding scientific knowledge has given human beings longer life spans, cures for diseases, and even **vaccinations** that prevent people from getting certain diseases. But we can still get blindsided by new **viruses** and **bacteria**. When a new germ comes along, often through an animal, people are not **immune** and they can get very sick and pass the disease to others.

**Vaccinations:** Vaccinations are the shots you get to prevent diseases. They are an important way the world stays healthy!

**Virus and Bacteria:** A virus is a highly infectious agent that can spread disease. Bacteria are germs, good or bad. Scientifically, there are differences between these terms, but in the context of history, both have been responsible for widespread disease.

**Immune:** If you're immune to something, that means it can't affect you. Being immune to a disease means it can't get you sick. Remember vaccinations? Those are one way humans can gain immunity to different illnesses.

## A GLOBAL PROBLEM

This is when the world's interconnectedness does not serve us so well. With all the international exchange going on, deadly diseases can spread across continents within days. When a disease spreads rapidly in one area it's called an epidemic, but when it spreads to the entire world it's called a pandemic.

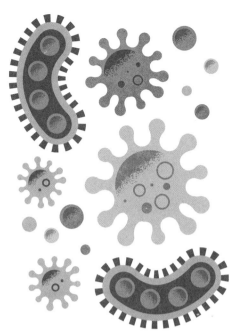

# COVID-19

The COVID-19 pandemic burned through the world beginning in 2019, killing more than 2.6 million people and infecting more than 117 million as of March 2021. People across the world were confined to their homes, businesses and schools closed, and most travel halted. Many people wore face masks to prevent the spread of a disease that anyone could be carrying, even if they looked and felt healthy.

*Mask-wearing helped prevent the spread of the deadly COVID-19 virus.*

# GLOBAL PANDEMICS

| COMMON NAME OF DISEASE | WHEN | WHERE | DEATH TOLL |
|---|---|---|---|
| HIV/AIDS | 1981–present | First identified in Democratic Republic of Congo; spread globally | 33 million |
| HONG KONG FLU | 1968–1970 | Started in Hong Kong, spread through Southeast Asia, Australia, Europe, and the United States | 1 to 4 million—500,000 in Hong Kong |
| ASIAN FLU | 1957 | Began in China, spread to Singapore, Hong Kong, and United States | 1 to 2 million |
| SPANISH FLU | 1918–1920 | First observed in U.S. military during WWI, spread globally | 25 to 50 million |
| THIRD CHOLERA PANDEMIC | 1852–1860 | Started in India, spread thru Asia, Europe, North America, and Africa | 1 million |
| BUBONIC PLAGUE ("BLACK DEATH") | 1347–1351 | Believed to have started in Asia, spread through Europe and Africa | 50 to 200 million |

# DISEASE MEETS OTHER CHALLENGES

This is a good time to think about how challenges in this section connect to each other. Historians will be watching for and analyzing those connections. For example, COVID-19 had a huge effect on global supply chains, as people stayed home from work, and shipping and travel became restricted, creating shortages of some manufactured items.

# INSTANT INFORMATION. . . AND DISINFORMATION

Social media impacted people's knowledge of the virus, both positively and negatively. People could get up-to-the-minute information on the number of cases, and plenty of information on how to prevent the spread of COVID-19.

# SOCIAL MEDIA ACCELERATES EVERYTHING

On the other hand, lots of misinformation flew around the Internet, some stories even claiming that the pandemic was being exaggerated, or that it was created on purpose as part of a secret plan to benefit drug companies. On social media, people could get accurate or confusing information about the COVID-19, depending on which stories got to them and which they chose to view.

# REFUGEES

If you are reading this in the comfort of your home, you might not know there are more than 80 million people in the world who have no homes, and half of them are children. In some places, right now, all you can see for miles are huge camps, where thousands of people are living, side by side, in long rows of tents or shacks.

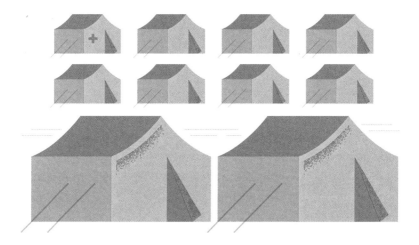

## DRIVEN OUT BY WAR, FAMINE, AND DISASTER

These homeless people, or refugees, are camped out because they had to leave their homes quickly and find a temporary place to live. They are among the poorest and most vulnerable of the world's people. Often a war drives them out, violent groups threaten their lives, they don't have enough food, or a natural disaster like a flood or a hurricane destroys the area in which they live. Sometimes people are forced out of their homes, or they decide to leave for their own safety and seek asylum (safety) in other countries.

Asylum: In the context of this chapter, asylum refers to the safety that refugees seek in other countries. It is a legal designation granted by the countries that refugees enter.

# REFUGEES' COUNTRIES OF ORIGIN, 2019

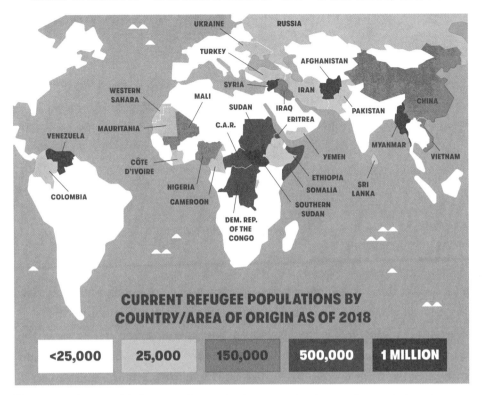

**CURRENT REFUGEE POPULATIONS BY COUNTRY/AREA OF ORIGIN AS OF 2018**

| <25,000 | 25,000 | 150,000 | 500,000 | 1 MILLION |
|---|---|---|---|---|

The map shows which areas have the largest numbers of people leaving them as refugees. Typically, refugees flee to neighboring countries, but some go to Europe. A fairly small number (30,000 in 2019) settle in the United States.

## ARE WEALTHY NATIONS DOING ENOUGH?

Countries place limits on the number of refugees they will take in. In 2020, 80 percent of all refugees were taken in by poorer, developing countries, while 20 percent went to richer, developed countries like the United States As of 2020, Turkey, Pakistan, Uganda, Sudan, and Germany were taking in the most refugees. Historians will continue to track how and why vast numbers of people get displaced, and how the world responds.

Many refugees end up unable to return to the countries they had to leave. It's an unsolved problem that the world will need to get better at addressing.

# INCOME INEQUALITY

Like most of today's challenges, income inequality is nothing new. We saw how the French peasants revolted in 1789 when the gap between rich and poor became too much to bear. We saw how communist governments tried to put all wealth in the hands of the state, often through force, which ultimately failed. Historians will continue to follow how income inequality affects government, culture, and human progress in general.

## A LOOK AT INEQUALITY IN THE WORLD

Worldwide, the gap between rich and poor is huge and it's getting bigger. In general, you could say that the very rich are getting richer and the rest are either staying where they are or getting poorer. Seventy percent of the global population today lives in countries where the gap between rich and poor is widening. Take a look at the following charts, which will give you an idea of who owns what part of the world's total wealth.

### WEALTH INEQUALITY WORLDWIDE, 2016

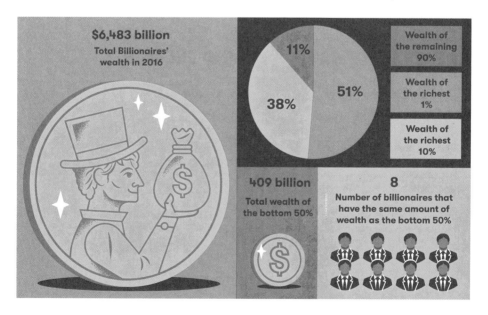

$6,483 billion
Total Billionaires' wealth in 2016

11%

38%

51%

Wealth of the remaining 90%

Wealth of the richest 1%

Wealth of the richest 10%

409 billion
Total wealth of the bottom 50%

8
Number of billionaires that have the same amount of wealth as the bottom 50%

Countries with more wealth and technology are called developed countries, while poorer countries, with less access to technology are called developing countries. Just to give you an idea of how differently people live in developed versus developing countries, only 35 percent of people living in developing countries have access to the Internet, while 87 percent of people in developed countries have access. In 2017, here's how the world map looked for human development.

**Developed and developing countries:** Countries with more wealth and technology are called developed countries, while poorer countries, with less access to technology, are called developing countries.

## HUMAN DEVELOPMENT INDEX, 2017

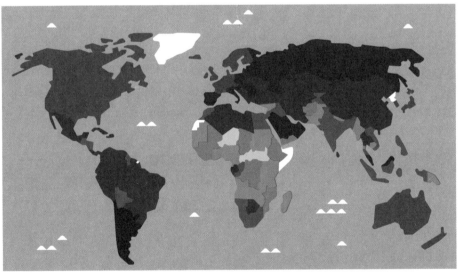

| LEAST DEVELOPED | NO DATA | .2 | .3 | .4 | .5 | .6 | .7 | .8 | .9 | 1 | MOST DEVELOPED |

What do you notice about the differences in development worldwide? How does what you've read in earlier chapters explain some of these differences?

_____

_____

_____

Experts warn that poverty, hunger, and suffering will worsen if countries don't reverse the current trends in income inequality. In developing countries, people (especially women) can get caught in what's called subsistence living.

> Subsistence living: Subsistence living means working to supply only the resources necessary for survival (food, water, and somewhere to live).

## THE TRAP OF SUBSISTENCE LIVING

Subsistence is like survival, and it sets up a cycle of no progress. Because these poorer countries don't have good roads, reliable electricity, even running water sometimes, people have to spend time doing basic things like fetching water just to survive. They can't get educated, start a business, or develop in other ways which would, in turn, help their communities to develop.

We saw in early civilizations how important it was to have the basics covered so that people could move on to education, innovation, and art. Today, there are many places where people are stuck because the basics for a decent modern life are still missing.

## INCOME INEQUALITY WITHIN DEVELOPED COUNTRIES

In a few modern-day countries, like Sweden and Norway, wealth is distributed fairly evenly, which means very few people in these countries are poor. But in many countries that we think of as wealthy, the hold on wealth is lopsided. The country with the world's most severe inequality is South Africa. (Check back to Postwar History in Chapter 7 for a refresher on why.)

## MIRROR, MIRROR ON THE WALL, WHO IS THE MOST UNEQUAL OF ALL?

The United States has been named as the most unequal country of all the G7 (developed) countries. In 2019, about 34 million people in the United States were living in poverty. From 1989 to 2016 the wealth gap between the poorest and richest U.S. families more than doubled.

# RACISM

Racism is the belief by people of one race that they are superior to another race due to their skin color, culture, or nationality. Racism also applies to the systems that uphold that belief. If you read only certain parts of history (and you also happen to be white and don't experience racism yourself), you *could* think that racism is a problem of the past.

 Put the brakes on! The U.S. civil rights movement did abolish Jim Crow laws, and apartheid did finally end in South Africa. But the sad truth is, racism remains an evil of modern life. Here are a few pieces of evidence:

• In the United States, between 2015 and 2020, police fatalities of Black people occurred at a rate of 2.5 times higher than did police fatalities of white people.

• White supremacists in Europe, the United States, Russia, and other countries communicate on the Internet and spread ideas of hate against Blacks, Jews, Muslims, immigrants, and other minority groups. Even some politicians adopt their anti-immigrant attitudes.

• More than 60 percent of all Roma people applying for jobs in the Czech Republic experience discrimination because of their race.

• In 2018, four-in-ten Latinx in the United States had experienced some kind of racism in the past year, like someone making fun of them for speaking Spanish or being told to go back to their home country.

• In 2019, during the COVID-19 pandemic, some people across the world became aggressive and violent toward Asians from all countries because COVID-19 began in China.

It's important to know there are four kinds of racism that plague our world. These forces will continue to shape history and impede human progress until we overcome them:

# THE FOUR KINDS OF RACISM

| | |
|---|---|
| **INDIVIDUAL RACISM** | This refers to the ideas of racism for an individual, as well as actions that may result. Examples are telling a racist joke, or being scared of someone just because they are Black. |
| **INSTITUTIONAL RACISM** | This kind of racism is government policies that exclude or make life harder for people of color. For example, the majority of toxic waste dumps are put into communities of color rather than white communities. The number of traffic stops for Black and nonwhite drivers are higher than white people. Even if a racist law is abolished (like Jim Crow), the effects of institutional racism are felt long afterward. |
| **INTERNALIZED RACISM** | This occurs when racist ideas are accepted by people, even people of color, so that they don't speak up and they conform to racist structures and ideas that have limited them. |
| **INTERPERSONAL RACISM** | This is racism that takes place person to person, like aggression, insults, violence, or even just avoiding someone. |

There's much work to be done. Groups like Black Lives Matter, the Anti-Defamation League, and the European Network Against Racism are fighting racism worldwide. In 2020, when an African American man named George Floyd was killed by police in Minnesota, people all over the world took to the streets in huge protests against police brutality and racism.

Big corporations responded by donating to racial justice groups, pledging support for Black-owned businesses, and promising to hire and promote more people of color. Many businesses and schools now hire consultants to come into their organizations to help people face their own biases and bring the topic of racism out into the open. One important measure of human progress going forward—one country at a time, one person at a time—will be the degree to which we can confront racism and stamp it out for good.

# GENDER DISCRIMINATION

*"Truth is the only safe ground to stand upon."*

—Elizabeth Cady Stanton, *The Women's Bible*, 1895

Let's consider these words, written more than a century ago by a pioneering women's rights activist. What truth might Stanton have been referring to? Maybe it was the basic truth that women are people, too. Or that women are smart enough to vote, or that women deserve higher education. Most everyone today would admit to these truths, but as we saw with racism, a change in the law, or even people saying they agree, does not guarantee true equality. Let's take a look at some truthful statistics:

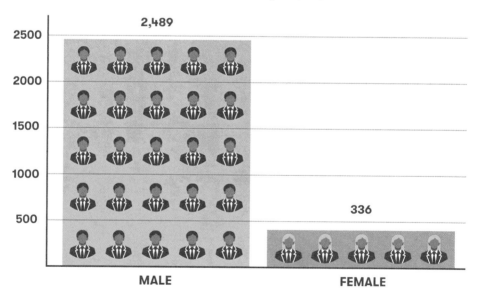

## NUMBER OF BILLIONAIRES BY GENDER, 2019

# TAKING STOCK OF WORLD LEADERS

The Council on Foreign Relations reports that in September 2020, twenty-one of the 193 world leaders (less than 11 percent) were women:

## WHO ARE THEY?

| COUNTRY | NAME | TITLE |
|---------|------|-------|
| Bolivia | Jeanine Áñez | Acting President |
| Bangladesh | Sheikh Hasina | Prime Minister |
| Barbados | Mia Mottley | Prime Minister |
| Belgium | Sophie Wilmès | Prime Minister |
| Denmark | Mette Frederiksen | Prime Minister |
| Estonia | Kersti Kaljulaid | President |
| Ethiopia | Sahle-Work Zewde | President |
| Finland | Sanna Marin | Prime Minister |
| Gabon | Rose Christiane Raponda | Prime Minister |
| Georgia | Salome Zurabishvili | President |
| Germany | Angela Merkel | Chancellor |
| Greece | Katerina Sakellaropoulou | President |
| Iceland | Katrín Jakobsdóttir | Prime Minister |
| Nepal | Bidhya Devi Bhandari | President |
| New Zealand | Jacinda Ardern | Prime Minister |
| Norway | Erna Solberg | Prime Minister |
| Serbia | Ana Brnabić | Prime Minister |

| Singapore | Halimah Yacob | President |
|---|---|---|
| Slovakia | Zuzana Čaputová | President |
| Switzerland | Simonetta Sommaruga | President |
| Togo | Victoire Tomegah Dogbé | Prime Minister |
| Trinidad and Tobago | Paula-Mae Weekes | President |

These numbers say a lot, don't they? Clearly, it's hard for women to become billionaires or world leaders. Overall, women tend to have lower-paying jobs than men. And in nearly every field, many women earn less than men for doing the same work.

Especially in developing countries, women face many forms of discrimination and oppression. As of 2020, about 61 million girls worldwide don't go to school at all because of poverty, war, and discrimination.

*Malala Yousafzai*

## MEET MALALA

Malala Yousafzai, a young activist from Pakistan, has worked to raise awareness about girls' education. Her organization, the Malala Fund, has raised millions of dollars for the cause. In 2014, at the age of seventeen, Malala became the youngest person to be awarded the Nobel Peace Prize.

## WOMEN'S HEALTH

Many women don't have decent healthcare, and very few countries offer adequate childcare programs for women who work. Women in developing countries often don't have access to birth-control methods, and thus have more children than they want. Many women die or suffer illness when they resort to illegal, unsafe abortions.

One in three women worldwide has been the victim of sexual or domestic violence. Each year millions of girls in developing countries are married off before they turn eighteen.

## STUBBORN IDEAS ABOUT WOMEN REFUSE TO DIE

Sometimes untrue attitudes about women run deeply, believed by women themselves. Just like people of color can internalize racist ideas and not speak up or question things, women can do the same with sexist ideas in society. For example, studies have found that, overall, girl students feel less confident in math than boys do, even though there is no evidence that girls' brains are any different as far as math goes.

So, the truths to stand upon today are truths about the actual state of gender equality, as well as the promise that a stronger female presence offers the world. We are not there yet, but there is progress. Historians will be watching the continuing rise of women.

# INTERNATIONAL RELATIONS

Looking across this chapter you can see that today's challenges have power at their core. Rich people have power, men have power, white people have power, businesses have power, and governments, especially those in developed countries, have power. We've seen through history how countries often compete for power but sometimes cooperate by building alliances.

# THE END OF THE COLD WAR

We saw in the Cold War how the United States and the Soviet Union formed two opposite forces in the world, and other countries ended up on one side or the other. When the United States and the Soviet Union spied on each other, badmouthed each other, threatened each other, and even came to the brink of war, the world was watching.

To understand the international scene today, you need to know that the two-sided game is long over. The Cold War ended in 1989 when the visionary leader Mikhail Gorbachev lifted the iron curtain. He broke apart the Soviet bloc into independent states, permitted a certain amount of capitalist commerce in Russia, and allowed in Western ideas and goods.

## GLOBAL ALLIANCES

Now that the two opposing "superpowers" are no more, global alliances are much more flexible, and they exist for lots of purposes. The world still has military alliances, but they can shift.

Countries also form coalitions to work on global issues like climate change, human rights, and ending poverty. Trade alliances and economic power continue to be important.

# THE RISE OF CHINA

And guess which country is winning on the economic front? China. Yes, the same country that suffered one of the worst famines in history is now the world's richest country. India is also gaining ground as an economic world power, though projected growth diminished during the coronavirus pandemic.

# COMPETITORS AND ALLIES

The relationship between China and the United States provides a good example of the way two countries can be both competitors and allies. China and the United States compete in international trade, and have plenty of disagreements. But when it comes to dealing with China's totalitarian neighbor, North Korea, the United States and China mostly support one another.

Members of alliances can also come and go, depending on a country's leadership or a vote by the people. For example, in 2008, the United States participated in talks to create treaties to address climate change, but when a new presidential administration stepped in eight years later, the United States withdrew.

**Coalitions:** Coalitions are strategic alliances. They can be between activist groups who see their work as interconnected or between countries who want to tackle global issues jointly. Try to identify coalitions as you read this chapter!

**Treaties:** Treaties are formal agreements between countries.

# BREXIT

In 2016, a big change occurred in the European Union, a coalition of twenty-seven countries that share the same money system and follow similar laws so that goods, people and services move freely within Europe.

*The flag of the European Union*

When the United Kingdom held a vote about whether to leave or stay, 52 percent of people voted to leave the European Union (EU).

Many thought businesses in the United Kingdom would be better off, and some people wanted to avoid having lots of immigrants come in from Europe. The decision got the nickname Brexit (**Br**itish **exit** from the EU).

# A LAST WORD

Our journey through time ends here, folks. We hope you've been amazed, amused, inspired, and occasionally grossed out. And we hope you've gotten angry when grown humans have behaved like babies or demons—or worse. We know it's gotten ugly, and we purposely didn't sugarcoat the bad parts. But we also hope you'll hang on to the good parts.

When humans have done brave, bold, brilliant things, can you see yourself in these individuals? Who says you can't make history, too? As we send you off to survive middle school, or keep surviving it, we think you're taking with you some important knowledge. But we cannot possibly give you all the knowledge. It's your job to keep finding out about the things that beg to be explored. And you must, must keep questioning.

You might even go back through this book and question it. What's missing? Whose story is left out? What have historians, archaeologists, scientists, and journalists discovered that makes something in this book now wrong or outdated?

That's how you'll continue to survive—into high school, college, and beyond. And don't forget the tools that will help you on any journey of learning. You've got a GPS, boots, binoculars, a magnifying glass, and a pickaxe to uncover the truth, find patterns, root out bias, and dig for causes.

Today's world presents you with some big challenges, no doubt about it. It might feel a little scary to face so many issues, even with all your equipment, but we know you've got this. Here's some sage advice from Nelson Mandela:

*"May your choices reflect your hopes, not your fears."*

Keep to your hopes and you'll do more than survive. You'll shape a better world for everybody.

# CHAPTER VOCABULARY

**Artificial Intelligence:** Artificial intelligence, or AI, allows computers to take on tasks that we normally think of as human: thinking, making decisions, understanding speech, and more.

**Asylum:** In the context of this chapter, asylum refers to the safety that refugees seek in other countries. It is a legal designation granted by the countries that refugees enter.

**Coalitions:** Coalitions are strategic alliances. They can be between activist groups who see their work as interconnected or between countries who want to tackle global issues jointly.

**Developed and developing countries:** Countries with more wealth and technology are called developed countries, while poorer countries, with less access to technology, are called developing countries.

**Digital:** If something is digital, that means it has to do with computers and technology. This current era is often referred to as the Digital Age because computer technologies are a central force shaping modern history.

**Epidemic:** An epidemic is the wide and rapid spread of a disease in a particular area.

**Era:** An era is a big chunk of time in history.

**Global supply chain:** The global supply chain is the process by which many goods are made using materials and labor from around the world. Any one of the stages of production or distribution can take place in any part of the world.

**Grassroots:** When activism or organizing is called grassroots, that means it's making change from the bottom up. It's often based in connecting with and organizing local community members.

**Immune:** If you're immune to something, that means it can't affect you. Being immune to a disease means it can't get you sick. Remember vaccinations? Those are one way humans can gain immunity to different illnesses.

**Privacy:** Privacy is the ability to be free from observation and surveillance by other people or from the government. There are many laws that determine what is protected as private, and conversely, what information and spaces are public.

**Profit:** Profit is the money made after expenses have been accounted for.

**Subsistence living:** Subsistence living means working to supply only the resources necessary for survival (food, water, and somewhere to live).

**Tariffs:** A tariff is a tax issued by a government on imports from other countries.

**Treaties:** Treaties are formal agreements between countries.

**Vaccinations:** Vaccinations are the shots you get to prevent diseases. They are an important way the world stays healthy!

**Virus and Bacteria:** A virus is a highly infectious agent that can spread disease. Bacteria are germs, good or bad. Scientifically, there are differences between these terms, but in the context of history, both have been responsible for widespread disease.

# NOTES

# 9

# HOW TO THINK LIKE A HISTORIAN

Out in the real world of research, news, and social media, all kinds of information flies around at lightning speed. What's true? What's important? What's fair? Answering questions like these takes clear thinking. Read on for some lessons from historians on the art of critical thinking. It's more challenging than you'd thought!

PRIMARY SOURCES
SECONDARY SOURCES
BIAS

As you move through middle school, you're going to need to learn lots of things on your own. Your teachers will ask you to write papers, make projects, and create podcasts and slideshows, all based on your own research.

The Internet is there to help you, but it's a big, big place. As of early 2021, there are about 1.8 billion websites on the Internet, and more are being added by the minute. Gobs of information comes at you on social media—some of it worthwhile, much of it not. That can be overwhelming, especially for a kid. In fact, a study of seventh graders found that 70 percent of them did not know how to evaluate the quality of sources or check to see if a claim was true.

> **Claim:** A claim is something that can be proved or disproved.
>
> **Skeptic:** A skeptic is someone who questions the things that they read or hear.

## GETTING SMARTER ABOUT SOURCES

It's clear that adults and kids need to get smarter about sources. Guess who's been dealing with sources all along, even before the Internet (like a *lot* before the Internet)? Guess which people keep on thinking critically and digging for the truth? Historians. So if you can think the way historians think, you'll be ahead of the game. It's not hard. It just takes some practice and some detective skills. Luckily, you've already got the tools.

# IMPORTANT THINGS TO KNOW (AND EMULATE) ABOUT HISTORIANS

## 1. HISTORIANS CARE ABOUT TRUTH

Historians have an extremely important job. They piece together what happened in the past and try to understand why. They have to sort through many versions of events. Before they put anything out to the world about what happened, they need to be as sure as they can be.

You could say that historians are in the "truth profession" because they need to be as accurate and fair as they can. It pays to care about the truth, even if you're still a student. It's more work, and it requires more thinking. But what's the point of "might be true" history?

## 2. HISTORIANS ARE *SKEPTICS*

Historians don't believe everything they read, and neither should you. They know the Internet is powerful but also riddled with misleading information and even lies. They check and recheck their facts. They are suspicious of one-sided accounts. They look for real stories, and they trust the words of scholars they respect. They always consider whose story might be missing and which accounts could be understated or overstated.

## 3. HISTORIANS USE MANY KINDS OF SOURCES

Historians use lots of different sources, some of them primary and some secondary.

## PRIMARY SOURCES

If you turn back to the introduction, you'll recall that primary sources are firsthand accounts of events, written by people who actually lived during the time period. Primary sources can also be images—artwork, photographs, ads, posters, films, anything made or written during a certain time period. Historians mainly use primary sources, and you can understand why, right? If someone was actually there, chances are they can describe events accurately. (But not always—remember, *everyone* has a point of view!)

## SECONDARY SOURCES

You could think of secondary sources as secondhand information, but they are still important. Just remember that some secondary sources are better than others, and that's where your thinking comes in.

Most often, historians and other experts create the best secondary sources, based on primary sources. In secondary sources (such as books, articles, and video sources), historians analyze cause and effect. They also find meaning in patterns and form theories about why things happened the way they happened. A historian might also consult a secondary source to find out how other scholars have interpreted a time period, person, or event.

So the first step toward researching like a historian is to use multiple sources, both primary and secondary. It's more work, but there's just no other way to get a full picture. If you don't believe us, these examples might convince you.

# CASE STUDIES ON SOURCES

## PRIMARY SOURCES: THE CONGO "FREE STATE"

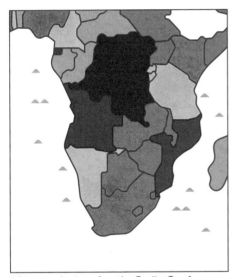

African colonies after the Berlin Conference of 1884 (detail)

Remember the Scramble for Africa, back in Chapter 5? Go back and review it. You'll recall how at a conference in Berlin, Germany, in 1884, the European imperial powers basically carved up the continent of Africa among themselves. They did so without consulting anyone who lived in Africa. Thereafter, Europeans colonized Africa, often brutally. (Check Chapter 4 if you're at all fuzzy about this concept of colonization.)

What we didn't tell you in Chapter 5 was that the scramble started with King Leopold II of Belgium. He wanted to create what he called the "Congo Free State" by taking control of a huge area in the center of Africa. He said he was doing it to help the people of the Congo. But his real goal was to become personally wealthy from rubber production. So he sent in some "explorers" to set up industries.

King Leopold II of Belgium

It doesn't sound so bad, bringing industry to an area. But there's much more to it. If you only used a certain textbook to understand this topic, you would find two paragraphs that deal with the Congo Free State specifically. An excerpt from the first paragraph is below.

> *King Leopold II was the real driving force behind the colonization of Africa. He rushed enthusiastically into the pursuit of an empire in Africa. "To open to civilization," he said, "the only part of our globe where it has not yet penetrated, to pierce the darkness which envelops entire populations, is...a crusade, if I may say so, a crusade worthy of this century of progress." Profit was equally important to Leopold. In 1876, he hired Henry Stanley to set up Belgian settlements in the Congo."*

The second paragraph is entirely about the Europeans and their competition to grab territories (we haven't printed it, you'll have to trust us on this). If you only read two paragraphs about the colonization of the Congo in this particular textbook, what would you come away thinking about?

You might remember that Leopold was "enthusiastic," which sounds positive. A lot of space is given to the quotation by Leopold, so you might remember some of what he said about his "crusade." If you didn't know much about Africa, you might assume that the Congo area of Africa was uncivilized because Leopold describes it as being in "darkness." But if you know about African civilizations (and you do—check Chapter 3!), you can see that Leopold is making a racist and inaccurate assumption about the people of Africa.

Is someone's story left out here?

If you also consulted primary sources, you would learn that the conquest of the Congo caused severe harm and humiliation to the people living there. One African American man (who happened to be a historian) named George Washington Williams visited the Congo in 1890, the time period in question. He wrote a letter to King Leopold to tell him about all the many abuses he saw there. Williams includes detailed evidence of the "deceit, fraud, robberies, arson, murder, slave-raiding, and general policy of cruelty" that he witnessed by those King Leopold had appointed. Witnessed firsthand? That's a primary source!

Other primary sources also describe how the king's representatives tricked and tortured the Congolese into giving away their land, their rights, and their labor. Henry Stanley and his men cut off people's hands, beat them, and even killed them. Stanley's men also brought in diseases that were fatal to the Congolese. Some historians estimate that 10 million people, or half of the total Congolese population, died between 1885 and 1908. These are not small details, but they didn't make it into the textbook.

Had you not gone back and checked primary sources, you might never have known the whole story!

**Fraud:** Fraud is a crime that involves being dishonest in order to take something valuable from someone else.

**Arson:** Arson is the crime of setting fire to something.

**Hearsay:** Hearsay is information that you hear secondhand, which means it comes from someone who didn't directly witness an event and can't positively confirm if it's true or not.

**Verify:** To verify something is to make sure that it's accurate or true. You might already recognize this word from Instagram or TikTok, where accounts can request to be verified.

# SECONDARY SOURCES: DID CALIGULA REALLY MAKE HIS HORSE A CONSUL?

Sometimes secondary sources can contain mistakes and exaggerations. Back in Chapter 2, you learned about a famously bad Roman emperor named Caligula. Most history books will tell you Caligula made his horse a consul—an important official—in the Roman government. But Mary Beard, a professor of classics at Cambridge University and an expert on Roman history, disagrees. Here are her reasons:

1. People have not read the primary sources accurately. According to Dr. Beard, no Roman ever wrote that Caligula made his horse a consul. They only wrote that he *planned* to do it. (Notice how we phrased it on page 103 in the "Who Was the Worst Roman Emperor?" sidebar: "He wanted to make his horse a consul.")

2. Sometimes history is based on hearsay. Someone writes down what they hear someone say, and it's not necessarily verified.

3. Historians wrote about Caligula eighty years after his death, and they didn't like him (and for some very good reasons). Even today, people love to hate Caligula. They enjoy the outlandish tales about him so much that, as Beard says, "he gets worse and worse" as time goes on. She also doubts that Caligula was insane, as many history books claim.

So why would Caligula say he wanted to make his horse a consul if he wasn't insane? Dr. Beard's theory is that one day he got so fed up with those in the Senate that he taunted them by saying something like: "You guys are all so hopeless that I might as well make my horse a consul!" It's a guess, but it's a good guess because Beard has spent her life studying ancient Rome, and so her theory is based on research.

# ARE ALL TEXTBOOKS CREATED EQUAL?

Textbooks can be useful for an overview. They cover a lot of ground and offer a big picture of history. But when you cram the whole history of the world or a country into one book, lots has to be left out.

Historically, the stories of Black people, Indigenous people, women, and poor people have been left out. And instead, the textbook writers give space to, say, a king's enthusiasm.

You should also know that U.S. textbooks can vary in their telling of history, depending on the publisher and the state in which the textbook is used. After a textbook is written, a **panel** of people from the state reviews it and might ask for certain changes. The textbook company then makes those changes to the books that students will use within that state. That's why a textbook from California, for example, might contain some details that are different from a textbook in Texas.

**Panel:** A group of people brought together to discuss, investigate, or decide a specific issue or subject.

Vocabulary Focus: Objective vs. Subjective

We can define these words as follows:

Something that is objective presents or deals with facts as they actually are, without distortion from personal feelings, prejudices, or interpretations.

Something that is subjective presents facts that are colored or skewed by personal views, experiences, or beliefs.

We've already said that one big objective truth is not really a thing because a person (with a personal view) is always telling the story.

That's why you consult a few different sources. But there are degrees of subjectivity, and there are also facts.

Let's think back to our soccer game in the introduction. Different people are observing different parts of the game, and they're probably rooting for one team or the other. Still, there are certain objective facts—for example, the score! Some people might not like the score, or they might want to disagree with it. But there is still a score by the end of the game. What other examples of soccer game facts can you think of?

The subjective part comes in with people's personal viewpoints—in other words, what they identify with, their background, and their beliefs. For example, if one player's grandfather explained the game to you, he might carry on about his granddaughter's incredible footwork (which someone else might consider average). There's nothing wrong with the grandfather's loving viewpoint. But you shouldn't expect him to give you an objective picture of the whole game. For a more complete view, you would need to talk to lots of people, including those from the other team.

# DETECTING BIAS

We've established that all accounts of history (or current events) will have a perspective depending on who wrote them. And this will be true for both primary and secondary sources. So you'll also need to be alert to bias, which is related to perspective, but different.

Bias means a piece of writing is favoring only one side of an issue. Sometimes people write biased accounts on purpose, to persuade their readers to see the subject from a certain point of view. Sometimes people have what's called unconscious bias. When someone is unconscious they are asleep or knocked out, right? So unconscious bias means the writer might believe they are telling the full story, but they're really telling only part of it, or they are telling it through a point of view they themselves are unaware of. In a way, these writers or speakers are asleep to their own perspective!

Readers can be asleep to bias, too. They might read something and take it in as true, not realizing they are getting a slanted version of things. For example, on social media, opinions fly around, and we know they're opinions. But in some news stories, or other sources that are supposed to be unbiased, subjectivity can be harder to detect.

There are many reasons to avoid sleepy reading, writing, or speaking. Most importantly, you can get foggy about what's fact and what's opinion. Historians certainly do not settle for it, so you'll want to keep your eyes wide open. You'll need to be alert to clues that reveal bias. And your tools are here to help!

## BECOMING A BIAS DETECTIVE

 Slow down and read carefully. Reread often.

 Be on the lookout for words that carry an opinion, express an emotion, or make a judgment.

## BIAS BUZZ WORDS

| | | |
|---|---|---|
| amazing | fanatical | surprising |
| angry | genius | terrible |
| best | hero | unbelievable |
| better than | radical | unfair |
| brave | sadly | weak |
| coward | shocking | worst |
| dangerous | smart | |

As you read, ask yourself: Is this author trying to get me to feel a certain way about the topic, a person, or a group of people? Is the message trying to make me feel angry at someone? To feel sorry for someone? To admire someone?

Is only one side being presented here? Whose perspective is missing?

# CASE STUDY: CHRISTOPHER COLUMBUS

Let's try this out with a common topic in world history: Christopher Columbus.

## SAMPLE 1

Read this excerpt from *The Life of Christopher Columbus*, written by John S.C. Abbott in 1875:

*[Columbus] was thoughtful, studious, pensive; of a deeply religious nature; ever pondering the mystery of this our sublime earthly being.... He was modest, sensitive and magnanimous. He was a natural gentleman, exceedingly courteous in his bearing, without a shade of vanity.*

How do you feel about Columbus after reading this excerpt? Do you find yourself admiring him?

_____

_____

_____

_____

 Let's notice which words and phrases create these feelings:

| | |
|---|---|
| sublime (beautiful or excellent) | sensitive |
| thoughtful | magnanimous (generous) |
| studious | natural gentleman |
| deeply religious | courteous (polite and respectful) |
| modest | |

We can tell from this positive language that the author wants to present a positive image of Columbus.

Now try it with two more paragraphs about Columbus from other authors:

## SAMPLE 2

Howard Zinn (2007):

> *Columbus's men searched Haiti for gold, with no success. They had to fill up the ships returning to Spain with something, so in 1495 they went on a great slave raid. Afterward, they picked five hundred captives to send to Spain. Two hundred of the Indians died on the voyage. The rest arrived alive in Spain and were put up for sale by a local church official. Columbus, who was full of religious talk, later wrote, "Let us in the name of the Holy Trinity go on sending all the slaves that can be sold."*

—from *A Young People's History of the United States*

Now how do you feel about Columbus? Which words contributed to those feelings?

_____

_____

_____

_____

_____

_____

_____

_____

_____

_____

# SAMPLE 3

Henry Eldridge Bourne and Elbert Jay Benton, D.C. Heath (1913):

> *As he failed to gain great riches for himself and others, [Columbus] became unpopular. Once he was taken back to Spain in chains like a common prisoner. Though his last days were saddened by misfortune, everyone now regards him as the greatest of discoverers.*
>
> —from *A History of the United States* (textbook for grades 6–8)

How do the authors of this passage want you to feel toward Columbus? How do you know?

_____

_____

_____

_____

_____

_____

_____

Let's work on separating facts from opinions in all three excerpts.

Which sentences are only facts?

_____

_____

_____

_____

_____

_____

Which sentences are biased?

_____

_____

_____

_____

_____

_____

_____

_____

_____

_____

_____

Do you have any theories about how the different times in which these texts were written (1875, 2007, and 1913) might affect the different biases?

_____

_____

_____

_____

_____

_____

_____

_____

_____

_____

_____

_____

Did you notice Abbott's and Zinn's very different perspectives on religion?

| ABBOTT | ZINN |
|---|---|
| "[Columbus was] of a deeply religious nature, ever pondering the mystery of this our sublime earthly being" | "Columbus, who was full of religious talk, later wrote, 'Let us in the name of the Holy Trinity go on sending all the slaves that can be sold.'" |

Can you name the two attitudes at play here? Which words and phrases are key?

_____

_____

_____

_____

Great work! You're getting good at being a bias detective! When you can notice authors' opinions within a text, you have the power to form your own opinion.

# EVALUATING INTERNET SOURCES

With more than a billion websites online and bias lurking everywhere, you can see why serious historians are careful about which sources they use. Before they even think about using a source, they check into it to make sure it's reliable.

What do we mean by "reliable"?

Another word for reliable is trustworthy. You probably know people who are trustworthy. Those are the people you choose as true friends, right? They're the ones who tell the truth and have your back. They are also responsible and keep their word. It's the same with sources, especially on the Internet. Some you can trust, and some you can't. The challenge is to figure out which is which.

## LOOK BEFORE YOU CLICK

 As soon as you type a search into your browser and press Enter, you can start deciding which links to check out and which ones to pass by. Follow these tips to avoid unreliable websites:

- **Beware of ads**. When you do an Internet search, sometimes the links at the top of the search results are there because the organization paid the search engine to give them a spot at the top. Most of the time, the word "Ad" will appear in boldface before the link. The sites could be selling something or promoting an opinion, so it's best to scroll past them.

- **Examine the name of the website or URL**. When you are looking for facts, it's important to rely on experts. Usually, experts work at universities, colleges, government agencies, and major news organizations. Let's face it—not everyone is an expert.

- **Take a close look at the ending of the URL.** This ending, or suffix, can give you clues to the site's reliability. There used to be restrictions on what kind of suffixes different groups could use, but now there are only two with restrictions. Only approved universities can use .edu. Only U.S. government agencies can use .gov.

- **If you see two letters, it means it's a site from another country.** For example, .uk tells you the organization is based in the United Kingdom.

# COMMON URL SUFFIXES AND WHAT THEY MEAN

| URL SUFFIX | WHAT IT MEANS | EXAMPLE | WHICH GROUPS CAN USE THIS SUFFIX? | RELIABILITY FACTOR |
|---|---|---|---|---|
| .edu | University or college | columbia.edu | Only higher education institutions | Probably reliable |
| .gov | U.S. governmental agency | nasa.gov | Only U.S. governmental agencies | Probably reliable. Might have a pro-government bias. |
| .org | Nonprofit organization | PBS.org (public broadcasting system) | any | Usually reliable, but could be political |
| .com | Company | natgeo.com | any | Widely used by schools as well as companies. Use caution. |

| .net | member of a network (like an Internet service provider) | historyforkids. net | any | Like ".com"— widely used. May or may not be reliable. |
| --- | --- | --- | --- | --- |

## Also look carefully at the main URL name (the part before the dot).

The words in the URL can sometimes give you clues. Does the name seem emotional, one-sided, or out to prove something? If so, chances are you won't find objective information there. For example, a site called www.attackallsystems.com might be coming from one side of an issue, right?

Try it out now. Which of these URLs seem to be reliable, and which would you have doubts about?

- www.factcheck.org
- redalertpolitics.com
- www.history.com
- www.100percentfedup.com
- www.nasa.gov/stem/forstudents

 Names can be tricky. Some names might sound objective, but in fact they promote one side of politics or the interests of a certain group. For example, Aim.org (Accuracy in Media) and Americanpeopledaily.com sound objective, but both organizations describe their sites as conservative, which means they lean to one side of politics. In the United States today, this means they are more likely to support Republican positions and interpretations of events.

Once you click on a site, check to see if there are links within it to other sources. If not, that may be a sign that the site is not reliable. Good sources usually connect to other good sources, which help you verify the information.

# WHAT IS WIKIPEDIA?

 Let's look closely at the word:

# WIKI    PEDIA

A wiki is an Internet space where people can share their knowledge on something. Sometimes wiki spaces are private to one organization. Other times they are public, meaning anyone can add to the wiki and edit it. The wiki can be updated as people discover things. One person can correct another. (The word wiki is Hawaiian and means "fast.")

It comes from the word "encyclopedia." An encyclopedia is a collection of information about many topics. Back in the day, an encyclopedia was a collection of hardcover volumes. The topics were arranged alphabetically. So there would be a book with all the "A" topics and a "B" book and so on, filling up a bookshelf with 26 or more volumes.

Wikipedia is a public wiki that gathers information from anyone about millions of topics. Over the years, Wikipedia has sometimes gotten a bad rap. You may have been cautioned against using it. The main thing to remember, as with any source, is not to use Wikipedia only. The nice thing about Wikipedia is it provides many links you can follow. So it can be a good place to start—especially the Simple English version, which is easier to understand for students.

# PROS AND CONS
# OF WIKIPEDIA

| PROS | CONS |
|---|---|
| Covers millions of topics | Dense and very detailed—can be overwhelming |
| Contains many links you can follow for further info and that verify the information | Can contain difficult vocabulary (even the Simple English version) |
| Bots (automated computer programs—computer "robots") continually comb through and delete entries with suspicious features, such as all caps or dramatic punctuation. | Entries are not necessarily from scholars or experts. That's why you shouldn't cite Wikipedia as a source, but you can get sources from the links and at the end of entries. |
| People are constantly updating the information and monitoring the site for false information. | |
| Available in many languages | |
| The Simple English version is easier for kids and learners of English to use. | |

# SHORTCUTS TO RELIABLE, READABLE SOURCES

| LISTS FROM YOUR TEACHER OR SCHOOL | SAVE YOURSELF SOME TROUBLE AND GO TO THESE FIRST! |
|---|---|
| www.kidzsearch.com | Google created a search engine called **Kidzsearch** just for kids. It uses safety filters to screen the sites, and it moves educational sites up on search results. It has a Kidztube tab, a wiki tab, games, cool facts—and ads. |
| www.commonsense.org/education/ top-picks/most-reliable-and-credible-sources-for-students | **Common Sense** was created by parents for parents, but you can use it too to find good sources. |
| mediabiasfactcheck.com | On **Media Bias/Fact Check**, you can enter the name of a source and find out how reliable it is based on the site runners' measures of objectivity. |
| teacherrebootcamp.com/2020/12/ stemadvent19/ | Author and educator Shelly Sanchez Terrell has assembled a list of quality research websites and search engines for students on a special page of her **Teacher Reboot Camp** site. |
| simple.wikipedia.org | **Simple English Wikipedia** was created especially for students and for adults learning English. In this version of Wikipedia, the articles are easier to read. |

# CLICKBAIT

If you've been on the Internet or social media even a little bit, you've seen clickbait. It's there to distract you, to lure you in, to make you so urgently curious that you just have to click on the link. That way, the site (supported by advertisers) gets more views, which means more people see their ads. The more people click, the more money they make.

## TAKING CHARGE OF YOUR ATTENTION

The creators of these links and sites are banking on your attention, so that's why they will do almost anything to get it. Justin Rosenstein, a former engineer at Facebook and Google, thinks it's gotten out of hand. He says these sites and their links are controlling people. "We're the product," he says. "Our attention is the product being sold to advertisers."

So, you need to decide: Do you want other people controlling your attention, or do you want to be in charge of it? We hope you choose the second option. To be in charge of your own attention, you need to know clickbait when you see it. Here are some common signs:

- Big, bold lettering

- Bright colors

- Over-the-top punctuation, such as !!!! and ??

- Attention-grabbing photos and GIFs

Clickbait intends to be obvious. It screams out at you, offering some secret or some amazing thing that will change your life. Does the site actually deliver what it promises? Almost never.

Common kinds of clickbait:

- Promises of money or moneymaking schemes

HERE IS THE MONEYMAKING SECRET THAT
BANKS DON'T WANT YOU TO KNOW!

- Miracle products or cures for illness

## THIS PRODUCT WILL CURE A HEADACHE IN SECONDS!

- Hyped-up headlines

## GIRL RESCUES MOM FROM LION ATTACK! YOU WON'T BELIEVE WHAT HAPPENS NEXT!

- How-to's that play on people's desires and emotions

## FIVE EASY STEPS TO BEING THE MOST POPULAR KID IN YOUR SCHOOL—#3 WILL SHOCK YOU!

Notice how these phrases are asking you to get emotional, crave the information, and then click? When you see lures like this, think: Do I really want to take this bait?

# FAKE NEWS

We hear a lot about fake news. We're going to divide fake news into two categories: Funny Fake News and Not Funny Fake News.

## FUNNY FAKE NEWS

Funny fake news has been around for many years. A newspaper called *The Onion*, founded in 1988, is one example. The headlines were beyond ridiculous—and on purpose! Often, they were making fun of the real news to give people a laugh or just creating bizarre stories to entertain people. A few people did believe the stories because the newspapers looked real, and the articles were always written as though they were true. But the publisher didn't intend to fool people. The idea was to publish wild stories for the fun of it. The writers also wanted to make a point through satire, by making fun of things they observed in society. Here's an example of a headline from *The Onion* from December 2020:

> "CDC Announces Children Will Be Last to Receive Covid Vaccine because What Are Those Little Twerps Going to Do about It"

You can see how the topic is real. The vaccine was actually being rolled out at the time, and in fact children were going to be the last to get vaccinated. But the last part is meant to make people laugh. People still subscribe to *The Onion* online and enjoy its twist on current events.

## NOT FUNNY FAKE NEWS

In recent years, people have begun to create fake news that is not intended to be funny at all, and it's a serious threat to our society. All fake news is nonsense, but it can be disguised as real news. It even sometimes contains a kernel of truth.

Fake news goes out onto the Internet and tries to grab people's attention, just like clickbait. When fake news plays on people's beliefs, prejudices, or fears, they can start to believe untrue stories about political figures, events in the world, health cures, diseases, and other hot issues. Some people even believe in conspiracy theories, which tell them that individuals or groups (usually the government) are carrying out secret schemes that are dangerous to them. Sometimes the claims are outrageous, like the government is making fake snow to trick people. But it's hard to argue with someone who thinks they have discovered a secret truth. A secret truth can make the real truth seem false. In this way, conspiracy theories can turn the world upside down for those who believe in them.

Let's consider the consequences of people not knowing how to tell true information from made-up information. How will they make choices in their lives? How will they treat other people who believe something different? How will they vote?

> **Conspiracy theories:** Conspiracy theories are beliefs that individuals or groups (usually the government) are carrying out secret schemes that are dangerous to people.

# HOW DOES A FAKE NEWS STORY SNOWBALL?

Have you ever made a snowman? You start by packing a little snow in your hands. Then you make a ball and pat on more snow. Then your friends might add more. Once the snowball is big enough, you can roll it on the ground. As it picks up more layers of snow, rolling along the ground, the snowball gets bigger and bigger and bigger.

Fake news stories can grow on the Internet like a snowball, but it happens in minutes. Over the course of hours, a phony story can travel worldwide, picking up hundreds of thousands of views. This is where some people's reasoning goes wonky: They think the story is true because it's all over the place. They figure it's real because so many people know about it. Does that sound like the way historians think? Pretty much the opposite!

## FAKE NEWS CASE STUDY: THE 5G HOAX

Let's look at how a false claim started out in a local newspaper article, snowballed into a big story on the Internet, and resulted in people setting more than twenty cell towers on fire. (This is not fake news—the fires really happened. Go ahead and fact-check it!)

In 2019, 5G cell towers started going up around the world to provide faster mobile connections. 5G is the latest and fastest technology for mobile networks, and it's gradually replacing older, slower 4G. Some people don't trust new technology, so there were people who didn't like 5G. (There were also people who didn't like towers and antennae going up when cell phones came into widespread use in the 1990s.)

Around the same time that 5G towers were being built near Wuhan, China, the first coronavirus cases occurred in Wuhan. Diseases don't spread through radio waves. Coronavirus and other viruses are spread only through droplets that come from human noses and mouths. However, some people decided to believe that radio waves and a virus were connected—and many, many people fell for it.

Scientists say, "Correlation is not causation." That's a fancy way of saying that just because two things happen around the same time, it doesn't mean that one caused the other.

# HOW A FAKE NEWS STORY WENT VIRAL

**JANUARY 22, 2020:**

A doctor in Belgium told a reporter from a small local newspaper that new 5G cell towers built in Wuhan, China, could be related to the coronavirus outbreak.

**HOURS LATER:**

The newspaper took down the article because the claim was false and embarrassing.

But it was too late. Anti-5G groups and individuals had already quoted the article and made links to it on Facebook in Belgium and the Netherlands.

**DAYS LATER:**

Quotes from the article appeared on English-speaking Facebook.

Talk show hosts on YouTube started discussing the theory and got tens of thousands of views.

**A FEW WEEKS LATER:**

Bots (Internet robots) picked up on the trend and automatically sent the theory to an even wider audience.

**MARCH 2020:**

Celebrities—some with more than a million followers—started to post on social media about the 5G-coronavirus conspiracy theory.

**APRIL 2020:**

Believers in the theory tried to destroy more than 20 cell towers in the United Kingdom, setting them on fire and posting videos on the Internet. Videos of the fires went viral and spread the fake news even farther.

Many fake stories that go viral follow this pattern: from hearsay to websites to YouTube to bots to targets with many connections. The result is a "news" sensation that happens to be completely false.

# WHY DO PEOPLE CREATE FAKE NEWS?

- To make money (see pg. 444). The more people visit a site, the more money it brings in.

- To promote a certain idea, political party, or opinion. But often the fake news is targeted at the people who already share those beliefs. Why? Because it will spread faster.

- To turn one group of people against another group.

- To harm the reputations of people they don't like or disagree with. If you harm someone's reputation, you make that person seem bad or untrustworthy.

- To sell products.

# WHY DO PEOPLE BELIEVE FAKE NEWS?

- It confirms what they already believed.

- They are afraid of something they can't control (such as coronavirus) and they like the certainty the fake news provides (even if it's unproven).

- It's exciting! They feel like they're in on a secret.

- They feel part of a group that believes it.

- Their friends or relatives send it to them, and they trust those people.

- They don't trust the government.

- They don't know how to fact-check.

> **Fact-check:** A fact-check is just what it sounds like; it means investigating and checking to make sure your facts or the facts that someone else is presenting are all true.

# GETTING REAL ABOUT FAKE NEWS

It's easy to think that the people who fall for fake news are somehow "dumb," but in fact, anyone can fall for a fake news story. Usually, it's for one of two reasons. One, it fools people whose own biases make them too eager to agree with or believe a story. But most often, fake news fools people because they read it without thinking critically. Taking the time to think about the trustworthiness of your source and possible bias is the key. The good news is that anyone can get better at spotting and avoiding fake news. You can start now!

## TIPS FOR SPOTTING FAKE NEWS

If something makes you suspicious—whether it's big lettering or a claim that doesn't sound right—slow down and think.

Let your own knowledge ground you. Trust your common sense. If something seems outrageous, silly, exaggerated, or impossible, it probably is!

Do some digging to see if it's true.

- Check out the author of the story or post. Is the person knowledgeable on the subject? Do they work for an organization that studies the subject in an objective or fair way, like a university, research group, or government agency? (If the story or post doesn't name the author, that could be a clue, too.)

- Consult reliable sources (see above) to see if those sources give the same information. This is called cross-checking, and it's vital if you have any doubts.

- Consult one of these fact-checking sites. They may have already checked the facts for you.

- apnews.com/hub/not-real-news

- mediabiasfactcheck.com

- www.politifact.com/

- www.factcheck.org/

- www.washingtonpost.com/blogs/fact-checker/

- www.snopes.com/

- truthbetold.news/category/fact-checks

 Look for signs of bias or one perspective (see above).

# THE FUTURE OF FAKE NEWS

Some experts warn that the fake news problem will get worse before it gets better. Around the world, people are growing more stubborn in their opinions and more untrusting of those who disagree with them. Technology continues to evolve, which will always bring new challenges.

You may have seen some deepfake videos. New apps can imitate the appearance of a person and have them say or do things they never said or did. Most people believe what they see, but with deepfake technology, even images can be phony. You'll need to be on the lookout from here on. Use our tools to evaluate sources, detect bias, and filter out fake news.

# YOU ARE A FUTURE HISTORIAN

Let's sharpen our skills for looking back at the past. Thinking like a historian takes some practice! You need to observe carefully and notice tiny details so you don't miss anything. Most important is to ask lots of questions and think carefully before reaching any conclusions.

You need to avoid making any assumptions that can lead to biased conclusions. You also need to consider the time period and its people from many points of view. But you can also be creative in making connections. As long as your guesses are reasonable and based on what you see, you'll be rehearsing some great thinking.

It's often low-tech work. The only things you need are your mind, an artifact, and some good questions.

> **Assumptions:** An assumption is something that is accepted as true, even without any proof.

## YOUR MISSION AS A FUTURE HISTORIAN

Here is your task:

Imagine you are a historian, archaeologist, or anthropologist living 200 years in the future. Your job is to examine an artifact used by people 200 years ago (our time period). You will then form some theories about our culture, our values, and our way of life.

# PEOPLE WHO STUDY THE PAST

| | HISTORIAN | ARCHAEOLOGIST | ANTHROPOLOGIST |
|---|---|---|---|
| What they study (sources) | Written sources: primary and secondary | Physical artifacts made by people of the past, often found in the earth | Both written sources and artifacts, depending on the time period. Anthropologists who study present-day cultures also observe people and conduct interviews. |
| Their purpose | Put together a picture of events, their causes, effects, and the various points of view of many people of the time. | Understand how people lived and what they could and couldn't do. | Understand people's beliefs, customs, and ways of life— both present and past. |
| Questions they ask | Who wrote this? When and where was it written? Why was it written? | Who made this? How was it made? When and where was it made? Who used it? How and why was it used? What kinds of technology was available to these people? | What does this tell me about these people's culture, belief systems, social structure, or way of life? How did people use technology? How did it affect their lives? |

1. Decide whether you'll be a historian, an archaeologist, or an anthropologist (take a look at the chart on the previous page). You can be all three if you want!

2. Find an artifact to analyze. Choose something lying around your house. It could be your sneaker, a backpack, a water bottle, your phone, a newspaper, some earbuds, a shopping list, a penny, a Rubik's cube, or a bag of chips. Anything.

3. Pretend you know nothing about the time we're living in now. Therefore, you aren't sure what the object or document is.

4. Begin by observing it or reading it very carefully. Just write down what you notice, with no interpretation.

5. Refer to the chart for questions to ask for interpretation. Jot down your answers. Again, try to forget what you know about our time and our culture so you can practice not making assumptions.

6. Now come back to today. How do your answers compare to our world right now? Do you have any new insights into our culture?

# CHAPTER VOCABULARY

**Arson:** Arson is the crime of setting something on fire.

**Assumptions:** An assumption is something that is accepted as true, even without any proof.

**Bias:** Bias is prejudice or slant in favor of one side of an issue over another, usually in a way considered to be unfair.

**Cite:** To cite something is to use it as evidence for your claim.

**Claim:** A claim is something that can be proved or disproved.

**Conspiracy theories:** Conspiracy theories are beliefs that individuals or groups (usually the government) are carrying out secret schemes that are dangerous to people.

**Encyclopedia:** An encyclopedia is a collection of authoritative information about many topics.

**Fact-check:** A fact-check is just what it sounds like; it means investigating and checking to make sure your facts or the facts that someone else is presenting are all true.

**Fraud:** Fraud is a nonviolent crime that involves intentionally lying or misrepresenting the truth in order to take something valuable from someone else.

**Hearsay:** Hearsay is information that you hear secondhand, which means it comes from someone who didn't directly witness an event and can't positively confirm if it's true or not.

**Objective:** Something that is objective presents or deals with facts as they actually are, without distortion from personal feelings, prejudices, or interpretations.

**Panel:** A panel is a group of people brought together to discuss, investigate, or decide a specific issue or subject.

**Reputation:** Someone's reputation is the general opinion that other people have about them.

**Satire:** Satire is a kind of comedy that uses irony and exaggeration to poke fun at something.

**Skeptic:** A skeptic is someone who questions the things that they read or hear.

**Subjective:** Something that is subjective presents facts that are colored or skewed by personal views, experiences, or beliefs.

**Verify:** To verify something is to make sure that it's accurate or true. You might already recognize this word from Instagram or TikTok, where accounts can request to be verified.

**Wiki:** A wiki is an Internet space where people can share their knowledge on something.

# ADDITIONAL READING

Interested in learning more? We've put together this list of reading resources (from short articles to full-length fiction and nonfiction books) that will help round out your perspective on the issues in each chapter.

# CHAPTER 1—ANCIENT CIVILIZATIONS

"Archaeologists Find Mummies With Golden Tongues," by Jacey Forton, *The New York Times*, February 3, 2021.

www.nytimes.com/2021/02/03/science/egypt-mummy-golden-tongue.html

"Civilizations," *National Geographic Society*, March 4, 2019.

www.nationalgeographic.org/encyclopedia/civilizations

"Hammurabi's Code: An Eye for an Eye," by USHistory.org, *Ancient Civilizations Online Textbook*, 2021.

www.ushistory.org/civ/4c.asp

"Introduction to the Black Pharaohs of the Kush Empire: Rise of the Black Pharaohs," PBS LearningMedia, 2012.

www.pbslearningmedia.org/resource/rise-of-the-black-pharaohs-1/introduction-to-black-pharaohs/

*National Geographic Kids Everything Ancient Egypt: Dig Into a Treasure Trove of Facts, Photos, and Fun*, by Crispin Boyer, National Geographic, 2012.

*Mummies Exposed!: Creepy and True #1*, by Kerrie Logan Hollihan, Abrams Books for Young Readers, 2019.

"Sacred Journeys: Three Religions, One City (Jerusalem)," PBS LearningMedia, 2014.

www.pbs.org/video/sacred-journeys-three-religions-one-city-jerusalem/

# CHAPTER 2—CLASSICAL CIVILIZATIONS

*Big Thinkers and Big Ideas: An Introduction to Eastern and Western Philosophy*, by Sharon Kaye, PhD., Rockridge Press, 2020.

*D'Aulaires' Book of Greek Myths*, by Ingri d'Aulaire and Edgar Parin d'Aulaire, Delacorte Books for Young Readers, 1992.

*The Emperor's Silent Army: Terracotta Warriors of Ancient China*, by Jane O'Connor, Viking Books for Young Readers, 2002.

*How Ganesh Got His Elephant Head and Other Stories*, by Vatsala Sperling and Harish Johari, Bear Cub Books, 2020.

*Percy Jackson & the Olympians* series, by Rick Riordan, Disney-Hyperion, 2005.

*Tools of the Ancient Greeks: A Kid's Guide to the History and Science of Life in Ancient Greece*, by Kris Bordessa, Nomad Press, 2006.

*You Wouldn't Want to Be a Roman Gladiator!: Gory Things You'd Rather Not Know*, by John Malam, Franklin Watts Inc., 2012.

# CHAPTER 3—POST CLASSICAL CIVILIZATIONS

*1001 Inventions and Awesome Facts from Muslim Civilization*, National Geographic Society, 2012.

"Africa's Great Civilizations," hosted by Henry Louis Gates, Jr., PBS, 2017.
www.pbs.org/show/africas-great-civilizations/

*The Byzantine Empire: A Society that Shaped the World*, by Kelly Rodgers, Teacher Created Materials, 2012.

*Castle Diary: Journal of Tobias Burgess*, by Richard Platt, Candlewick Press, 2003.

*DK Eyewitness Books: Ancient China: Discover the History of Imperial China from the Great Wall to the Days of the Last Emperor*, by Arthur Cotterell, DK Publishing, 2005.


# CHAPTER 4—EARLY MODERN HISTORY

*Before Columbus: The Americas of 1491*, by Charles C. Mann, Atheneum Books for Young Readers, 2009.

*The Enlightenment: A Revolution in Reason*, by Patrice Sherman, Teacher Created Materials, 2012.

*Inside the Reformation*, by Mark Sengele, Concordia Publishing House, 2012.

*The Renaissance Inventors: With History Projects for Kids*, by Alicia Z. Klepeis, Nomad Press, 2018.

*Science Year by Year: A Visual History, From Stone Tools to Space Travel*, DK Publishing, 2017.

*The World Made New: Why the Age of Exploration Happened and How it Changed the World*, by Marc Aronson, National Geographic Kids, 2007.

# CHAPTER 5—LATE MODERN HISTORY I

*100 Inventions That Made History: Brilliant Breakthroughs That Shaped Our World*, DK Children, 2014.

*The 1619 Project: Born on the Water*, by Nikole Hannah-Jones and Renee Watson, Kokila, 2021.

*Copper Sun*, by Sharon M. Draper, Atheneum Books for Young Readers, 2008.

*Fannie Never Flinched: One Woman's Courage in the Struggle for American Labor Union Rights*, by Mary Cronk Farrell, Abrams Books for Young Readers, 2016.

*Growing Up in Slavery: Stories of Young Slaves as Told by Themselves*, edited by Yuval Taylor, Chicago Review Press, 2005.

*Hands-On History! Ancient Japan*, by Fiona Macdonald, Armadillo, 2014.

*Kids on Strike!*, by Susan Campbell Bartoletti, Houghton Mifflin Harcourt, 2003.

*Roses and Radicals: The Epic Story of How American Women Won the Right to Vote*, by Susan Zimet and Todd Hasak-Lowy, Puffin Books, 2020.

# CHAPTER 6—LATE MODERN HISTORY II

*The Diary of a Young Girl: The Definitive Edition*, by Anne Frank, Bantam Books, 1993.

*Navajo Code Talkers*, by Stuart A. Kallen, Lerner Publications, 2018.

*Spies, Code Breakers, and Secret Agents: A World War II Book for Kids*, by Carole P. Roman, 2020.

*Treaties, Trenches, Mud, and Blood: A World War I Tale*, by Nathan Hale, Amulet Books, 2014.

*The Untold History of the United States: Young Readers Editions, Volume 1 (1898-1945)*, by Oliver Stone and Peter Kuznick, adapted by Susan Campbell Bartoletti, Atheneum Books for Young Readers, 2014.

*World War II for Kids: A History with 21 Activities*, by Richard Panchyk, Chicago Review Press, 2002.

*We Had to Be Brave: Escaping the Nazis on the Kindertransport*, by Deborah Hopkinson, Scholastic Focus, 2020.

# CHAPTER 7—THE POSTWAR WORLD

*Africa Is Not a Country*, by Margy Burns Knight and Marc Melnicove, First Avenue Editions, 2002.

*A Night Divided*, by Jennifer A. Nielsen, Scholastic, 2018.

"If the Mango Tree Could Speak," by Patricia Goudvis, 1993.
    vimeo.com/200986886

*Nelson Mandela: The Authorized Comic Book*, by Umlando Wezithombe and the Nelson Mandela Foundation, W.W. Norton & Company, 2009.

*Red Scarf Girl: A Memoir of the Cultural Revolution*, by Ji-li Jiang, HarperCollins, 2018.

*Spies: The Secret Showdown Between America and Russia*, by Marc Favreau, Little, Brown Books for Young Readers, 2019.

*The Untold History of the United States: Young Readers Editions, Volume 2 (1945-1962)*, by Oliver Stone and Peter Kuznick, adapted by Susan Campbell Bartoletti, Atheneum Books for Young Readers, 2019.

# CHAPTER 8—CHALLENGES TODAY

*After Gandhi: One Hundred Years of Nonviolent Resistance*, by Anne Sibley O'Brien and Perry Edmund O'Brien, Charlesbridge Publishing, 2009.

*I Am Malala: How One Girl Stood Up for Education and Changed the World*, by Malala Yousafzai and Patricia McCormick, Little, Brown Books for Young Readers, 2016.

*Queen of Likes*, by Hillary Homzie, Aladdin Paperbacks, 2016.

*Refugee*, by Alan Gratz, Scholastic Press, 2017.

*Stamped: Racism, Antiracism, and You*, by Ibram X. Kendi and Jason Reynolds, Little, Brown Books for Young Readers, 2020.

*Voces Sin Fronteras: Our Stories, Our Truth*, by the Latin American Youth Center Writers, Shout Mouse Press, 2019.

*We Are All Greta: Be inspired by Greta Thunberg to Save the World*, by Valentina Giannella, Laurence King, 2019.

*We Are Displaced: My Journey and Stories from Refugee Girls Around the World*, by Malala Yousafzai, Little, Brown Books for Young Readers, 2019.

# GENERAL READING

*The Fierce 44: Black Americans Who Shook Up the World*, by The Staff of The Undefeated, Houghton Mifflin Harcourt, 2019.

*Rad Women Worldwide: Artists and Athletes, Pirates and Punks, and Other Revolutionaries Who Shaped History*, by Kate Schatz, Ten Speed Press, 2016.

*Stories for Boys Who Dare to Be Different: True Tales of Amazing Boys Who Changed the World without Killing Dragons*, by Ben Brooks, Running Press Kids, 2018.

*Timelines of Everything: From Woolly Mammoths to World Wars*, DK Publishing, 2018.

# TEXT CREDITS

Page 11: "On the Pulse of Morning" from *On the Pulse of Morning* by Maya Angelou, copyright © 1993 by Maya Angelou. Used by permission of Random House, an imprint and division of Penguin Random House LLC. All rights reserved.

Page 99: From *SPQR: A History of Ancient Rome* by Mary Beard. Copyright Mary Beard Publications, 2015. Used by permission of Liveright Publishing Corporation. Used in the U.K. with permission from Profile Books.

Page 303: "Dreamers," Copyright Siegfried Sassoon by kind permission of the Estate of George Sassoon.

Page 401: Data from "World Refugee Day, June 20, 2019," by Humanitarian Information Unit and the U.S. Bureau of Population, Refugees, & Migration. Retrieved from: 'https://reliefweb.int/sites/reliefweb.int/files/resources/World_RefugeeDay_2019Jun19_HIU_U2094.pdf'.

Page 402: Data from "The World's Staggering Inequality," compiled by Dyfed Loesche, Statista. Retrieved from: 'https://www.statista.com/chart/7585/the-worlds-staggering-wealth-divide/'. Original data sourced from Oxfam.

Page 403: Data from "Human Development Index (HDI)," by Max Roser. Published online at OurWorldInData.org. Retrieved from: 'https://ourworldin data.org/human-development-index'. Original data sourced from the United Nations Development Programme (UNDP).

Page 408: Data from "Number of billionaires around the world in 2019, by gender," by M. Szmigiera, Statista. Retrieved from: 'https://www.statista.com/statistics/778577/billionaires-gender-distribution/'.

Page 425: Republished with permission of McGraw Hill LLC from *Glencoe World History Modern Times Student Edition*, 2009, permission conveyed through Copyright Clearance Center, Inc.

Page 434: Howard Zinn, excerpt from *A Young People's History of the United States: Columbus to the War on Terror*, adapted by Rebecca Stefoff. Copyright © 2007, 2009 by Howard Zinn. Reprinted with the permission of The Permissions Company, LLC on behalf of Seven Stories Press, sevenstories.com.

# ABOUT THE CREATORS OF HOW TO SURVIVE MIDDLE SCHOOL: WORLD HISTORY

**Elizabeth M. Fee** is currently Assistant Principal at the Ella Baker School, a Pre-K through grade 8 public school in New York City. During thirty years as an educator, she has served as a middle school Humanities teacher, ELA Instructional Coach, Social Studies Core Curriculum writer, and an advisor to principals. She holds a Master of Arts from Teachers College at Columbia University and New York state certifications in building level and district level leadership.

**Sideshow Media** is a print and digital book developer specializing in illustrated publications with compelling content and visual flair. Since 2000, Sideshow has collaborated with trade publishers, institutions, magazines, and private clients to deliver well-crafted books on a wide variety of subjects, in virtually every format. Sideshow excels at making complicated subjects accessible and interesting to young readers and adults alike. Sideshow is led by its founding partner, Dan Tucker. www.sideshowbooks.com

**Carpenter Collective** is a graphic design and branding studio led by partners Jessica and Tad Carpenter. They focus on bringing powerful messages to life through branding, packaging, illustration, and design. They have worked with clients ranging from Target, Coca-Cola, and Macy's, to Warby Parker, Adobe, and MTV, among many others. They've earned a national reputation for creating powerful brand experiences and unique visual storytelling with a whimsical wink. See more of their work at carpentercollective.com

# NOTES

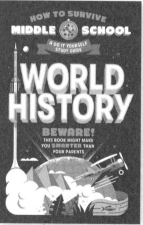